ISBN 978-1-330-83663-7
PIBN 10111862

For support please visit www.forgottenbooks.com

1 MONTH OF
FREE
READING

at

www.ForgottenBooks.com

By purchasing this book you are eligible for one month membership to ForgottenBooks.com, giving you unlimited access to our entire collection of over 700,000 titles via our web site and mobile apps.

To claim your free month visit:
www.forgottenbooks.com/free111862

English
Français
Deutsche
Italiano
Español
Português

www.forgottenbooks.com

Mythology Photography **Fiction**
Fishing Christianity **Art** Cooking
Essays Buddhism Freemasonry
Medicine **Biology** Music **Ancient
Egypt** Evolution Carpentry Physics
Dance Geology **Mathematics** Fitness
Shakespeare **Folklore** Yoga Marketing
Confidence Immortality Biographies
Poetry **Psychology** Witchcraft
Electronics Chemistry History **Law**
Accounting **Philosophy** Anthropology
Alchemy Drama Quantum Mechanics
Atheism Sexual Health **Ancient History**
Entrepreneurship Languages Sport
Paleontology Needlework Islam
Metaphysics Investment Archaeology
Parenting Statistics Criminology
Motivational

MADAME DE STAËL;

A STUDY

OF

HER LIFE AND TIMES:

THE FIRST REVOLUTION and THE FIRST EMPIRE.

By A. STEVENS, LL.D.

IN TWO VOLUMES.—VOL. II.

WITH PORTRAITS.

LONDON:

JOHN MURRAY, ALBEMARLE STREET.

1881.

CONTENTS

OF

THE SECOND VOLUME.

CHAPTER XXVI.

LIFE AT COPPET—CONTINUED.

CHAPTER XXVII.

THE 'ALLEMAGNE'—RENEWED PERSECUTION.

CHAPTER XXVIII.

SHE RETURNS TO COPPET.

CHAPTER XXIX.

HER SECOND MARRIAGE.

CHAPTER XXX.

INCREASED PERSECUTION.

CHAPTER XXXI.

FLIGHT FROM SWITZERLAND.

CHAPTER XXXII.

HER PASSAGE THROUGH AUSTRIA TO RUSSIA.

CHAPTER XXXIII.

IN RUSSIA.

CHAPTER XXXIV.

IN ST. PETERSBURG.

CHAPTER XXXV.

IN SWEDEN.

CHAPTER XXXVI.

IN ENGLAND.

CHAPTER XXXVII.

IN ENGLAND—THE ' ALLEMAGNE.'

CHAPTER XXXVIII.

LITERARY AND OTHER HABITS.

CHAPTER XLIII.

LAST SCENES—DEATH.

Madame de Staël.

CHAPTER XXIII

COPPET—'CORINNE.'

She returns to Switzerland—Letters to the Grand Duchess of Weimar
—Guests at Coppet—Returns to France—Finishes 'Corinne'—Its
great Success—Its Character—Bonaparte's Resentment—The
Countess of Albany—Sismondi's Letters to her.

SHE arrived again in Switzerland in the summer of
1805, and spent a year, at Coppet and Geneva,
preparing her new book as a relief to the mental
suffering which her return to these localities revived. Writing, August 24, to the Duchess Louise
of Weimar, she says: 'After my long tour in
Italy, I am again in Coppet, where I have been
seized by a sadness which distresses my imagination and nerves. There is something very grievous
in the suffering which is renewed by the aspect of
places; I have this feebleness; my natural rest-
lessness causes in me some distraction, and yet
bitter repentance for this relief. But, amidst all
these impressions, I have thought, without ceasing,

of you, and I frequently feel anxious to depart for Weimar. I will yield to this desire as soon as my claim on the government treasury is paid, but (whatever the journals may say) there are only vague words from the Emperor on the subject, and he does not permit me to go to Paris to attend to it in person. My eldest son is there at school; I make this sacrifice for his education. But will not Germany, the land where they recognise your virtues, be as good for his education? What shall I say of France? Everything is controlled by one man, and no person can take a step, or form a wish, without him. Not only liberty but free will seems banished from the earth. How I mourn for Schiller.[1] There is now in the world one less of the grand motives of emulation for all that is noble and true.'[2]

During the preparation of the 'Corinne,' the guests of the château, if fewer than formerly, were those who were dearest to her. The chief of them were, Madame Rilliet-Huber, the companion of her childhood; Madame Vernet-Pictet, 'still very young,' says Steinlen, 'but already the mother of the poor,'—whose daughter became the wife, and long survived at Coppet as the widow, of Baron Auguste de Staël, maintaining its hospitalities down to our own day; Madame Necker de Saussure, Schlegel, Constant, and Sismondi. The latter was ripening

---

[1] Schiller had been dead some four months.
[2] *Coppet et Weimar*, iii.

there in all his faculties. 'He is,' wrote Frederica Brun, 'a young man of serious and persevering activity ; he unites a strong sense and a sound head to that richness of the heart which is the appropriate companion of both.' He read to them chapters of his 'Italian Republics of the Middle Ages.' Madame de Staël was his beloved critic ; her good sense guided his pen. 'His style,' continnes Frederica Brun, 'is vigorous and clear ; his manner of presenting facts simple and vivid ; all is animated by noble thoughts and by the action of a free spirit, which the pressure of our epoch has not led astray.' She admires above all the cousin of Madame de Staël, the daughter of Saussure—her 'noble features, which strikingly resemble those of her father,' the 'purity of soul which is evident in all her being.' She dislikes Schlegel and Constant ; they are too iconoclastic for her romantic tastes. The favourite recreation of the château is still the drama. Ida, the daughter of Madame Brun, afterwards Countess of Bombelles and honoured by Madame de Staël in the 'Allemagne,' had, though now but a child, extraordinary dramatic talent. 'Readily affected,' says Steinlen, 'by a touching scene, she would immediately reproduce it in the dance—Alcestis, Andromache at the tomb of Hector—with an art in drapery, a life and nobleness in attitudes, worthy to inspire a sculptor or painter, and which drew tears from the spectators. Madame de Staël liked to act in tragedy. She had contrived a small theatre at Coppet, where she appeared sometimes as Merope, Zaïre, Phædra; sometimes in small pieces sketched by herself, and played by her children and herself before enthusiastic assemblies. Her defects in art were redeemed by the majesty of her mien, and the truthfulness with which her passionate soul seized and represented characteristic ideas.'[3]

She sent Schlegel with her son to Paris to superintend his studies; but she again longed to be there herself, for the education of her children and her own gratification, and especially for the publication of 'Corinne.' She approached the city furtively, keeping for some time at the prescribed distance of forty leagues. She established herself at Auxerre, a small place no inhabitant of which she knew, but whose Prefect treated her with great consideration. Thence she removed to Rouen, some leagues nearer to the capital, where she could receive letters from Paris every day. She had thus penetrated within the interdicted circle, and as no remonstrance was made by the Government, she began to hope for still greater indulgence. The Prefect of the Seine-Inférieure (M. de Savoie-Rollin) showed her much courtesy. His subsequent dismissal and persecution by the Government was attributable to his friendship for her.

Prussia had now fallen before Napoleon; no

[3] Steinlen's *Bonstetten,* chap. viii.

government on the Continent could make any effective stand against him, and France was utterly and submissively under his control. Fouché thought, therefore, that the rigour of her exile might be somewhat relaxed. He tacitly permitted her to reside at Acosta, near Meulon, about twelve leagues from Paris, on the lands of Madame de Castellane, a lady of considerable culture, who could sympathise with her sufferings. The exile made Acosta memorable by completing there her immortal romance.[4] She could observe there also the reception of the work. A few of her old friends dared cautiously to visit her.

She lived, however, in the closest retirement. But her genius was again to triumph. Suddenly there broke in upon her almost utter solitude the burst of enthusiasm, the *éclat,* with which Europe hailed the appearance of '*Corinne.*' It was published in Paris in 1807, in three volumes 12mo and in two volumes octavo. Vinet says it was 'one of the greatest literary events of the day.'[5] Sainte-Beuve says 'its success was instantaneous and universal.'[6] Another of her critics remarks that, 'far from incurring the objections with which "Delphine" was assailed, "Corinne" carried all suffrages—such diverse tastes are satisfied by the book; it offers at

---

[4] *Coppet et Weimar,* iii.; and 'Avertissement' to second part of *Dix Années.*

[5] *Littérature Française au* 19e *Siècle,* i. 1.

[6] *Critiques et Portraits Littéraires,* iii.

once a romance, a picture the fidelity of which a prac-
tised eye can discern through all its dazzling colours,
and a record of subtle and precious thoughts. It
places her in the rank of great writers. Dominated by her subject, her step is more free,
her manner more natural, than in her previous
writings.'[7] 'As a work of art, as a poem,' says
Sainte-Beuve, 'the romance of "Corinne" is an immortal. monument.' Chenier describes 'Corinne'
as '"Delphine" perfected, free, giving to her faculties
their highest flight, and always doubly inspired by
genius and love.'[8] Vinet, whose high moral standpoint gives additional value to his fine critical judgment, says that, 'considered as a work of art, I
estimate it far above "Delphine." The author of
"Corinne" is less an able painter than an euthu-
siastic thinker and a passionate moralist. It is a
composition full of art; the purity equals the splendour of its style; and it must be remembered among
the monuments of the French language. It is above
all remarkable for the rich suggestions which it
affords for moral meditation. How many strong
ideas, how many profound views, how many fine
and piquant observations, jet out from all its parts,
and spread over all its subjects! "Corinne" alone,
of all the productions of Madame de Staël, appears
to me the work of an artist. It is, nevertheless, in
the "Allemagne" that she shows herself the poet,

[7] *Biographie Universelle,* xl.
[8] Chenier's *Tableau de la Littérature.* Paris, 1818.

especially in the last part.'   Villemain speaks with
equal enthusiasm of its merits : ' " Corinne," he
says, ' is an original, an inspiring work ; a romance,
a poem, a philosophic treatise.   We see in it the
character of Madame de Staël's genius, which excelled, above all, in painting the world and the
human heart, in appreciating and expressing social
life even more than the spectacle of nature and the
arts.   What new and profound interest we feel in
the chief character of this eloquent drama !   What
a charm attaches to this poetic fiction, which seems
the confidence of a superior soul, the history of her
own sufferings ! What enchanting contrasts ! What
vivacity of emotion and of courage ! The alliance
of imagination and of meditative genius gives to
this work originality which never flags.' [9]

Modern readers of fiction are generally dissatis-
fied with ' Corinne,' notwithstanding its transcen-
dant qualities.   Doudan, one of the best critics,
alluding to this failure of the work to meet the expectation of later readers, remarks that ' time has,
on Romances, an effect like that of the sun on beautiful clothes.   When everything changes—manners,
habits, turn of mind, tone of imagination, even the
forms of language—the general character of a fiction must appear very different from what it was to
contemporary readers.   Romances suffer more from
these revolutions of taste than any other kind of
literature, because their principal charm arises from

[9] Villemain's *Cours de Littérature Française*, iv.   Paris. 1873.

their attempt to combine the ideal with everyday life. When a costume has become old-fashioned it is likely to be ridiculous. A man the most distinguished for manners would appear awkward in a modern *salon* clothed in the fashion of Louis XIV. The shades of sentiment have been replaced by other shades which prevail in a new society.' [1]

Happily ' Corinne ' does not require the extent of apologetic criticism which we have given to ' Delphine.' The world is familiar with it, and has determined its rank, moral as well as literary. Madame Necker de Saussure remarks that only from the time of its publication did the great authoress find real satisfaction in her works ; ' envy pardoned her under the name of Corinne ; and she obtained what had been withheld from her, and what she most needed, admiration mixed with sympathy. " Corinne " had a prodigious success. It was adapted to all readers ; artists could draw from it new enthusiasm and new means of expression ; the learned, new and ingenious illustrations ; travellers, happy directions ; critics, observations full of subtlety ; the coldest souls were inspired by its enthusiasm ; in short there was pleasure for malice itself in its characteristic pictures of nationalities. There was only one voice, one cry of admiration, throughout lettered Europe, on its appearance.' [2] Even in critical Edinburgh this enthusiasm prevailed. In spite of the war

[1] Doudan's *Mélanges et Lettres,* ii. Paris, 1876.
[2] *Notice,* etc. i.

some copies reached that city, and produced an inconceivable sensation. Its metaphysicians and geologists, its professors of every kind, stopped one another in the streets to talk of the book. Jeffrey pronounced its authoress, in the 'Edinburgh Review,' the greatest writer in France since the time of Voltaire and Rousseau, and the greatest female writer of any age or country.

Sir James Mackintosh read it with enthusiastic admiration. 'It has been said,' he writes, 'to be a tour in Italy, mixed with a novel. The tour is full of picture and feeling, and of observations on national character so refined that scarcely any one else could have made them, and not very many will comprehend or feel them. What an admirable French character is D'Erfeuil; so free from exaggeration that the French critics say the author, notwithstanding her prejudices, has made him better than her favourite Oswald. Nothing could more strongly prove the fidelity of her picture and the lowness of their moral standard. She paints Ancona, and above all Rome, in the liveliest colours. She alone seems to feel that she inhabited the Eternal City. It must be owned that there is some repetition, or at least monotony, in her reflections on the monuments of antiquity. The sentiment inspired by one is so like that produced by another, that she ought to have contented herself with fewer strokes, and to have given specimens rather than an enumeration. The

attempt to vary them must display more ingenuity
than genius. It leads to a littleness of manner
destructive of gravity and tenderness. In the
character of Corinne, Madame de Staël draws an
imaginary self—what she is, what she had the power
of being, and what she can easily imagine that she
might have become. Purity, which her sentiments
and principles teach her to love; talents and accomplishments, which her energetic genius might
easily have acquired ; uncommon scenes and inci-
dents fitted for her extraordinary mind ; and even
beauty, which her fancy contemplates so constantly
that she can scarcely suppose it to be foreign to
herself, and which in the enthusiasm of invention
she bestows on this adorned as well as improved
self, these seem to be the materials out of which
she has formed " Corinne " and the mode in which
she has reconciled it to her knowledge of her own
character.'—' I read " Corinne " slowly that I may
taste every drop. I prolong my enjoyment, and
really dread the termination. Other travellers
had told us of the absence of public amusements
at Rome, and of the want of conversation among an
indolent nobility ; but, before Madame de Staël, no
one has considered this as the profound tranquillity
and death-like silence which the feelings require
in a place where we go to meditate on the great
events of which it was once the scene, in a magnificent museum of the monuments of ancient times.
How she ennobles the most common scenes ! '—

Again : 'Read the fourth and fifth volumes of
"Corinne." Farewell, "Corinne," powerful and extraordinary book ; full of faults so obvious as not
to be worth enumerating, but of which a single
sentence has excited more feeling and exercised
more reason than the most faultless models of
elegance. To animadvert on the defects of the
story is lost labour. It is a slight vehicle of ideas
and sentiment. The whole object of an incident
is obtained when it serves as a pretext for a reflection or an impassioned word. Yet even here
there are scenes which show what she could have
done if she had been at leisure from thought.
The prayer of the two sisters at their father's
tomb (the opposition of their characters) is capable
of great interest if it had been well laboured.
The grand defect is the want of repose, too much
and too ingenious reflection, too uniform an ardour
of feeling. The understanding is fatigued, the
heart ceases to feel.'—'There is sometimes as
much truth and exactness in Madame de Staël's
descriptions as in those of most cold observers.
Her picture of stagnation, mediocrity, and dulness ;
of torpor animated only by envy ; of mental superiority dreaded and hated without even being
comprehended ; and of intellect gradually extinguished by the azotic atmosphere of stupidity, is
so true ! The unjust estimate of England, which
this Northumbrian picture might have occasioned,
how admirably is it corrected by the observations

of Oswald, and even of poor Corinne, on their second journey—and how, by a few reflections in the last journey to Italy, does this singular woman reduce to the level of truth the exaggerated praise bestowed by her first enthusiasm on the Italians!'[3]

Napoleon was not too much absorbed in his own greatness to be indifferent to so much enthusiasm for the object of his persistent and paltry malice. The official journal of Paris attacked 'Corinne,' and, if we may credit Villemain, the Emperor himself wrote the criticism in the 'Moniteur.' But neither his sceptre nor his pen could touch the indefeasible honours of her genius. She stood out before Europe crowned, like her own heroine, on the capital of the world. But he could still annoy and oppress her, and he now resumed his persecutions, not only of herself, but of her dearest friends, with incredible minuteness, cruelty, and perseverance. 'Hardly,' says her son, 'had " Corinne " appeared, when a new exile commenced for my mother, and she saw all the hopes with which for some months she had consoled herself vanish.

---

[3] *Life* etc., by his Son, vol. i. chap. viii. London, 1836. Her generous heart led her to commemorate some of her friends in *Corinne*. ' I am immortalised in the Prince *Castel-Forte*, the faithful, humble, unaspiring friend of Corinne,' said Schlegel to Mrs. Jameson. (*Sketches of Art, Literature, and Character*, i.) A. Humboldt, Sismondi, Goethe, Madame Récamier, Frederick Schlegel, Frederica Brun, Talma, Alfieri, and particularly Necker, her father, are not only mentioned, but especially honoured, in either her text or her notes.

By a fatality which rendered her anguish the more bitter, it was on the 9th of April, the day of the anniversary of the death of her father, that the order which separated her from her country and friends was sent to her. She returned to Coppet, and the immense success of " Corinne " could hardly mitigate her grief.' [4]

She had contracted (in 1787) an intimate friendship with the Countess of Albany, the unhappy wife of Charles Stuart, the Pretender, and the friend of Alfieri, the tragic writer. The ' royal countess ' was a faithful correspondent of the authoress, and of Sismondi, Bonstetten, and other members of the coterie of Coppet; [5] and the *élite* circles of the château on the shore of Lake Leman and the Casa d'Alfieri at Florence maintained familiar relations during the remainder of the life of Madame de Staël. Sismondi wrote to the Countess (June 1807) : ' Fifteen days ago I was with Madame de Staël at Coppet ; she has ordered her librarian to send you " Corinne." I flatter myself that your approbation will be complete, and that, if France has been only just towards her, Italy will be grateful. You have probably learned that our friend has experienced new grievances. They had allowed her

---

[4] 'Avertissement' to second part of the *Dix Années* etc.

[5] *La Comtesse d'Albany*, par Saint-René Taillandier. Paris, 1862. Compare *Die Gräfin von Albany*, von Alfred von Reumont, 2 vols. Berlin, 1860. For the true character of the relations of the Countess with Alfieri, and later with Fabre, see the entertaining *Souvenirs de Massimo d'Azeglio*, vol. i. 2 vols. Paris, 1876.

to purchase a country place in the valley of Mont-morency by giving her deceitful hopes ; and in-stead of permitting her to inhabit it, they have exiled her to beyond thirty leagues from Paris. She, therefore, returned to Coppet, where I have spent a month with her.'—'Her friends, some per-sons dear to her heart, and who alone can fully understand her, are irrevocably fixed in Paris. Away from Paris, she finds herself exiled from nearly all that can take the place of her family as well as her country. Sensitive as she is, she has maintained a courage which has never belied itself. She has consented to be silent, to wait, to suffer the loss of all things dear to her ; but she refuses a word of homage to power. The Minister of Police (Fouché) demanded only the insertion of a flattery in " Corinne." She answered that she was ready to take out of it anything offensive, but not to add anything to make her court to the government. You see, Madame, that she is devoid of flattery ; and in our times of base-ness and shame this is a real merit.'[6]

She was not to be long so isolated as Sismondi feared. If some of her best friends were for the present ' irrevocably fixed in Paris,' the attractions of Coppet were to be irresistible to them in the coming Parisian summer vacation.

[6] Sismondi's *Lettres inédites*, par Saint-René Taillandier. Paris, 1863. See also Taillandier's *La Comtesse d'Albany*.

CHAPTER XXIV.

COPPET—GERMANY.

At Coppet again—Its Society and Entertainments—Madame Récamier and Prince Augustus of Prussia—Benjamin Constant—Theatricals at Coppet—Bettina von Arnim's Account of her at Mainz—At Frankfurt—Goethe's Mother—Madame de Staël and Fichte—She goes to Vienna—Letters to Madame Récamier—Letter to Talleyrand—Again at Weimar—Interview of her Son with Napoleon—Returns to Coppet.

AGAIN expatriated, Madame de Staël returned to the quiet but saddened scenes of Coppet. A circle ·of select minds [1] soon gathered around her there, and dispelled its melancholy impressions. Among her guests were her old and faithful friend Mathieu de Montmorency; the eccentric but talented Marquis, afterwards Duke, de Sabran, the last heir of one of the most illustrious families of Provence, and destined to be a prisoner for his friendship for her; Lemontey, author of a 'History of the Regency,' and of an 'Essay on the Monarchy of Louis XIV.,' 'censor of the imperial police,' a sordid but a superior man, whom she could consult with advantage; Prosper de Barante, the accomplished critic and historian;

[1] *Coppet et Weimar,* iv.

Benjamin Constant; Madame Récamier; and Prince Augustus of Prussia, who having been liberated as a prisoner of war, made Coppet his home during several weeks, fascinated and retained there by the charms of Madame Récamier. He proposed to marry her, and thus introduce her into the royal family of Berlin. It would not have been difficult, in those times, to obtain a legal release from the obligations of her former, merely nominal, marriage; but, on due reflection, she declined the splendid temptation, yet continued through life the friend and correspondent of the Prince. 'There remains,' says Chateaubriand, 'a monument of this passion in the picture of Corinne which the Prince obtained from Gérard; he presented it to Madame Récamier as an immortal souvenir of the sentiment she had inspired in him, and of the friendship which united Corinne and Juliette.'[2] Besides these guests from a distance, Sismondi, the elder Barante, and many others from Geneva and Lausanne, mingled frequently in the circle.

We have already had some glimpses of the life and society of Coppet. Its attractions were now greater than ever. Its hostess was in improved health and spirits; her fame was European; her *salon* was crowded; the highest subjects were discussed there daily; and music and dramatic performances relieved the graver occupations of the company. In a letter to the Duchess Louise of

[2] *Mémoires d'Outre-Tombe*, viii.

Weimar, she writes (October 13, 1807), 'I shall remain here a month longer; the Prince Augustus of Prussia is still with us. He is about to leave, after spending six weeks here. We have acted tragedies during this period—Madame Récamier, Benjamin Constant, and M. de Sabran taking parts. Benjamin is preparing a piece for the Théâtre Français, on the death of Wallenstein; he has written three admirable acts. We wish to play it on our theatre before our company disperses; then I will depart. Constant will go to Paris to try his drama. It is possible I may commence my journey by the south of Germany, and not reach you till spring.' The niece and adopted daughter of Madame Récamier tells us that Madame de Staël had a passion for the drama, and could throw into her performance 'soul and fire.' 'Though not beautiful she had a good figure, beautiful arms and hands and magnificent eyes; these were advantages on the stage.'[3] They played Racine's 'Phèdre.' 'The illustrious châtelaine herself took the part of the heroine; she claimed her beautiful and timid friend, Madame Récamier, for that of Aricie, Benjamin Constant was Theseus, and Count Sabran was Hippolytus. These amusements attracted to

---

[3] Madame Lenormant does not mention, however, that she had large feet—a fact which gave origin to a pun that mortified her a little. On one occasion she represented a statue the face of which was veiled. A gentleman being asked to guess who the statue was, glanced at the block of marble on which she stood, and answered: 'Je vois *le pied de Staël*' (*le piédestal*).—Mrs. Child's *Memoirs* &c.

Coppet a crowd of curious, critical, and satirical spectators. Imagine Benjamin Constant, with his red hair, his pale blue eyes impaired by his use of glasses, and his gawky German-student appearance, personating the heroic vanquisher of the Minotaur! The Count de Sabran was equally inapt. But these representations amused Madame de Staël.'[4]

Sismondi had become an authority in the circle on subjects of history and political philosophy, but could take no part in its dramatic performances. An unconquerable *gaucherie* kept him from the boards. He was often, however, an oracular arbiter in the high discussions of the table; always acknowledging, nevertheless, the supremacy of Madame de Staël. His friend, Pictet de Sergy, remarks that, ' notwithstanding all that has been written about him, he has never been exactly appreciated. The noble qualities of his heart have never received full justice, while his serious political qualities have, perhaps, been overrated. He was essentially a man of tender affections; an excellent son, loving passionately his remarkable mother; an equally affectionate brother; a more or less sentimental lover; and, in short, after marrying in advanced years an English lady much younger than himself, the best and most gallant of husbands. His opinions were eminently conscientious, but impetuous rather than judicious and well considered. One fact had a strong influence on his life, especi-

[4] *Coppet et Weimar,* **iv.**

ally at its outset ; he was extremely awkward, and
this disadvantage was rendered somewhat grotesque
by an uncontrollable passion for dancing. As with
other men of genius to whom nature has been
unfavourable, this defect led him to take refuge
in prodigious studies which indemnified him for
the absence of the graces. His courageous loyalty
was another and still more honourable title to
the esteem of his friends. Though he was apparently pacific by nature, he on more than one occasion confronted formidable aggressions rather than
compromise a friend. He was connected with a
celebrated Review in which was inserted an article
that wounded the feelings of a man who was too
vain of his nobility. He accused Sismondi of its
authorship, and required him to acknowledge the
charge or name the real author. Sismondi refused
him any answer. A challenge was sent ; Sismondi accepted it, received the fire of his adversary,
and fired his own pistol into the air, declaring, for
the first time, that he was not the writer of the
article. He retired from this ridiculous conflict
with all the honours of war. He had a fine talent
for poetry—a fact unnoticed by his numerous
critics. He figured in the first rank of the faithful
friends of Madame de Staël.'[5]

The two magical charms of the château life
were the conversation of Madame de Staël and the
beauty of Madame Récamier. Chateaubriand

[5] Manuscript *Souvenirs.*

speaks of them with enthusiasm. ' A superb appearance,' he says, ' a sweet smile, an habitual expression of benevolence, the absence of all minute
affectations and of all disagreeable reserve, occasional words of flattery, praises a little direct, but
which seemed to escape from her enthusiasm, an
inexhaustible variety in her conversation, astonishing, attracting, and conciliating all who approached
her, such were the characteristics of Madame de
Staël. I know no woman more convinced of her
own immense superiority over all the world, and
who made others feel the weight of that conviction
less. Nothing was more attractive than the conversation of Madame de Staël and Madame Récamier. The rapidity of the one in expressing a
thousand new thoughts, and of the other in seizing
them and judging them ; the strong and masculine
spirit which unveiled all things, and the fine and
delicate spirit which comprehended all ; those revelations of a trained genius communicated to a
young intellect worthy to receive them—all formed
a combination which it is impossible to describe
without having had the happiness of witnessing it.'[6]

At the approach of winter the circle of the
château dissolved. Montmorency and Madame
Récamier returned to Paris ; the Prince Augustus
re-entered Prussia ; and Madame de Staël, accompanied by her daughter, her youngest son, Schlegel,
and Sismondi, set out for Germany, where she pro-

[6] *Mémoires d'Outre-Tombe,* viii.

posed to resume her studies, begun at her former
visit, preparatory for her next great work, the
' Allemagne.' We get a glimpse or two of her
journey there in Bettina von Arnim's ' Correspondence of Goethe with a Child.' [7] Bettina wrote to
Goethe's mother—' I will just tell you that I supped
with Madame de Staël at Mainz. No lady would
undertake to sit beside her at the table, and un-
comfortable enough it was. The gentlemen stood
around the table and planted themselves behind us,
elbowing one another, only to speak with her or
look at her. They leaned quite over me, and I said
in French, " Your adorers quite suffocate me ; " at
which she laughed. There came at last so many
who all wanted to speak with her across and over
me, that I could endure it no longer and said,
" Your laurels press too heavily upon my shoulders."
I got up and made my way through her admirers.
Then Sismondi, her companion, came and kissed
my hand, and said I had much talent. This he
said over again to the rest, and they repeated it at
least twenty times, as if I had been a Prince from
whom everything sounds clever be it never so
commonplace. I afterwards listened to her conversation about Goethe. She said she had expected
to see a second Werther, but was mistaken, for
neither his manners nor person answered the character ; and she regretted there was nothing of
Werther about him. I was angry at such talk, and

[7] Goethe's *Briefwechsel mit einem Kind.* 3 vols. Berlin, 1835.

turned to Schlegel and said to him in German, ' she has fallen into a two-fold error, first in her expectation, and then in her opinion.' We Germans think Goethe can shake out of his sleeve twenty such heroes, quite as imposing for the French, but that he himself is quite another sort of hero.'

Bettina, the rather mature ' child correspondent' of Goethe, was not the most veracious of writers, and her capricious fancy played tricks with her narrations; but, in her next allusions to the French travellers, we doubtless have an indication, at least, of the almost fantastic prejudice with which intellectual Germany, which had now effectively broken away from the trammels of French literary authority, and detested French political authority, beheld in the person of a turbaned woman the supreme living authority of French letters, attended by a *cortège* of intellectual idolators. The sight was hardly compatible with German notions of either literature or woman. Bettina's next letter was addressed to Goethe himself. ' My ill-luck,' she writes, ' took me to Frankfort exactly as Madame de Staël passed through. I had already enjoyed her society a whole evening at Mainz. Your mother was well pleased to have my assistance, for she had been already informed that Madame de Staël would bring her a letter from you, and she wished me to play the interpreter, if she should need relief during the great catastrophe. The interview took place in the apartments of Maurice Bethmann.

Your mother, either through irony or fun, had decorated herself wonderfully, but with German humour and not in French taste. I must tell you that when I looked at your mother, with three feathers upon her head, which nodded on three different sides, one red, one white, and one blue—the French national colours—rising from out a field of sunflowers, my heart beat with joy and expectation. She was deeply rouged, and her great black eyes fired a burst of artillery. Round her neck she wore the celebrated gold ornaments given her by the Queen of Prussia; magnificent old-fashioned lace (a perfect heirloom) covered her bosom. Thus she stood, with white kid gloves. In one hand was a curiously wrought fan, with which she set the air in motion; the other hand, which was bared, was quite covered with sparkling stones. From time to time she took a pinch out of a gold snuff-box in which was set a miniature of you, representing you with powdered ringlets, thoughtfully leaning your head upon your hand. The party of distinguished elder ladies formed a semicircle in Maurice Bethmann's bedchamber. On the purple carpet, in the centre of which was a leopard on a white ground, the company looked so stately that it might 'well be imposing. On the walls were ranged beautiful Indian plants, and the apartment was lighted by shaded glass globes. Opposite the semicircle stood the bed, upon a daïs of two steps, also covered with purple tapestry; and on each

side was a candelabrum. I said to your mother,
" Madame de Staël will think she is summoned
before the Court of Love, for the bed yonder looks
like the covered throne of Venus." It was thought
that (in that case) she might have much to answer
for. At last the long-expected personage came,
through a suite of lighted apartments, accompanied
by Benjamin Constant. She was dressed as Corinne.
Her turban was of aurora or orange-coloured silk ;
her dress of the same, with an orange tunic, girdled
so high as to leave little room for her heart. Her
black brows and lashes glittered, as did also her
lips, with a mysterious red. Her long gloves were
drawn down, covering only her hand, in which she
held the well-known laurel-sprig. As the apartment where she was expected is on a much lower
level, she was obliged to descend four steps. Un-
fortunately she held up her dress before instead of
behind ; this gave the solemnity of her reception a
terrible blow ; it looked very odd as, clad in complete oriental style, she marched down towards the
stiff dames of the virtue-enrolled Frankfort society.
Your mother darted a few significant glances at me
whilst they were presented to each other. I had
stationed myself apart to observe the whole scene.
I perceived Madame de Staël's astonishment at the
remarkable decorations and dress of your mother,
who displayed immense pride. She spread out her
robe with her left hand ; with her right she saluted ;
playing with her fan, and, bowing her head with

great condescension, she said, with an elevated voice, " Je suis la mère de Goethe "—I am the mother of Goethe. " Ah, je suis charmée "—Ah, I am charmed—answered the authoress ; and then followed a solemn stillness. Then ensued the presentation of her distinguished suite, Schlegel, Sismondi, and Constant, all curious to become acquainted with Goethe's mother. Your mother answered their civilities with a new year's wish in French, which, with solemn curtsies, she kept murmuring between her teeth. In short I think the audience was perfect, and gave a fine specimen of the German *grandezza.* Soon your mother beckoned me to her, and I was forced to play interpreter between them.'

In this whimsical picture the stately Frau von Goethe appears to much less advantage than Madame de Staël herself. Her ceremonious irony must have been the perfection of affectation and discourtesy ; she was growing senile, and was vain of her importance as the ' mother of Goethe ; ' but we must make much allowance for the exaggerating humour of Bettina, though the child correspondent was now about twenty-three years old.[8] The Germans were disposed at first to wonder àt the French authoress, then to be equivocally sarcastic, but at last both to wonder and admire. They could never, however, entirely get rid of their first opinion, that there must be something

8 Her correspondence with Goethe began in the preceding year.

inadmissible in such high intellectual claims on the
part of a woman, and she a Frenchwoman! Her
books, indeed, surprised them, and her conversation fairly dazzled their slower wits ; but she was
so subtle, so oracular! The Pythoness might belong to classic Greece, but could not come out of
France.

The American scholar George Ticknor met at
Berlin, some thirty years later, the old prime
minister Ancillon, who told him a characteristic
anecdote of her visit to that city. ' When she was
here,' he said, ' she excited a great sensation, and
had the men of letters of her time trotted up and
down as it were before her,. successively, to see
their paces. I was present when Fichte's turn
came. After talking a little while, she said, " Now,
Monsieur Fichte, will you be so kind as to give me,
in fifteen minutes or so, a sort of idea, or *aperçu,* of
your system, so that I may know clearly what you
mean by your *ich* (I), your *moi* (me) ; for I am
entirely in the dark about it?" The notion of ex-
plaining, in a little quarter of an hour, to a person
in total darkness, a system which he had been all
his lifetime developing from a single principle
within himself, and spinning as it were from his
own bowels till its web embraced the whole universe, was quite shocking to the philosopher's
dignity. However, being much pressed, he began,
in rather bad French, to do the best he could..
But he had not gone on more than ten minutes

before Madame de Staël, who had followed him with the greatest attention, interrupted him with a countenance full of eagerness and satisfaction. " Ah ! it is sufficient ; I comprehend, I comprehend you perfectly, Monsieur Fichte ; your system is perfectly illustrated by a story in Baron Munchausen's Travels." Fichte looked like a tragedy, the faces of the rest of the company like a *comédie larmoyante.* Madame de Staël heeded neither, but went on. " For, when he arrived once on the banks of a vast river, where there was neither bridge nor ferry, nor even a poor boat or raft, he was at first quite confounded, quite in despair, until at last, his wits coming to his assistance, he took a good hold of his own sleeve and jumped himself over to the other side. Now, Monsieur Fichte, this, I take it, is just what you have done with your *ich,* your *moi,* is it not? " There was so much truth in this, and so much *esprit,* that of course the effect was irresistible on all but poor Fichte himself. As for him he never forgave Madame de Staël, who certainly, however, had no malicious purpose of offending him, and who in fact praised him and his *ich* most abundantly in her " De l'Allemagne." ' [9]

She arrived at Vienna in December 1807, where, as she wrote to the Duchess of Weimar, she received a ' marvellous reception ' at the Court. Placing her youngest son in the Military School of

[9] Ticknor's *Life and Letters,* i. 198.

that city, she remained there to attend his examinations. Meanwhile Schlegel gave, before an applauding audience, his course of lectures on Dramatic Literature, the three volumes of which have been recognised by the literary world as one of his most remarkable productions.

The lavish attentions of courtiers were not what she wished at Vienna; she complained of its lack of 'distinguished men' at the time. She wrote to Madame Récamier: 'I have need of a summer to indemnify me for this winter; for I declare to you that I am *ennuyée*. The attraction of novelty sustained me at first. One becomes disgusted here with frivolities. I assure you that with the exception of my companions, the Prince Tuffiakin is at the top of all the world here; he reigns in conversation. They say the Prince Sapieka is in love with you; you are the only woman of whom such a fact could be true without wishing it. Adieu, dear angel. Ah! it is sad to be in a strange land. "Happy those who have not seen the stranger at their feasts." Exile weighs heavily upon me. The Prince Tuffiakin has your portrait. He is to bring it to me to-morrow, I will make a fête over it! It ought to please you that I have heard you spoken of universally as a person of perfect conduct. Such is your reputation; don't trouble yourself for wounded enemies; be satisfied with what you are in the general opinion. Adieu! adieu! Speak to me, above all, of our next meeting.' Again she writes, on receiving a robe from her beautiful correspondent : ' How this gift touches me ! I gaze on it to find the imprint of your beauty. I will wear it on Tuesday, when I take leave of the Court. I will say to everyone that I have received it from you, and make all the men sigh that you do not wear it here yourself. I have not enjoyed myself this winter. The Prince Augustus writes me a letter full of you. He speaks with enthusiasm of your letters, of your intellect, of your character. I declare you are the happiest person in the world, though you will not believe me. In leaving this city I feel as if I were saying a last adieu to you, for it seems that your memory has inhabited it with me for these five months. I shall be at Coppet on June 30 (1808), where I hope to find Mathieu de Montmorency. How could he suppose I would remain in Germany when I can have the chance of seeing him ? All Germany is not worth two days in his company. Adieu, dear angel ! The Prince Tuffiakin will be with you in fifteen days. Ah, how I envy all who approach you ! '

From Vienna she wrote to Talleyrand (April 3, 1808) : ' You will be astonished to receive a letter from me, whom you have forgotten. At this distance it seems to me that I address you as from another world, and my life has changed so much that I can readily fall into this delusion. I have requested my son to see you and demand of you frankly and simply to interest yourself in the pay-

ment of our claim of two millions, which consti-
tutes more than half our fortune and the inheritance
of my children.   It is a cruel pain for me to think
that I injure my family—that they would be paid
to-morrow, if I no longer existed,   This debt has
a character so sacred, that the Emperor's prejudice
against me can alone prevent him from settling it.
I have said sufficient for you to divine all.   You
wrote me thirteen years ago from America, " If I
must remain even one year more here, I shall die."
I could say as much of my exile.   I succumb beneath it, but the time of pity is past ; necessity has
taken its place.   See, meanwhile, if you can render
any service to my children.'   She adds her usual
lamentations over her sufferings, and the impossibility of satisfying Bonaparte, and concludes as
follows : ' Adieu, shall I never again talk to you ?
I think of going to America ; a country is necessary
for my sons ; I will inquire in New York where
you have lodged.   There are moments in which,
notwithstanding my profound disgust of life, I am
somewhat amiable ; then I think I have learned
this language from you ; but with whom can I
speak it? Having so superior a mind, do you
not sometimes recognise sorrow as inseparable
from all things?   As for me, I wish to distract
myself but cannot ; that which afflicts me above
all else is my inability to give to my children either
their country or their patrimony.   If you can
rescue me from this sorrow I will join this moment

to our last conversation, and the interval shall be filled and crowned.'[1]

Again she writes to Madame Récamier, from Weimar, where, in 1804, she received the first news of the death of her father : ' I suffer cruelly here ; you may imagine what memories seize me. But I believe it a duty to make this sacrifice for the admirable woman who is the sovereign of this little state. I found her ill. Her heroic courage during the battle of Jena has, I fear, permanently prostrated her health. Alas, how unhappy is all this world ! I have been received in Saxe-Weimar in an astonishing manner ; as I passed a gate, the officer of the barrier stopped my carriage and said that for years his chief desire has been to see me, and that he would die content after having at last had that pleasure ; and this scene under various forms has been renewed many times in the hotels. See what I have, dear Juliette, as the only indemnity for the loss of all the happiness of my life.'

Little Weimar had for her attractions which eclipsed all the glories of the Austrian capital. Of the latter she writes : ' It has no arts save music ; its grand assemblies are characterised more by ceremony than pleasure, by a politeness which is mere obsequiousness to an unpolished aristocracy. The line of demarcation between different classes is more inflexible than in other parts of Germany ;

---

[1] Larousse's *Grand Dictionnaire Universel du* 19ᵉ *Siècle,* xiv. Paris, 1875.

the sovereign has no taste, but rather a disdain
for letters, and consequently there is an absolute
absence of emulation in the labours of the mind.'
She had obviated, however, in her own household
circle, these disadvantages. Sismondi lodged with
her and was, says his biographer, ' surrounded,
especially at her Monday suppers, with an *élite*
society which comprised men and women who were
most distinguished by rank and talent—persons
of polished manners and sparkling language. He
there played comedies with princes, dukes, and
counts, of Germany and Russia.' But they are
described as otherwise ' inert, without motives,
without will, discouraged and depressed by the
condition of the Court.'

While she was still in Germany, her eldest son
(then about seventeen years of age) had an interview with Bonaparte as the latter passed through
Savoy, and entreated him to mitigate, at least, the
proscription of his mother. The youth made a
record of the conversation; it shows much good
sense and generous temper on his part, in contrast
with the imperious selfishness of the Emperor.
' Your mother,' said the latter, ' could not be six
months in Paris before I should be compelled to
send her to Bicêtre, or the Temple. I should regret this necessity, for it would make a noise and
might injure me a little in public opinion. Say,
therefore, to her, that as long as I live she cannot
re-enter Paris. I see what you wish, but it cannot

be ; she will commit follies ; she will have the world around her ; she will make jokes about me,' &c.[2]

In June, 1808, she was again at Coppet working on the 'Allemagne.' Baron von Vohgt, a man of intellect, was there, assisting her by his conversations ; Sismondi was there, preparing the fifth volume of his 'Italian Republics ;' Schlegel was there, busy in the preparation of his lectures on Dramatic Art, for publication at Heidelberg ; Constant was there, preparing his 'Wallenstein' for the press ; Mathieu de Montmorency spent some time there, and no man was more welcome ; Etienne Dumont, the associate of Mirabeau (some of whose best speeches he composed), afterwards the friend and editor of Jeremy Bentham, was there, occasionally at least.[3] Madame Récamier cheered her friend by frequent letters, and by the promise of a visit, and of her company in another journey to Vienna. Letters passed often between Weimar and Coppet ; the Duchess Louise, esteemed, since the battle of Jena, even by Napoleon's own admission, as one of the great characters of the time, kept up her correspondence with the authoress, and the marble bust of the latter, by Tieck, was honoured with a place in the palace of Weimar.

[2] *Œuvres diverses de la Baronne de Stäel.* Paris, 1829.

[3] The controversy excited by Dumont's posthumous *Souvenirs* (1832) about the composition of Mirabeau's speeches by Dumont, Reybaz, Clavière, and Du Roveray—all Swiss—has been conclusively settled by more than fifty letters of Mirabeau, left by Reybaz to the public library of Geneva, where they are deposited.

CHAPTER XXV

LIFE AT COPPET.

Madame Récamier—Religious Conversation with Madame de Krüdner —The Duchess of Saxe Weimar—Werner—His Account of Coppet —Oehlenschlaeger a Guest there—Ritter's Visits—Her Opinion on Preaching—Her Distinction between Morality and Religion.

THE years 1808, 1809, and 1810 were devoted to the preparation of her work on Germany; but the hospitalities and amusements of Coppet went on as usual. We are dependent on casual letters, and other contemporary but mostly ephemeral sources, for some glimpses of the interior of the château during this period. Soon after the return of its hostess Madame Récamier proposed to visit her in the coming autumn; but she declined the offer, fearing it might involve her friend in her own per-sccntions, a calamity which subsequently befel her. 'It is kind of you,' she wrote, 'to think of relieving my sad winter months. No, indeed, I cannot accept such a sacrifice. Should there not be war, I will return to my son at Vienna. It is next year that I hope to see you somewhere; it will be too much to pass two years away from you. Mathieu de Montmorency has been here ten days; in ten days more I shall lose him. It is thus that life passes; friendship for me is only suffering. Perhaps in case of war Prince Augustus will remain at Koenigsburg. I have received a letter from his sister, who wishes to see me at Toeplitz. Can you be tempted to accompany me? They expect you there. But only exiles need to travel; I am always struggling between the desire of seeing and the fear of injuring you. I send you a Vienna robe; it is not as magnificent as your gift to me, but you will look well in it.'—'I have met the Prince of Bavaria' (afterwards King Ludwig), 'who eagerly demanded news of you; he tells me that the Government disapproves his friendship for both you and me. He has intellect, but it is enclosed in an inferior casket.'[1]

In 1808 she had another interview with Madame de Krüdner, who was now animated with the intensest ardour for her new life, and had gone to Geneva in prosecution of the religious mission which she pursued with unabated zeal over much of Europe through the remainder of her years. She spoke with fervour to Madame de Staël of her spiritual consolations, of the delicious calm she enjoyed after so many storms. 'Ah, yes,' responded Madame de Staël, 'it is this repose that I need, this calm after which I sigh, and that I cannot obtain.' Madame de Krüdner's daughter, who shared her mother's devout zeal, replied: 'Never-

---

[1] *Coppet et Weimar,* v.

theless, Madame, it is not in repose that one advances.' ' Pardon me, Mademoiselle,' rejoined Madame de Staël, with her characteristic readiness and courtesy, ' pardon me, you are precisely a proof of the contrary.' Her clear and candid reason could not fail to perceive the weaker elements of Madame de Krüdner's nature ; but sincere piety always commanded her reverent interest, and she could not conceive of piety as destitute of enthusiasm. In the ' Allemagne,' which she was now writing, she says : ' If enthusiasm intoxicates the soul with happiness, it also, by a singular prestige, sustains the soul in misfortune. It leaves behind it some profound and luminous trace. It serves as a refuge against the bitterest sorrows, and it is the only sentiment which can calm without chilling us.' [2] A year later Madame de Krüdner's biographer says that her relations with Madame de Staël had become more intimate since the interview at Geneva. They corresponded ; and Madame de Krüdner wrote her ' of her consolations, her calm, the joys of prayer and of the love of God.' She recounted to her her life, but without relating the extraordinary facts which would have astonished without edifying her. She had a high idea of the sincerity of Madame de Staël, and believed that she would discover the truth. She admired the vivid sensibility, the good sense and uprightness of her passionate soul, so apparent in all her life and

[2] *De l'Allemagne*, iv. 12.

writings, and, confiding in the ultimate success of her appeals, did not press them with indiscreet zeal. 'Madame de Staël,' she wrote, 'feels herself to be very far from the haven. She is frank and true. I fear the effect of over much zeal with her; this is useless, it is necessary to let her take her own way; it is necessary to pray; time is necessary, and the disgust of the world, and a thousand things which cannot be hastened. She cannot be compelled; God alone can draw her; she will not escape him.'[3] Madame de Staël could be an enthusiast, but hardly a mystic, still less a fanatic.

To the Duchess of Saxe Weimar she wrote (February, 1809), 'I have sent you "Wallenstein," and am impatient to know your estimate of it. Has the Duke received the "Duke de Ligne," edited by me?[4] I should like to have his opinion of it. "Wallenstein" makes a great sensation in Paris; it is a literary event; the critics contend for and against it with furor. My son Auguste will leave in May for America; I look with great emotion to such a separation.[5] I shall pass the summer at Coppet, and I hope to publish my book in the following winter. This is all I know of my sad future. Have you been told that we acted one of Werner's pieces here, and that the lady of honour of your sister the Queen' (Dowager of Prussia)

[3] *Vie,* &c. i.

[4] She published in 1809 *Lettres et Pensées du Prince de Ligne.* See her Preface, *Œuvres,* ii.

[5] The young Baron did not go to America.

'acted the part of the wife? The piece is singular
and produced extraordinary effects. I pray you
continue to remember me kindly. Whenever a
profound discouragement seizes me, I think that
you love me and my soul is relieved.'

Werner was one of her most interesting guests
at this time. In another letter to the Duchess she
says: 'I am singularly attached to him; such a
union of intellect and heart, of nature and enthusiasm, of gaiety and sadness, is quite unique, and
what tact combined with force he has.' Werner was a ' character '—eccentric, capricious, vivid
with enthusiasm, a lyrical poet and author of
numerous tragedies, a mystic, ' half socialistic, half
religious,'[6] and singularly devoted to Freemasonry,
which, with his other hobbies, he endeavoured to
promote by his dramatic talents. His youth was
spent in excessive dissipation; a few years after our
present date he renounced Protestantism in Rome,
became a Catholic priest, and devoted himself
with his characteristic ardour to preaching. His
passionate and poetic style in the pulpit rendered
him extremely popular. Some of his sermons
remain in print. His tragedy on the ' Death of
the Maccabees' was written after he became a priest,
as were also some good examples of his religious
poetry. Oehlenschlaeger wrote: ' One day Werner
entered the hall with a profound reverence, having
a large snuff-box in his narrow vest pocket, and

[6] *Coppet et Weimar*, v.

his nose full of tobacco. He spoke French badly, but that did not annoy him in the least. He daily discussed, in his patois, at the table, his mystic æsthetics; they listened to him very devoutly, and he did not fail to make converts.'[7] Werner wrote to Counsellor Schneffer that 'Madame de Staël is a queen, and no man of intelligence who comes within her circle can escape from it, for she retains us by a sort of magic. These men are not, as is foolishly supposed in Germany, busied in assisting her literary works; on the contrary they receive from her a social education. She possesses an admirable talent for harmonising the most divergent elements, and all who approach her, however divided in opinions, are united in adoring this idol. She is of middle size, and her figure, without having the elegance of a nymph, is very well proportioned. She is vigorous and a brunette; her face is certainly not very beautiful, but you forget all else as soon as you see her superb eyes, in which a great divine soul not only sparkles but shoots out fire and flame.'

Oehlenschlaeger, the Danish poet, was a guest at Coppet about this time, and recounts his impressions of its cultivated society. He was still a young man, full of genius, but with the usual sensitiveness and caprices of the artistic temperament. He was now rapidly producing those great works which soon made him the 'national poet' of

[7] Morell's *Karl von Bonstetten* &c. Winterthur, 1864.

the Danes, and the acknowledged Scandinavian chief of the Romantic school. Besides his dramatic talent, he was already distinguished by that varied culture which rendered his æsthetic lectures at the University of Copenhagen a centre of attraction to crowded assemblies down to the middle of our century. Before his present visit to Coppet, he had mingled with youthful enthusiasm in the literary society of Madame de Staël in the Rue du Bac at Paris, and she had invited him to spend a summer at her château. In the capital he had found consolation, while struggling with pecuniary embarrassments, in her unrivalled conversation and that of Schlegel and Constant, and composed, in his 'humble chamber,' three of his 'most noble tragedies,' his 'Hakon Jarl,' 'Palnatoke,' and ' Axel and Walborg,' which he sent to Copenhagen, where they were received with acclamation.[8] Of his visit to Coppet he writes: ' Madame de Staël greeted me with cordiality and entreated me to spend some weeks with her, indulging in graceful pleasantries meanwhile on the faults of my French. I then addressed her in German, which she understood very well, as did also her two children. I found with her Benjamin Constant, Augustus Schlegel, the old Baron Vohgt of Altona, Bonstetten of Geneva, the celebrated Sismondi, and the Count de Sabran, the only person in all the com-

---

[8] *Oehlenschlaeger, le Poète National du Danemark,* par J. Le Fevre Deumier, iv. Paris, 1854.

pany who did not know German. Schlegel seemed
to me polished but cold. Madame de Staël was not
beautiful, but there was in the lustre of her black
eyes an irresistible charm ; and she possessed in
the highest degree the power of subduing opinion-
ated men, and of reconciling repellent characters.
Her voice was strong, her face was somewhat
masculine, but her soul was tender and delicate.
She was writing at this time her book on Germany,
and read to us parts of it every day ; she has been
accused of not having studied the books of which
she speaks in this work, and of being completely
subject to the dictation of Schlegel. This is false.
She read German with the greatest ease. Schlegel
had doubtless some influence wtih her, but she
often disputed his opinions and accused him of partiality. Schlegel, for whose erudition and intellect
I have great respect, was in fact imbued with
partiality. He placed Calderon above Shakespeare ;
he severely blamed Luther and Herder. He was,
like his brother, infatuated with aristocracy. If
you add to all the qualities of Madame de Staël
her wealth and her generosity, you will not be
astonished that she lived in her enchanted château
as a queen or a fairy. Her magic wand was a
little branch of a tree, which a domestic placed
every day on the table by the side of her plate,
and which she handled during the conversations.'
A fan, an ivory or silver paper-knife, or a simple
roll of paper, was sometimes her sceptre.

Coppet was not entirely an intellectual heaven; its little court, like all other courts, like that of Olympus itself, had its internal disturbances, and both the head and heart of its queen were sometimes tasked to maintain its tranquillity amidst the varied and aspiring courtiers who, though always ready to bow under her gracious sway, were sensitive rivals and tenacious of the creeds of their respective political, literary, or philosophical schools. Two such susceptible and eccentric characters as Werner and Oehlenschlaeger could hardly contribute to its good order. They were both consummately vain. The Dane was incessantly presenting his unfledged literary productions for criticism, or rather for admiration. The German was mysteriously reticent of his until he could give them flight in full plumage. Oehlenschlaeger resented this lack of confidence and reciprocity, and a whimsical scene ensued which required the best management of the hostess. 'What do you think?' cried the Dane. 'I have submitted my new piece to him, and he will not say a word to me about his own; is not this a shame?' 'Why?' asked Madame de Staël, gaily; 'Werner feels independent of everybody, and can be so; his talents justify him. With you, my friend, the case is otherwise; you are developing yourself.' The answer was frank but not impertinent. The offended poet said not another word, but suddenly quitting the place, retreated to his chamber and prepared to leave the château. As he did not re-appear at the accustomed hour, she sent to in-quire what detained him. On learning that he was about to depart she went to him herself, and ap-peased him at last by her fascinating influence. ' Acknowledge,' he cried, as his irritation gave way, ' that I have reason on my side ; you do not know my works, perhaps ; I have written as much as Werner ; I do not believe that I have much to learn from him. If I had to return to school, it would not be to him.' Madame de Staël did not attempt to justify her preference, but acknowledg-ing that her friendship for Werner might have carried her too far, she won again the heart of the exasperated poet, and led him back to the com-pany. He lost, as we have seen, none of his good opinions of his hostess ; on the contrary, he worked diligently in the château during several weeks on a composition which he designed to be a ' Souvenir of Coppet '—his ' Correggio,' which has been called (not altogether justly), ' the richest gem in the jewel-casket of Oehlenschlaeger.' [9]

Karl Ritter, travelling in Switzerland about this period, says : ' Her hospitable château stands open for all intelligent foreigners. I was diffident of introducing myself there, but I was deeply inte-rested to visit this lady and her guests, so educated and so educating.' He met her in Geneva, and afterwards, by invitation, at Coppet. 'Led on by

[9] Deumier's *Oehlenschlaeger,* iv.

Schlegel,' he continues, ' we came quickly to speak of German history, art, and language. I found out her knowledge of them. We went to the table, where we were lively enough, and *bons mots*, puns, witticisms, flew right and left. Madame de Staël appeared to me more interesting than when I saw her at Frankfort. I am sure she must always gain by a more intimate acquaintance. She has rare goodness of heart and a charming simplicity. She pronounced German very well, and cited our authors readily. She conversed also in English and Italian, and quoted Latin sometimes, but without affectation. I have seen her often brilliant and at times truly inspired.' He mentions an instance of her inspiration in a conversation in which Sismondi undertook the defence of a preacher whom they had recently heard, and whose discourse was more didactic than religious. Sismondi's faith was that of his American friend and correspondent, Channing of Boston.[1] Religion, he contended, must be substantially morality ; otherwise it will rest only in feeling, and, having no principle, it will become isolated, and therefore fanciful and fanatical, and produce those excesses from which Europe has suffered for ages so many evils. Religion needs firmness ; the understanding can alone give it firmness. Madame de Staël responded, and her ' inspiration,' continues Ritter, ' lasted nearly an

---

[1] See his letters to Channing, *Fragments de son Journal et Correspondance.* Genève, 1857.

hour.   Never in the whole course of my life have
I felt more nervous agitation ; I had cramps even
to the ends of my fingers.   There was in her something of that power which Alcibiades attributes, in
the Banquet, to the word of Socrates.'

This conversation was profoundly interesting to
the earnest mind of Ritter, more even for its theological significance than for its extraordinary eloquence.   It confirmed in him that spiritual tendency
which, contrary, as he says, to his early habits of
thought, ripened at last into the pure, simple, rich
moral life which consoled and beautified the declining years of the great geographer. 'Sismondi,'
he remarks, ' had been very emphatic at first, but
his words were to Madame de Staël's mind like fire
falling upon tinder.   She attacked his narrow view
of religion on all sides with overwhelming arguments
and examples.   She showed the higher relation of
religion to the nature of man, as the source of all
virtue, the condition of all morality ; how morality
is a necessity of our ordinary life, religion a necessity of our higher life ; morality directs us, but it
presupposes a force, a power to be directed ; morality is didactic and appeals to the understanding,
religion inspires, pervades our whole being, and
brings us into direct communion with the Deity.
This is the true function of public worship.   This
elevation of the whole man is at the same time an
ennobling of each part in detail.   A strong religious
sentiment may be the source of all moral principles

and actions. The subject was so entirely congenial
to her, her analysis was so clear, her illustrations so
luminous, her positions so crowded with ideas, that
I consider this conversation one of the most interesting facts in my life. Sismondi, who could no
longer defend himself, exclaimed : " But would
you not have morality in sermons ? To what
will all feeling lead if not directed by reason ? "
She agreed with him heartily, and replied, " I would
have reason, but not *reasoning*, in every sermon."
But I find it impossible to reproduce such a conversation. I have found that she appears to much
more advantage in conversation than in her writings. She is regal, queenly in the former.' Ritter
alludes to many other interesting discussions with
the select minds of Coppet, especially with Schlegel,
who was now deep in the study of the Nibelungenlied,
and disposed to talk about it; but none of them, he
says, made so deep an impression upon his mind as
this magnificent conversation. Though chiefly on
preaching, it related to ' the essence of religion, and
her thoughts and feelings were expressed with a
captivating power, a fire, and an irrefutable logic,'
before which no opposition could stand. ' If she
has not the first imagination in Europe, she is
certainly one of the most gifted of women;'—'all
Geneva was talking about her '—' a lady who is
banished from her country by an Emperor who
does not fear all Europe, yet is frightened at her.'

'Her intimate friends are all fascinated by her. Apart from her amiability, her misfortunes, and the inward power with which she confronts the scoffing of fate, give her the greatest claim to our admiring sympathy.' [2]

[2] *Carl Ritter : ein Lebensbild, nach seinem handschriftlichen Nachlass dargestellt,* von G. Krammer, i. p. 290. 2 vols. Halle, 1864.

CHAPTER XXVI.

LIFE AT COPPET—CONTINUED.

Madame le Brun, the Artist, at Coppet—Her Portrait of Corinne—Sis-- mondi's Letters to the Countess of Albany about Coppet—Bon- stetten in love with the Countess—Madame de Stäel and Talma— The ' Allemagne '—Sismondi's Opinion of it—Theology at Coppet —Baron Vohgt there—Chateauvieux—Bonstetten's Account of Coppet.

MADAME LE BRUN, the artist, travelled in Switzerland in 1808 and 1809, and spent some time at Coppet, greatly enjoying its society, and making one of the most noted portraits of the authoress. In a letter to the Countess Potocka, she writes: ' I have passed a week with Madame de Staël, and have read her last romance, " Corinne, ou l'Italie." Her face so animated and so full of genius has given me the idea of representing her as Corinne seated on a rock with a lyre in her hand. I paint her in antique costume. She is not beautiful, but the animation of her visage takes the place of beauty. To aid the expression I wished to give her, I entreated her to recite tragic verses while I painted. She declaimed passages from Corneille and Racine. I propose to take the portrait to

Paris and there give it the last touches. I find many persons established at Coppet: the beautiful Madame Récamier, the Count de Sabran, a young Englishwoman, Benjamin Constant, &c. Its society is continually renewed. They come to visit the illustrious exile who is pursued by the rancour of the Emperor. Her two sons are now with her under the instruction of the German scholar Schlegel; her daughter is very beautiful, and has a passionate love of study. Madame de Staël receives with grace and without affectation; she leaves her company free all the morning; but they unite in the evening. It is only after dinner that they can converse with her. She then walks in her *salon*, holding in her hand a little green branch; and her words have an ardour quite peculiar to her; it is impossible to interrupt her. At these times she produces on one the effect of an improvisatrice. I have seen "Semiramis" played at Coppet. Madame de Staël acted as Azema; she was very successful in some passages of this *rôle*, but her acting was unequal. Madame Récamier, her friend, nearly died with fear in her part of Semiramis; M. de Sabran was not too much at home in his *rôle* of Arsace. I have always observed that comedies and proverbs can be tolerably well played in society, but never tragedies.'[1]

[1] *Souvenirs de Madame Vigée le Brun*, ii. Paris, 1869. The portrait here mentioned was during many years in the family of Madame Necker de Saussure, but is now in the Musée Rath of Geneva.

One of her most appreciative guests, who still lives, insists that she was as successful in tragedy as in comedy. 'The great *salle* of the *rez-de-chaussée* of the château was,' he writes, 'converted into a complete and permanent theatre; and there she and her friends acted not merely comedy, but more frequently tragedy. The Marquis de Sabran, being small of stature, appeared nearly crushed under the helmet of Pyrrhus; Madame Récamier represented Andromache, and Madame de Staël personated with marvellous effect Hermione. The Counts de la Bédoyère threw their youthful French vivacity into the plays. From time to time Madame de Staël left her feudal home and transported all her noble *cortège* to Geneva, where they gave representations in the great building called the Douane, on the Place du Molard. All the best society of the city descended from the Rue des Granges or the Taconnerie into this large hall of the common people, borne thither by an irresistible impulse—a place where they seldom deigned to be found, especially at night. There I still see Madame de Staël, imposing and terrible, in the *rôle* of Phædra; and Benjamin Constant, but not, as they have lately reported him, personating Hippolytus in blue spectacles which he absolutely refused to lay aside. The Genevese were enthusiastically grateful for the complaisance of Madame de Staël in thus bringing among them her actors and theatrical apparatus. I agree with her cousin that in tragedy she produced truly grand effects. When she could identify herself, by her predominant natural susceptibilities, with her characters, when the sentiments she was to represent on the stage were in perfect harmony with those which filled her own heart, she moved all her audience profoundly. Such, for example, I remember, was the effect of her Biblical play, in which she retraces the history of Hagar in the desert sustaining her child who was perishing of thirst. She personated Hagar, and her young daughter, Albertine, the child. Nothing could be more heart-rending than the despair of the mother beholding her child about to expire for lack of water which she could not discover in the desert. Madame de Staël and her daughter were sublime in the expression of their respective sentiments ; maternal and filial love were irresistibly affecting in the ardour of their reciprocal embraces.' [2]

Sismondi sent to the Countess of Albany frequent news of Coppet and of its principal guests, particularly of Bonstetten, who was a universal favourite by reason of the geniality of his heart as well as the originality of his mind. The ' royal countess ' had some tender recollections of the amiable philosopher, and her Coppet correspondents probably supposed that their tacit allusions to them would afford her pleasure. Bonstetten,

---

[2] Pictet de Sergy's manuscript *Souvenirs.*

in his old age,[3] records with evident feeling the romantic episode of his youth which kept her memory still fresh in his soul. 'The society of the Stuarts,' he says, 'had a great charm for me. The king'—her brutalised husband, Charles Edward, the Pretender—'showed me friendship. I was in love with the queen, without avowing it; she loved me without then acknowledging it.' They frequently corresponded. 'In 1780,' he continues, 'she separated from her husband, and retired into a convent (Santi Apostoli, Rome) whence she wrote me letters full of vivacity and affection. A few years later she appointed me a meeting at Baden, in Switzerland. I received at the same time a letter from Madame Necker, who invited me to visit her, her husband and daughter, at Lausanne. Uncertain which to accept, and when on the point of deciding for the queen, I was informed that she was accompanied by a young Italian, who was ardently in love with her. He was Alfieri, then without distinction. I decided for the Neckers.' It was in this visit that he saw again, after some years, the precocious child of St. Ouen now, as we have before cited, 'full of the charms of youth, of intellect, and of coquetry.' The 'queen of hearts,' as he named the Countess, 'was, when I saw her at Rome, of middling size, blonde, with dark blue eyes, a nose slightly turned up, a fair complexion like that

---

[3] His *Souvenirs* were written in 1832, when he was eighty-seven years old.

of the English, and was gay, piquant, and sensible enough to turn all heads. Thirty-three years later I saw again her whom I had left a budding rose. Happily it was in the twilight ; she had the same voice and a little of the same look ; all the rest was gone ; she was an old woman. But I forced my heart to enshrine as by magic her whom I had seen at Rome. My first care on returning to my lodging was to face the mirror and see whether I looked old. I was astonished not to find myself horrible. The Queen of England had, meanwhile, an air of dignity which befitted her age, and still more the buskin style of Alfieri with whom she lived.'

But let us return to the date of our narrative. Sismondi wrote to her from Coppet (August 12, 1808) : ' You have been impressed without doubt with the perfect amiability of Bonstetten, whom you have lost from view for so many years. The more I compare him with all whom I know, the more I am struck and confounded by the ever-fresh grace and activity of his mind. It is not the present generation nor the education of our times that can produce such a man.[4] We have

[4] There is a bust of him by Christen in the Rath Museum of Geneva—a head worthy of the classic Greek. This gallery has quite a collection of portraits and busts of the *dramatis personæ* of our narrative. Besides Madame le Brun's painting, and the bust of Bonstetten, there is a bust of Madame de Staël ; a bust by Houdan, and a miniature in enamel, of Necker ; busts of Sismondi (by Pradier), of Benjamin Constant (by Bra), of Etienne Dumont (by David portraits of Candolle, Dr. Tronchin, &c. There are examples also in the gallery of the neighbouring University.

passed the greater part of the summer at Coppet
with Madame de Staël, Constant, and Schlegel.
We frequently have guests worthy of such society,.
and forget there the beautiful sky of Italy ; nevertheless some of us think of returning some day or
other, and all those of us who have known you
entertain among their chief motives for revisiting
Florence their desire to see you.'   Later he writes :
'We have had at Coppet Werner the tragic poet,
author of " Luther," of " Wanda," of " Attila," and
one of the most distinguished men of Germany.   I
hope you will become acquainted with him if he
goes to Italy.   One is happy to know, through its
chief prophet, that mystic poetry which has completely assumed the ascendency in Germany, and
holds all that country in a sort of somnambulism.
Werner is a man of very much intellect, of exceeding
grace, of tact and gaiety of mind, to which he joins
sensibility and profundity.   He considers himself
called to go forth and preach love through the
world ; he is the apostle and professor of love.
His tragedies have no other object than to spread
the religion of holy love, and they ought to succeed,.
for he has the most admirable versification yet seen
in Germany, and an imagination so rich and so
original that in spite of his mental eccentricities
we cannot but admire him.'   In May, 1809, he
writes : 'We are at present reunited at Coppet.
Madame de Staël has all her children around her,
but the eldest is about to leave for America to

look after her estates there, and to make arrange-
ments for the voyage of his mother, for she wishes
next year to seek peace and liberty beyond the
Atlantic.   It is impossible to tell you how much I
suffer from this prospect, how deeply I am plunged
in misery at the thought of the solitude I must
then endure.   The eight or nine years that I have
known her, living always near her, and becoming
more attached to her every day, have rendered
her society a necessity of my life.   Ennui, sadness,
discouragement, oppress me whenever I am far
from her.   We have still here Sabran and Schlegel,
and Bonstetten will soon return.   We are assured
of the most brilliant company from Paris for the
next summer, but I am not anxious for it.   I
wish not to add to our circle.'

In the same month he writes: 'Madame de
Staël goes to Lyons, accompanied by her eldest son.
She will stay there as long as Talma continues to
play in tragedy at its theatre.   Alas! she goes to
seek distraction with little hope of finding it.   Her
son will soon leave for America; a considerable
portion of their fortune is beyond the Atlantic, and
at this moment, when all this old corrupt world is
falling into dissolution, it is more important than
ever to secure a retreat, a means of independence, a guarantee of liberty, beyond the circle of
our European revolutions.   However wise such a
voyage may be, she suffers intensely at the thought
of it.   But enough for our individual troubles; you

know what are the public ones, how every courier announces disasters upon the friends to whom we are attached, the hosts to whose hospitality we have been indebted, upon entire cities which are ruined or burned. You can judge what is our habitual sadness. No one of us has any more courage to labour. One takes a disgust for literature, for study, for thought, when life is so heavy; one feels himself in the midst of universal death. I would like to sleep always, to relieve myself of the impressions of the events of the day, and the useless effort which a powerless philosophy makes to turn in upon itself for comfort in such times.'

Some three weeks later he writes to the Countess from Lyons, whither he had gone to join Madame de Staël. 'If she goes' (to America) 'I will go immediately to Italy to attempt to relieve my mind of this immense loss, and to seek some distraction in a change of scene and of habits. I have told you that she is here to see Talma. I have followed with hardly an object—less to see the king of the French stage than not to be separated from her in the state of sadness and even of illness which she is now enduring. I will return to Geneva the day after to-morrow; she will return in about a fortnight. She has desired long and ardently to see Talma; she has spoken often of this privation as one of the great misfortunes of her exile; but now her mind is little free to enjoy the drama. Nevertheless, as she combines in herself tragic talent with that of declamation, it is of all things that which, apart from her affections, can most powerfully interest her. Bonstetten returned on the day I left. He appears so young that one thinks he must have deceived time by enchantment, and I fear that the least accident may break the charm.[5] You have learned what extraordinary success has attended the " Mélanges " of the Prince de Ligne, edited by Madame de Staël ; the work has already reached its third edition ; but all this glory can hardly console the old general for the misfortunes of his country.'

She studied thoroughly Talma's remarkable genius during this visit to Lyons, and has devoted several pages of her ' Allemagne ' to him. ' Madame de Staël alone,' says his biographer, ' has painted for posterity, with that powerful and original touch which is peculiar to her, this imposing dramatic figure.' [6]

Returning to Coppet, she resumed her literary labours with renewed vigour. Her ' Allemagne ' was the chief subject of interest and discussion in the circle of the château. Sismondi, writing to the Countess of Albany (Sept. 6, 1809), says : ' She has completed about a quarter of the work, but that which is written appears to me superior to all that we have yet had from her pen. It is not, like

---

[5] He was now fifty-four years old, and died at eighty-seven, after giving to the world some twenty-five volumes.

[6] *Mémoires Historiques et Critiques sur Talma*, par Regnault Warrin, chap. xviii. Paris, 1827.

"Corinne," the frame of a romance in which obser-vations on national character are presented ; she treats her subject directly, and handles it with a force that no one would expect in a woman. There is a truly admirable depth in its judgments of national traits, in its intellectual pictures, &c. Nothing so new, so impartial, and so incisive, has yet been written, I think, on the character of any nation.'[7]

The circle at the château 'presented,' says a Genevan writer, 'the aspect of a synod of quite novel character. The different systems of religion were strongly contrasted there. Catholicism was represented by Mathieu de Montmorency, Quietism by M. de Langallerie, Illuminism by M. de Divonne, Rationalism by Baron Vohgt, Calvinism by the pastor Maulinie. Even Benjamin Constant, then occupied with his work on Religions, brought his tribute to the theological conferences— conferences which borrowed no austerity from the accidents of the time or the place. The conversations at dinner and in the evening were chiefly on religious subjects of the most mystic nature, and were seldom changed even for the news of the day or for brief musical entertainments.'[8]

Baron Vohgt had been introduced to Coppet by Madame Récamier, for whom he entertained a passionate admiration. He was an enthusiastic

[7] *Lettres inédites,* &c. *passim.*
[8] M. Petit-Senn ; Vulliet's *La Famille.* Lausanne, 1873.

German, fond of the society of celebrities, devoted
to intellectual culture and to philanthropic and
agricultural experiments, which he pursued among
his peasants on his large estate near Hamburg,
and which led to intimate relations between him
and De Gérando and Camille Jordan—two other
occasional guests and correspondents of Coppet.[9]
The good and sentimental Baron was a favourite in
the circle of the château ; allusions to him have
already occurred several times in our pages ; they
recur constantly in the Coppet correspondence
about these times.   He fell in love with Madame
Récamier, and was a worshipper of Madame de
Staël, though he deserted her in the time of her
greatest sufferings at the hands of the government.
In the autumn of 1810, when the depression mentioned · by Sismondi had somewhat given way,
Vohgt wrote to Madame Récamier : 'It is to you
that I owe the perfectly cordial reception I have
had at Coppet.   Without doubt the favourable
opinion of me that you produced there has procured my acquaintance with this unique woman ;
by you I have been able to penetrate into the intimacy of this beautiful and sublime soul, and to
discover how far superior she is to her reputation.   She is an angel sent from heaven to
reveal goodness on earth.   She is irresistible ; a
pure celestial light embellishes her spirit and

[9] *Madame Récamier : les Amis de sa Jeunesse et sa Correspondance
intime.*   2 vols.   Paris, 1872.

renders her amiable in all aspects.   Both profound
and gay, revealing at one time a mysterious depth
of soul—showing at another the slightest shade of
sentiment—her intellect shines serenely, sometimes
as a brilliant summit, at others as a sweet twilight.
Without doubt some errors, some feebleness, veil
at times this celestial apparition ; the initiated
themselves are, perhaps, afflicted by those occasional eclipses which the astronomers of Geneva
attempt in vain to calculate and predict.   The life
which is led at Coppet agrees perfectly with me ;
its society still more.   I love the wit of Constant,
the erudition of Schlegel, the amiability of Sabran,
the talent and character of Sismondi, the simplicity,
truthfulness, and intellectual soundness of Auguste
the son, and the *spirituelle* gentleness of Albertine
the daughter.   I must not forget Bonstetten ; good,
excellent, full of varied knowledge—so facile in
mind and character, so rich in all that inspires
esteem and confidence.   Your great friend animates and enlivens all around her, and imparts
mind to all.   In every corner some one is at work
on some intellectual task.   Corinne herself writes
her delicious " Letters on Germany ; " [1] this will
doubtless be her best work.   She is also finishing
her " Shunamite," an oriental melodrama, which
will be played in October, and is charming.
Coppet will weep at the representation of it.   Con-

---

[1] The *Allemagne* was composed in the form of letters, but was
altered, before publication, to that of chapters.

stant and Auguste are each writing a tragedy,. Sabran a comic opera, Sismondi his history, Bonstetten his Philosophy, and I my letter to Juliette. Madame de Staël has read us many chapters of her work. It everywhere bears the marks of her talent. I wish you could induce her to omit politics ; she ought not to obtrude her republicanism. Mademoiselle Jenner has played a part in a tragedy of Werner which was acted before twenty persons on Friday. She, Werner, and Schlegel acted to perfection. I was exceedingly affected. You will not be curious, however, to hear more about a piece in which there were distributed among the three actors, three murders and one assassination. We were allowed to breathe a little between the acts, when Sabran and Auguste were admirable in some proverbs of M. de Chateauvieux. The arrival of Cuvier has been a happy distraction for Madame de Staël ; they have been well pleased with each other. Werner is about to leave us for Rome. There is a singular kind of folly and inaptitude in one so swayed by the imagination ; it is paying too much even for genius. I accompanied Corinne to Massat, the portrait painter. To relieve the tediousness of the sitting, a beautiful musical performance had been planned. A Mademoiselle Romilly performed very agreeably on the harp ; the *atelier* was a temple of the Muses. The portrait will be a likeness without that exaggerated inspiration which, among other faults,

disfigures the one by Madame le Brun. Bonstetten
has given us two readings of a memoir on the
Northern Alps, in which he was at first very good,
and then a little tedious. Madame de Staël resumed her readings and there was no more ennui.
It is astonishing how much she must have read
and how profoundly she must have meditated, to
produce the ideas, the beautiful things, which she
discusses. One may easily dissent from her
opinions, but no one can fail to admire her talents.
We have all been at Geneva, and we reproduced
Coppet there. Last evening the illusion of Coppet
was perfect. Madame de Staël and I visited
Madame Rilliet, who is quite charming, at her chimney corner ; on returning, I played draughts with
Sismondi ; Madame de Staël, Mademoiselle Randal,[2]
and Mademoiselle Jenner conversed on the sofa
with Bonstetten and the young Barante. We were
there as in all other days of our companionship—
those days which I shall regret without ceasing.'

Lullin de Chateauvieux, to whose proverbs,
acted at Coppet, Vohgt alludes, was now, and for
more than a quarter of a century, one of its *habitués*.
He admired Madame de Staël with a sort of idolatry,
and her influence formed his intellectual character,
as it did that of Sismondi, Constant, Barante, and
so many other young writers. After her death he
wrote, in an unpublished record, that 'her friend-

---

[2] A devoted English companion of Madame de Staël, who was
with her through many years down to her last hour.

ship has made, during twenty-five years, the charm
of my life ; my opinions, my sentiments, have been
formed on hers. I mourn her death with deepest
sadness; I have now no consolations but my recollections.'[3] He won literary distinction by his
Letters on Italy and many other productions.
Sismondi says he was 'the most amiable, the most
witty of all the parish of Calvin, and that his conversation was always animated, piquant, and new.'
Chateauvieux, alluding to the Coppet conversational discussions of this period, says that ' they
abounded in new and profound ideas on the
mysteries of our moral nature. No one was silent
in these debates; all questions were attacked and
analysed, even to their foundations. The German
philosophy and literature were then new, but we
have since seen them invade, by her " Allemagne,"
the ideas, the traditions, and even the literary
habitudes of France.'[4]

Vohgt wrote about this date to De Gérando :
'She has projected a great voyage to America; it
will take place as soon as her work on Germany
is printed. In vain do her friends write to deter
her. Her book will charm you by the richness of
its ideas, the force of its thoughts, the poetry of
its style, the sagacity of its observations, the profundity of its reflections. It appears to me more

[3] *Ecrits et Discours,* by the Duke de Broglie, i. 3 vols. Paris
1863.

[4] *Mémoires de la Duchesse d'Abrantès,* vii. 8.

correctly written than her romances. The return
of her company has contributed greatly to the
pleasure of my sojourn in Switzerland. I am
under the charm of her talent and her goodness ; I
pray sincerely for her happiness.'

The sage Bonstetten was bewildered amid the
scenes and discussions of the château at this time.
His vexation becomes ludicrous. He writes to
Frederica Brun : 'Nothing is more changed than
our world at Coppet. These people have become
Catholics, Boehmists, Martinists, Mystics, thanks
to Schlegel and the Germans. Three days ago
Vohgt read to us Lessing's "Nathan," in German.
For several days we have seen few besides Germans.
Oehlenschlaeger lives here, a handsome young
Dane ; Overbeck and Werner have arrived ; a very
great number of Germans and Americans come
here to ventilate their opinions. When Madame
de Staël is alone in her carriage she pores over
mystic books. They are rehearsing a Biblical
drama, the "Shunamite," in which Ezekiel [he
means Elisha] resuscitates B———. Schlegel would
explain the Trinity by my own book. All this
would be abominable to me, were not Madame de
Staël always full of kindness and tenderness for
me. When I am here I cannot tear myself away,
and she seems saddened when I leave. If you and
I are ever to live together, beware of becoming a
mystic. Madame de Krüdner has also touched
at Coppet in passing. She is quite crazy, and has

spoken to Madame de Staël of nothing but
heaven and hell. This nonsense repels me like
asafœtida ; but when they do not approach me too
nearly, these people amuse me. Vohgt says now
" yes," and then " no ; " it is too amusing to see his
magical gyrations. I will return in the spring. If
Geneva becomes mystic, I will go to Paris or to
Sicily. Tieck is coming. Nothing is more droll
than the manner in which they speak of this great
artist ; if you believe them, Canova and Thorwald-
sen are only dwarfs by his side.'[5] Coppet had,
however, irresistible attractions for the perplexed
philosopher ; if the German disputants disturbed
his. habitual amiability, it was but for a moment ;
Madame de Staël and the neighbouring scenery
restored his equanimity. He wrote, later, to his
favourite correspondent : ' I cannot describe to you
the beauty and magnificence of the autumn. My
chamber (it was also Benjamin Constant's) looks
out towards the Jura, on the park ; towards
Lausanne, on the Pays de Vaud, the Alps, the
lake and its enchanting borders. All the colours
of the creation shine in the park. I write to
you with my coat off, and with my windows open.
Why are you not here ? Poor Madame de Staël—
she is so sad ! you cannot imagine how her perse-
cutors have broken her life. She knows not how
to harden herself against misfortunes.'

The good Bonstetten was, indeed, one of the

[5] Steinlen's *Bonstetten,* chap. viii.

most interesting characters of the château circle. We never tire of his gossip. He came of a family of ancient lineage among the high Bernese noblesse ; for some time he was Bailiff of Nyon, on the shore of Lake Leman, and lived in its historical old castle, where he maintained the freest hospitality and the heartiest festivity, especially when joined by Matthisson the poet, Müller the historian, and similar friends. They were as frolicsome as boy-playmates, yet as speculative and profound as sages. Sublime discourse, varied learning, sentiment, and wit, prevailed at their repasts ; and it is to be for ever regretted that there was no Athenæus there to record their classic symposia. Nyon is but a few miles from Coppet, and their intellectual pyrotechnics played from one château to the other. There could be no dulness in the presence of Bonstetten. He never outgrew his youth. His relation with Frederica Brun was intensely sentimental to the last. He saw nearly all his innumerable friends pass away for ever, but continued to study, to write, and to love on, as if he were never to die. Few men have been more poetically sensitive to external nature and life, fewer have been more meditative. 'A habit of reflection,' he says, ' gave me an interior life which was animated and embellished by everything that I saw. In this disposition of the soul every object became a subject of thought.'

His still surviving friend, Pictet de Sergy,

says : ' It was not possible to live with him without remaining under a seductive charm : there was so much grace, gaiety, and spirituelle bonhomie about the amiable old man. It was difficult to be serious with him ; his very features, delicate, young, and humorously frank, even at eighty years, conspired against all gravity, though he might attempt to assume it in his speech. When he entitled one of his books, " The Man of the North and the Man of the South," he expressed beforehand the image which our memory retains of him. The distinctive traits of the two races could not be presented more saliently in one character. Although glowing with the most expansive and tender German sensibility, he was always frisking, prattling, sparkling like an Italian. His correspondence with his old friend Madame Brun (sister of the Bishop of Münster, and mother of the Countess Ida de Bombelles) is vividly interesting for its accounts of the society of the times, but more so for its revelations of the happiness of old age, upon which he obstinately insisted down to his eighty-seventh year. " One cannot be fully happy," he affirmed, " till after his sixtieth year." Surrounded by friends who were dear to him, and who appreciated him more every day ; animated by an insatiable curiosity for everything beautiful, original, or only new ; rich in a capacity for labour, having in his distant correspondent an auditor who was ever eager to learn his news, and to whom he opened his heart and mind without reserve, he enjoyed life completely in accordance with his organisation. He was always a young man, full of vitality, a sort of practical philosopher, combining Epicurus and Anacreon, and adding by his benevolence for his neighbour something of the Christian sage. " To resist with success," he said, " the frigidity of old age, one must combine the body, the mind, and the heart ; to keep these in parallel vigour, one must exercise, study and love." ' [6]

Such are a few glances at the interior life o the Coppet society which the correspondence of the time affords ; they are slight indeed, but the more precious for being so.

[6] Manuscript *Souvenirs.*

CHAPTER XXVII.

THE 'ALLEMAGNE'—RENEWED PERSECUTION.

Again in France—She writes to Bonaparte—Life at Fossé—The
Government suppresses her 'Allemagne'—She is banished from
France—Letters to Madame Récamier—Letter from the Minister
of Police—Bonaparte's Malice.

ABOUT six years of research and study were
spent on the 'Allemagne;' two of them in its
composition at Coppet.[1]   Her chief relaxation
from this laborious work was the writing, and playing on the stage of her château, of most of the
small dramas which are given in her collected
works under the title of 'Essais Dramatiques.'   On
completing the third volume of the 'Allemagne' she
determined to escape, after its publication, from
the power of her imperial persecutor, by sailing
for the United States of America, where, as we
have seen, she had already invested funds in real
estate.[2]   Before leaving Coppet, with her manuscript, she obtained a passport, hoping to find

---

[1] Baron de Staël's 'Advertissement' to second part of the *Dix
Années.*

[2] See her Letters in *Revue Rétrospective*, 1 série, tome iii.   Paris,
1834.

a passage in a frigate which was about to
bring to France a plenipotentiary from America.[a]
She wished to publish her 'Germany' at Paris,
but the order of her exile did not allow her to
approach within forty leagues of the city; she
therefore established her family near Blois, in
the romantic old château of Chaumont-sur-Loire,
which was notable as having been occupied by
Cardinal d'Amboise, Diane de Poictiers, Catherine
de Medicis, and Nostradamus. Its proprietor, M.
Le Ray, was in America, but soon returned with
his family, and, though he was proud of his tenant
and urged her to remain, she removed to an estate
called Fossé, belonging to M. de Salaberry, who
generously lent it to her.

She had submitted the first two volumes of her
work to the state censorship, and had obtained the
necessary authorisation for its publication after the
elimination of a few sentences. Her preference of
Goethe's 'Iphigenia' to that of Racine had to be
qualified; and among other suppressions was that
of a brief passage in which she described Germany
deprived of liberty as a temple which lacks columns
and roof. She now addressed a letter to the Emperor, in which she said: 'Ten years have passed
since I have seen your Majesty; during eight of
them I have been exiled. As I am soon to embark for America, I entreat your Majesty to permit
me to speak to you before I depart. I will allow

[a] *Coppet et Weimar,* vi.

myself but a single subject in this letter ; it is the explanation of the motives which induce me to leave the continent, if I do not obtain your permission to live in a country home near enough to Paris to render it convenient for my children to reside there. Persons in disgrace with your Majesty suffer from that fact throughout Europe. I cannot take a step without encountering its consequences ; some of my friends fear to compromise themselves by seeing me ; others defiantly brave that fear. The most ordinary relations of society thus become services that a proud soul cannot endure. I have passed my life for eight years between the fear of not obtaining these sacrifices and the pain of being their object. My sons are without careers ; my daughter is thirteen years old ; in a few years it will be necessary to establish her in life. It would be selfishness for me to force her to live with me in my banishment ; is it then necessary to separate me from her ? This life is not tolerable, and I see no remedy for it. What city on the continent can I choose, where my disgrace will not produce insurmountable obstacles to the settlement of my children, as well as to my personal repose ? ' &c.[4] The prompt answer to this appeal was, as we shall presently see, the destruction of the whole edition of her book, and her banishment from the entire territories of France.

Her faithful friends in Paris ventured to visit her

4 Chateaubriand's *Mémoires d'Outre-Tombe*, viii.

at Fossé, Madame Récamier, Adrien and Mathieu de Montmorency, Prosper de Barante, Benjamin Constant, and others ; and some days of sunny life were enjoyed by her in tranquil unconsciousness that they were the prelude of an approaching storm, the severest that broke upon her years of exile. She relates with minuteness, because with happiness, the most insignificant events of these few bright days.[5] ' This country house,' she says, ' was the abode of a Vendean soldier who had no anxious care about it, but whose loyal kindness made everything easy, while his originality gave us continual amusement. We had hardly arrived when my Italian musician began to play on his guitar, my daughter accompanying him on the harp, and the sweet voice of Madame Récamier joining them. The peasants gathered about our windows, astonished to find this colony of troubadours enlivening the solitary home of their absent master. It was there that I passed my last days in France with friends whose memory lives in my heart. Assuredly so private a reunion, so retired an abode, such innocent occupations, could harm nobody. We sang frequently a charming air, composed by the Queen of Holland, the refrain of which was " Do your duty, come what may." After dinner we placed ourselves round a garden table and wrote to one another instead of talking together. This *tête-à-tête*, varied from day to day, amused us so much that we were

[5] *Dix Années*, ii. 1.

impatient to go forth from the dining room in order to resume it. If by chance any visitor arrived, we would not suspend the recreation, and our little Post, as we called it, went on as usual. Our neighbours, astonished by this novel proceeding, mistook it for pedantry, while we found in it only a resource against the monotony of our solitude. One day a gentleman of the neighbourhood, who had no thought in life but for the chase, came to take my son into the woods ; he remained some time at our table, restless and silent. Madame Récamier wrote with her beautiful hand a little billet to this rough hunter, that he might feel more at home with us. He excused himself from receiving it by assuring us that he could not, in that dazzling light, read the writing. We laughed at the disappointment which the benevolent coquetry of our beautiful friend encountered, and thought that a billet from her hand would not always have met with the same fate.'

An opera which had excited much interest in Paris was to be given in the little theatre of Blois, and Madame de Staël was tempted to see it. On leaving the building she was followed by a crowd of people, more curious to see her as an exile than as an authoress. ' This sort of notoriety,' she writes, ' which arose more from my misfortunes than from my talents, irritated the Minister of Police, who wrote to the Prefect of Loir-et-Cher that I was surrounded by a court. " Certainly," I replied to

the Prefect, " but it is not power which gives it to·
me." '

On September 23 she corrected the last proofs
of the ' Allemagne.' ' After six years of labour, it
was,' she says, ' a real joy to me to place the word
Finis at the end of my third volume. I made a
list of a hundred persons, to whom I wished to
send the book ; I attached some value to it, for I
believed it would make known some new ideas to
France. Having received a letter from my publisher which assured me of the authorisation of
the censors, I had no fears, and I went with my
friends to the château of Mathieu de Montmorency,·
which is five leagues from Blois. It is in the·
midst of a forest ; I walked its paths with the man
that I respected more than any other in the world
since the death of my father. The beauty of the·
season, the magnificence of the forest, the historical
memories of the place, tranquillised my soul. My
worthy friend was occupied there only with his
preparation for heaven ; in our conversations he
thought not of the affairs of time, but sought to
do good to my soul. We left him the next day,
but lost ourselves on the way. About midnight we
were met by a young man on horseback, who
invited us to take shelter in the château of his·
family. We did so, and there, on the next morning, M. de Montmorency sent me a letter from my
son, urging me to return home immediately, for·
my book had met with some obstruction from

the government.   As I mounted the carriage, my honest old Vendean, whose own perils in battle had never moved him, pressed my hand with tears on his cheeks.   I understood then that new and serious persecutions threatened me.   Montmorency, whom I questioned on the way, told me that the Minister of Police had sent his agents to cut in pieces the ten thousand copies of my book, and had ordered me to leave France in three days.'

Her son Auguste had secured her manuscript. It was demanded by the police, but a rough copy which they had at hand was given instead of it, and the precious work was thus saved to the world.

She was stunned by this sudden and unexpected blow.   She had flattered herself with the hope of an honourable success in the publication of the 'Allemagne.'   'If,' she says, 'the censors had refused me their sanction, the case would have been simple enough ; but, after I had submitted to all their objections, after I had made the changes they demanded, to learn that my book was suppressed, and that I must separate myself from the friends who sustained my courage—it was too much for me, and I wept.'   It extorted from her 'a cry of despair,' says the biographer of Madame Récamier, who gives us the following indignant letter addressed, at the time, by the persecuted authoress to her beautiful friend.   'I have fallen into deepest sadness.   The thought of my departure has taken entire possession of my soul, and for the first time I have felt all the pain of a condition that I thought easy to bear. I reckoned on the success of my book to sustain me, when behold, six years of labour, of study, and of travel are nearly lost! And imagine the caprice of this affair. The volumes which have been seized are the first two, which had already been approved by the censors. Thus I am banished for having written a book which has been approved by the censors of the Emperor. This is not all. I could have printed my book in Germany; I voluntarily submitted it to the censors. The worst that ought to have occurred should have been the prohibition of the work. But can they punish anyone for having come voluntarily to receive orders from the censors? Dear friend, Mathieu is here, a friend of twenty years' standing, the most perfect being that I know, and it is necessary to quit him. You, dear angel, who have loved me for my misfortunes, who have shared with me only the period of my adversity, you who render life so sweet, it is necessary also to leave you. Ah! my God! I am the Orestes of exile, and fate pursues me. But it is necessary that the will of God be done; I hope he will sustain me. For the last time I have heard that music of Pestozza which recalls to me your sweet face, your charm which is superior to your beauty, and the many pure and serene joys of this summer. In June I shall press you once more to

my heart, and then the unknown future will begin.
Pardon me for writing you so sad a letter. I will
take fresh courage; but thus to die to all one's
memories, to all one's sentiments, this is a terrible effort. I have such a cloud of wretchedness
around me that I no longer know what I write
If I pass the winter, as I expect, in Switzerland,
dear friend — I dare not finish. I should be
tempted to say to you as M. Dubreuil to Pech-
meja: " My friend, thou above all shouldst be
here." '[6]

The three days allowed for her departure
from France were of course insufficient. The
requisition was a cruel impossibility for a mother
with three children, and no preparation, in money,
or otherwise, for so sudden a flight. It seemed
that the government might not be unwilling to
involve her in other liabilities; and, after the unpardonable crime at Vincennes against the Duke
d'Enghien, and other enormities of her persecutor,
she knew that he was capable of any inhumanity
which might be dictated by his resentful egotism.
She was not without apprehensions, as she later
tells us, of imprisonment, possibly lifelong imprisonment, within the walls which had witnessed
the tragedy of Vincennes. She was in despair,
and wished to escape by a vessel which was about
to sail for America from the port of La Manche.
But this would require more time. She appealed

[6] *Souvenirs de Madame Récamier*, i. 2.

to the Duke of Rovigo, the Minister of Police, and received an answer which has become infamous for its mendacity and insolence, and which allowed her to embark from certain ports, but not from La Manche. He granted her seven or eight days. 'These must suffice,' he said, ' for I can allow you no more. You must not seek the cause of the order I have conveyed to you in the silence you have kept regarding the Emperor, in your last work. This would be an error. No place worthy of him could be found in the book. Your exile is a natural consequence of the course you have constantly followed for many years. It has appeared to me that the air of this country does not agree with you, and we are not yet reduced to the necessity of seeking models in the people that you admire. Your last work is not French ; I myself had it suppressed. I regret the loss which your publisher must suffer, but it is not possible to allow the book to appear.'[7] Her son had waited on the Duke and received this letter ; she says that 'the Minister of Police had in fact shown more frankness in orally expressing himself on the affair ; he had demanded why I did not name the Emperor or the army ? The work being purely literary, such subjects were not relevant, was the reply. "Does she think," rejoined the Minister,

---

[7] This letter was inserted in her London Preface to the *Allemagne.* For the baseness to which Savary could descend—his ' brutality,' as the Duchesse d'Abrantès calls it—see her *Mémoires,* passim, particularly vol. xvi. ch. iii. ix. x.

" that, after we have fought Germany eighteen years, a person so well known can print a book without mentioning us ? The work shall be destroyed, and we ought to send its author to Vincennes." ' Her two sons attempted to see the Emperor himself, then at Fontainebleau, in order to plead for their mother ; but they were turned back with the threat that they should be arrested if they persisted.

These painful details can be tedious to no man of letters, to no woman of heart. With similar facts heretofore noticed, and worse ones to come, they present a spectacle for the contemplation of the intellectual world, at least of all students of human nature : the little great man of empire pursuing with minutest inhumanity and egotism a helpless woman of genius—helpless, yet the greatest of her age, if not of any age. Great enough to conquer Europe, this man was not great enough to conquer himself. He was conquered by his own pettiest passions. And the truest function of history regarding him is to hold him forth before all eyes with the admonitory lesson that there is no real greatness of genius without the moral greatness of the heart.[8] The German thinker, Fichte, says of Napoleon that, ' with his

[8] ' When Bonaparte insisted that the heart is one of the entrails, that it is the pit of the stomach that moves the world, do we thank him for the gracious instruction ? Our disgust is the protest of human nature against a lie.'—Emerson's *Letters and Social Aims.* Boston, 1876.

great clearness of views and firmness of will, he
might have been the liberator of humanity if the
least sentiment of the moral destiny of the human
race had inspired his mind ; but he never had this
sentiment ; he is for all ages an example of what
these two elements can produce when they are
left to themselves and joined to no idea of the
spiritual order of the world.' If we are not willing
to accept fully the opinion of an accomplished
English writer—that ' perhaps the greatest calamity
in history was the wars of Napoleon, in which
some incidental good may nevertheless be found,' [9]
—we can hesitate only because time is still requisite for a full estimate of the man and his influence upon Europe ; hitherto the nations (particularly France) have been able only to retrace
their steps back through the ruins which mark his
disastrous course.

After breaking down the whole political fabric
of the continent, for his own glory and that of his
family, after sacrificing millions of French and
other lives to his selfish ambition, he was to be
cast out of Europe as an unendurable political
nuisance. His restored dynasty was again to
corrupt France till it should dissolve in official
rottenness, and the bravest, most brilliant nation of
modern times be overrun by foreign troops and
trodden in the dust with a humiliation unparalleled
in the history of nations. The bewildered world

[9] Goldwin Smith, in *Contemp. Rev.* Dec. 1878.

still cries 'hosanna' to the memory of Napoleon; but in the coming ages of better light and juster sentiments, when the glory of war shall be rightly estimated as barbarism, which shall stand out worthiest and brightest in the recognition of mankind—the genius of the great military tyrant, or that of the great suffering writer? Which alternative will enlightened France then choose for her homage—her greatest man of blood, or her greatest woman of intellect? Should we brush aside such reflections as merely rhetorical, destiny itself will nevertheless reinstate them.

Alluding to her sufferings, Madame de Staël says: 'It may perhaps excite astonishment that I compare exile to death, but great men of antiquity and of modern times have sunk under it. Many a man has confronted the scaffold with more courage than he has been able to command in the loss of his country. In all codes of law perpetual banishment has been considered as one of the severest penalties; but here the caprice of one man inflicts, in a kind of sport, the sentence which conscientious judges have reluctantly pronounced on criminals.' But her wrongs were yet to be adjudicated by 'conscientious judges.' The conscience of the world is always right in its ultimate judgments, and wisdom and virtue have only need to wait. One of the finest thinkers of our times, or of any times, says that 'culture alters the political status of an individual. It raises a rival royalty in a monarchy. It is king against king. It creates a personal independence which the monarch cannot look down, and to which he must often succumb. The history of Greece is at one time reduced to two persons—Philip or the successor of Philip on one side, and Demosthenes, a private citizen, on the other. Kings feel that this is what they themselves represent. This is no red-kerchiefed, red-shirted rebellion, but royalty, kingship. This is real kingship, and theirs only titular. Literary history and all history is a record of the power of minorities, and of minorities of one.'[1] Ever since the epoch of the Revolution, France has been reeling between the alternatives of the personal government exemplified by Bonaparte and the constitutional liberty for which her greatest authoress pleaded and suffered. Destiny will infallibly decide at last for the latter; no other final decision is possible under the moral laws of the universe

[1] Emerson's *Letters and Social Aims.*

CHAPTER XXVIII.

SHE RETURNS TO COPPET.

Scenes on the route—Sismondi's Account of her—Letters to
Madame Récamier—Geneva—Madame du Deffand.

It was now the autumn of 1810; she could not
prepare for her proposed voyage to America in
time to escape the winter severities of the Atlantic;
she turned therefore again towards her asylum at
Coppet. On the route she stopped for a few hours
in Orleans, and walked the streets sadly pondering
her fate. ' I passed,' she writes, ' before the statue
of Jeanne d'Arc and thought that certainly, when
she delivered the country from the power of the
English, this France was freer, was much more
France, than it is to-day. It is a singular sensation
that we experience in wandering thus, in a city
where we know no one and are known by no one.
I felt a sort of bitter pleasure in regarding in my
isolation this land that I was about to leave, perhaps for ever, without speaking to anyone, without
distraction even from the impressions which the
country made on me. Some persons who passed
me stopped to look at me, because I had, I suppose,

in spite of myself, an expression of sorrow, but they soon continued their way ; for, alas, how accustomed we all are to see suffering ! At fifty leagues from the Swiss frontier the country bristled with citadels, with houses used as prisons ; everywhere we saw men constrained by the will of one man, unhappy prisoners and conscripts. At Dijon the Spanish captives, who would not renounce allegiance to their country, sunned themselves in the public squares ; their mantles were ragged, but they wore them with dignity ; they were proud of their sufferings. At Auxonne were the English prisoners ; at Besançon more Spaniards. Among the French exiles, whom one saw everywhere in the provinces, was an angelic girl, shut up in the citadel of Besançon because she would not part from her father. Mademoiselle de St. Simon shared the fate of him who gave her life. On the height of the mountains, at the entrance of Switzerland, is the Château de Joux, with its prisoners of state, the confinement there of many of whom is unknown to their families. There Toussaint Louverture perished by the cold.'[1]

As she approached Coppet, ' trailing the wing,' she says, ' like La Fontaine's dove, I saw the rainbow spanning the house of my father, and I dared to take hope from this sign of the covenant.' The presage was not to be entirely illusive.

She still hoped to go, sooner or later, to

[1] *Dix Années*, ii. 1.

America.[2] Sismondi wrote to the Countess of Albany that, 'before making her great voyage, she wished to traverse France slowly, and abide some weeks at the prescribed distance from Paris, in order to take leave of her friends. God grant that she may discover some among them sufficiently amiable or devoted to make her regret more vividly all that she is about to leave, and shake her determination. For myself I can do nothing more, and I am desolate. The ennui of America seems to me as gigantic as its forests, its lakes, its rivers. I can judge of the mercantile conversation of the Americans by their newspapers, in which fifteen columns are given to pecuniary and domestic interests, and the sixteenth only to subjects of thought.'[3] He had before written on what he considered the folly of this voyage. 'Without doubt,' he had said, 'America is a place of mortal sadness, especially for her, since she has become interested in German philosophy and poetry. Nothing could be more contrasted ; all is reverie, vague and without ob-

---

[2] Taillandier (*La Comtesse d'Albany,* livre iii.) remarks that neither Villemain nor Sainte-Beuve 'have mentioned this singular episode,' and that 'at first it was only a means of reaching England more easily.' Her mind wavered, in fact, between the two designs. Citations already given from her letters, and more still to be given, show that at times she seriously designed to escape to America ; there are, on the other hand, intimations in the *Dix Années d'Exil* that she wished to reach England by a vessel bound to America. Her one wish was, in fine, to escape anywhere from the power of Napoleon. Taillandier sees (in later letters of Sismondi) evidence that she desired to find refuge in America.

[3] *Lettres inédites,* &c.

ject, in Germany ; all is utilitarian and practical in
America.   Of all countries in the world it is in this
that the question is most asked, " of what use will
it be ? "   Nothing serves there better than money ;
it is their highest thought.   I have seen an American journal in which her voyage has already been
announced.   " She is a very rich woman," it says,
" and has lived in a noble manner in her château.
She has also written many books, which being read
in Europe, have afforded her much money."   It is
among such miserable calculators that she goes to
pass some years !   Oh, how much pain for both
those who go, and for those who see them go !'
Sismondi lived to learn better things of America.
However relevant some of his animadversions may
have been, Madame de Staël viewed that country
from a loftier standpoint.   'What is more honourable,' she wrote, ' for the human race than this new
world, which is establishing itself without the prejudices of the old ; this new world, where religion is
in all its fervour without needing the support of
the State for its maintenance ; where law is more
powerful by the respect which it inspires than by
military force ! Europe, alas, may some day present,
like Asia, the spectacle of a stationary civilisation,
which, having not power to perfect itself, must de-
generate.   But old and free England should be inspired with admiration by the progress of America.'[4]

Still later Sismondi writes that she is yet un-

----

[4] *Considérations* &c. vi. 7.

shaken in her resolution to leave Europe; she is but waiting for the equinox to pass. In November he writes, exultingly, that she has postponed her project. 'This,' he says, 'has changed all my existence; she is the being that I love the most, and one who, if you love her not, still sheds happiness on all who approach her, by an inexpressible charm. The season will not permit her to embark; the delay in the printing of her book has defeated her plan. The suppression of her admirable work is virtually an order to write no more; for the high questions of morality, religion, sentiment, which she treats with so much profoundness and nobleness, have never been more loyally separated from all that ought to displease the government. Never, in expressing a noble thought, has it been more guarded against abuse as an offensive weapon. She has had the kindness to show me this work from its beginning to its completion. I need not tell you how its suppression afflicts me for her; but it afflicts me also for the progress of the human mind. Great truths are established in it beyond all doubt, great fallacies refuted beyond all recovery. She is armed with pride to sustain such a terrible blow, and has borne it with a force which I could never command.'

On January 1, 1811, she wrote her new year's greetings to Madame Récamier in a letter which, though tinged with sadness, alludes to her returning tranquillity and to one of its chief sources.

' Do you not,' she says, ' experience with me, dear angel, a sentiment of seriousness in thinking that a new year has commenced? The happy moments that one has had in the year that has passed are readily effaced from one's thoughts, and we see, at least I see, only those cruel periods of suffering which have marked the course of 1810. There is also something unknown, mysterious, in the future, which chills one with fear. Without doubt all moments are equally mysterious; in all there is but one support, and, without this thought, the imagination would be overwhelmed with dread; but such solemn facts are well adapted to concentrate our thoughts. Alas! dear Juliette, shall I ever again see you? I know not; I know not even that I should wish it. Ah! how painful is this perpetual apprehension of bringing peril upon all who approach us! I war against my soul in endeavouring to keep myself from plunging into the bitterness of the miseries which thus attend exile. But they are friends indeed, the only ones to be cherished, who stand this test. I experience at times a sort of calm, which certainly comes not from myself, but from God. The agitated life which I have hitherto led, and from which his hand, and assuredly not my own, has drawn me, has at last some hope. I keep occupied, and the day is short if one shuns reverie. I believe that religious ideas are gaining more and more control over me. I have many evil presages at the com-

mencement of this year. Am I not to see you?
Dear friend, who of us controls anything in our
existence? There is but one thing clear and
fixed in the world ; it is *duty*. Adieu, dear angel ;
promise me to keep the friendship which has
afforded us some sweet days.'[5] A little later she
writes, deploring their unavoidable separation :—
'If I had been able to foresee that ties so intimate were to be broken, no literary success,
no celebrity, could have satisfied me for the loss.
But circumstances constrain us ; we know not
what we are doing for ourselves. Nevertheless, I
ought to say to you that the hand of God sustains
me, and I am no more in that state of despair
which almost annihilated my being. I know not
if this grace will be continued to me, but I perfectly believe it is grace, and not my own strength.
I thank God for the power to love which He has
given me, and you are the object of its most tender
regard.' Still later she writes from Geneva : 'I am
again in this city where I have suffered so much
ennui for ten years. Heaven grant that you may
not experience these sad returns of suffering, so incident to our troubled times ! I have been reading
a book which I recommend to you as a diversion.
It is the " Letters of Madame du Deffand to Horace
Walpole." They are souvenirs of the society which
preceded that which we have known. My father
and mother are frequently mentioned in them.

[5] *Coppet et Weimar*, ch. vi.

What peaceable times! And yet trouble found its way into them. This woman became blind, and that sort of exile is more frightful than ours. Ah! dear Juliette, where is the time when we could commune freely; when you gave me life in speaking of all that you appreciate with so much spirit, vivacity, and finesse? Each year has borne me a new misfortune. But this one—I know not that my enemies can add to its sorrows. I have received from one of our sister exiles, Madame des Cars,[6] a letter full of nobleness. Have they told you that the government has refused to Madame de la Trémoille[7] permission to visit the city nearest to her estate, where she wished to attend her sick husband? After the approaching springtime, improve your opportunities of travelling. Do not waste life in waiting and expecting. I have done so, and repent of it. Adieu, my angel, adieu! I shall believe the light of my life renewed when I see you, if I do ever see you, again.' She writes again from Geneva: 'Your reflections on Madame du Deffand are very fine, and I am perfectly of your opinion on her character; but she is natural, and I cannot express the interest which this fact alone gives me in her. It gives to her correspondence a life which makes me finish it as reluctantly as I would leave a person with whom I have long lived, and

---

[6] The Duchesse des Cars; she was banished to the island of Sainte-Marguerite.

[7] Another exile.

then that which is perfectly natural in others seems to bring back to us something in our own lives.' Her allusion is, probably, to the ardent ideal love of the aged Marquise for Walpole, one of the most remarkable examples of the kind in French literature. Madame de Staël was now entering into a similar, though a more serious experience with young Rocca, of Geneva. ' Madame du Deffand,' she continues, ' was a character whose defects have some relation with my own; I hope it is not thus, however, with my other qualities. A very curious thing in these letters is the magic lantern of names of persons whom we have known, I some of them, you their children, both of us their families. I have read the famous " Conaxa," but I like better the " Deux Gendres," [8] though its conclusion is not good. The great defect of the " Deux Gendres " is that its subject is bad. " Conaxa " is more a farce. Its immorality, like its sadness of subject, is lost in the old style, which makes all the personages so many buffoons. Dear Juliette, your letters are the only interest of my life at present.' She complains of the ennui of life in Geneva ; but she was subject to the melancholy of its capricious climate—a climate which, if it could not repress the natural gaiety of Voltaire, made even him a hypo-

[8] A drama received with great applause at the *Comédie Française* the preceding year; but which was found to be a plagiarism from the *Conaxa*, a production of a Jesuit of the seventeenth century. The plagiarist (Charles Guillaume Etienne) was the chief editor of the *Journal de l'Empire*, and one of the chiefs of police.

chondriac. In intervals of better health, and especially of genial weather, she enjoyed greatly the cultivated society of that city, and was as cheerful there as anywhere.

We have seen Sismondi's surprise at the restoration of her courage and good spirits. Early in 1811 he writes to the Countess of Albany that she is acting comedies in the château of Coppet, and has attained tranquillity if not gaiety. 'She has taken her part; she no longer thinks of Paris; she has forgotten her book, and has none other in prospect; she lives in the present without making projects. She confounds me more and more every day; I should never have expected such self-command.'

Sismondi did not know the chief secret of her cheerfulness—the romantic episode which was relieving her exile and filling her womanly heart. She was in love. The presage which she had seen, as she approached Coppet, in the rainbow that spanned her home, was not, as has been remarked, to be entirely illusive. A single streak of light was breaking through the clouds which shaded her existence, and she was at last to realise what had been 'the dream of her life—l'amour dans le mariage'—a love at once romantic and legitimate, and therefore satisfying alike to her sensitive heart and to her equally sensitive conscience.

CHAPTER XXIX.

HER SECOND MARRIAGE.

Resignation to her Fate—Sismondi's Account of her to the Countess of Albany—Rocca—Her Cousin's Account of him—Frederica Brun's Account of him—Rocca's Account of his Perils in Spain—Their Secret Marriage.

As there seemed to be no longer a possibility of her using the press, on the continent at least, Madame de Staël had now abandoned all further literary labours. Sismondi, writing again to their common friend, the Countess of Albany, repeats the expression of his wonder at the mysterious change which had come over her. 'She has borne her sufferings,' he says, ' with a courage that I admire, but do not comprehend. She has renounced all literary occupations; she banishes from her mind and her conversation all allusions to her afflictions; and in thus excluding two kinds of thoughts which have always held the strongest place in her life, she maintains a liberty of mind, a gaiety, a fire in conversation, which charm all who see her.' [1]

Her fame was now established: no woman of

[1] *Lettres inédites, &c.*

Europe had more; but she had found it unsatis-
fying to her soul, and perhaps few women in
Europe had suffered more. She now sought
happiness in her affections, and in the society of
her friends who had been tried and had been
found faithful.

Soon after her return from France to Coppet
she went to Geneva, where she had long been a
favourite in the best circles. There were her admired cousin, Madame Necker de Saussure; the
companion of her childhood, Madame Rilliet-Huber;
Sismondi, Bonstetten, and a host of others, appreciative of her genius as well as endeared by long
friendship. In these circles she noticed an accomplished young officer of the French army, who
had fought gallantly in Spain, and had returned
broken in health and also stricken with incurable
wounds. His was precisely such a case as could
not fail to command both the sympathies and the
admiration of women, especially of such a woman
as the author of 'Corinne.' Unconscious herself
of any stronger sentiment, she showed so tender a
sympathy for his sufferings that he was touched
not merely with gratitude, but at last with passionate love. The disparity of their ages, and her
pre-eminence of reputation and fortune, might well
have discouraged his affection, but he remarked
to one of his friends, 'I will love her so much that
I will finish by making her marry me.'

Her cousin, speaking of this romantic passage

in her life, says that 'her conversation produced
a prodigious effect on him. There was something
celestial in her language. Madame de Tessé said,
"Were I queen, I would order Madame de Staël
to talk with me without ceasing." This ravishing
music renewed the existence of the young man;
his head and his heart were inflamed by it. His
love was favoured by circumstances. Madame de
Staël had been extremely unhappy; she was tired
of grief; her soul, full of resources, tended to raise
itself again, and she demanded but a single hope.
At the moment when her exile was most restricting
her life, and sombre shadows were gathering from
all points over her head, a new day came to illuminate her. Happiness renewed itself in her desolate heart as from its own ashes, and her ideal of
love—love in marriage, seemed now to be within
her reach. The thought of such happiness had
never been foreign to her mind. In speaking of
her hope of finding some day an asylum in England, she had said: "I have need of tenderness, of
happiness, of support, and if I discover there a
noble character I will sacrifice my liberty." The
noble character was found suddenly nearer to her.
Without doubt she might have made a more suitable choice, but the inconvenience of marriages of
inclination is, precisely, that they are not matters
of choice. Nevertheless it is certain that this
union rendered her happy. She had well judged
the character of M. Rocca; extreme tenderness,

constant admiration, chivalric sentiments; and, what most pleased her, language naturally poetic, imagination, even talent (as his writings prove), graceful wit, a sort of originality of mind which excited hèrs and varied her life—these she found in him.' [2]

Rocca was, then, not without attractions for any woman of much sensibility. He was of good lineage. The Roccas had long been conspicuous in Switzerland. 'At Geneva,' says a Swiss antiquary, ' the family had enjoyed great consideration from its beginning.' [3] It had intermarried with the family of the Reformer, Theodor de Beza, and 'constantly maintained itself on the best footing.' It gave some creditable magistrates, divines, and soldiers to the republic.

The Danish authoress, and friend of Bonstetten, Frederica Brun, who was so intimate with the circles of Geneva and Coppet, has left us some details of the early life of the gallant young officer. She says : ' It was in the summer of 1806 that we made at Seligny the acquaintance of Rocca, a beautiful youth of from eighteen to twenty years of age. He had the most magnificent head that I have ever seen ; and we loved him for the purity of his soul and the noble candour of his being. He was educated at the Polytechnic School of Paris, whence he went to take part in the destructive

---

[2] *Notices* &c. ii.

[3] Galiffe gives some five pages to it. *Notices Généalogiques*, ii. Geneva, 1831.

war in Spain.   He was severely wounded in battle and lay unconscious on the field, where a Spanish woman saw him, and, struck by his beauty, would not believe that he was yet dead.   She immediately resolved to draw him away from the peasants who were killing the wounded, and, placing him, as a corpse, before the altar of a neighbouring church, she watched there by him till the crowd had vanished.   She had him secretly conveyed to her abode, where she dressed his wounds and re-called him to life by powerful remedies.   Through six weeks the kind young creature guarded and attended him.   When at times he suffered pain from his wounds, she diverted him with songs, accompanying them with her guitar.   Rocca, thus saved, returned to his country, bearing a wooden leg, and his arms and shoulders severely injured. Living in Geneva, he saw there, and espoused with his young enthusiastic heart, the first woman of her times.'[4]

We can accept Madame Brun's statements re-specting the beauty and accomplishments of the young officer, for they are given from her personal recollections of him as she saw him in 1806; and allusions to him by other writers confirm her statements respecting his 'magnificent head,'[5] the

---

[4] Taillandier's *Lettres inédites de Sismondi.*

[5] Byron saw him in London, and says he 'is remarkably hand-some.'—Moore's *Byron*, ii.   Mrs. Jameson, visiting Coppet, says of his marble bust there, 'I was more struck with it than anything I saw,

'purity of his soul,' and the 'noble frankness' of
his manners; but the remainder of her romantic
story is made up of fictitious reports current
among her Genevan correspondents, and naturally
enough founded on the more prosaic facts which
Rocca himself has recorded.[6] She ended her
nearly twenty years of travel in 1810, and never
saw Rocca after his return from Spain. The story
of the 'wooden leg,'[7] as well as all the legend of
the Spanish maiden's discovery of the unconscious
soldier, and the 'neighbouring church,' are romantic exaggerations. After many perilous adventures
he was attacked at the head of a foraging party
by an overwhelming force of Serranos, in a dangerous defile about four leagues from Ronda: two
balls struck him, the first traversing his left thigh,
the other lodging in his body. One of his hussars conducted him back towards his quarters at

---

not only as a *chef-d'œuvre*, but by the perfect and regular beauty of
the head and the charm of the expression.'—*Sketches* &c.

[6] Taillandier, usually an admirably exact writer, cites Frederica
Brun's statement without correction (*Lettres inédites de Sismondi*,
p. 347). Rocca's *Mémoires sur la Guerre des Français en Espagne*,
which gives the real facts of the case, has been out of print more than
half a century, and may have escaped his attention. Matthisson's
Briefe von Bonstetten (ii. 160), Galiffe's *D'un Siècle à l'autre* (ii. 6),
Morell (*Bonstetten*, viii.) and, indeed, nearly all other writers about
Madame de Staël, give Madame Brun's story. I regret that I am
compelled to despoil it of so much of its romance.

[7] 'Rocca had no wooden leg. His wounded leg was simply stiff,
"ankylosée," as we say in French, and did not prevent him from being
a remarkably good rider to the end of his life.'—*Mons. Pictet de
Sergy to the Author.*

Ronda. 'I was obliged,' he says, 'to collect all my remaining strength, rapidly diminishing by loss of blood, to save myself from fainting: had I fallen from my horse I should probably have been poignarded. I held on to the saddle with both hands, and spurred forward my horse by the only leg that I could still use. The poor animal plunged along falteringly, a ball having passed through him from side to side. He gave out a quarter of a league from the city, and my hussar galloped forward for aid. Left alone, the mountaineers fired at me from the woods. I was at last saved by some of our soldiers, and conducted to my quarters.' His hosts had, before this, entertained him with reluctance as an enemy of their country, but their sympathies were now touched by his sufferings; they would not allow him to be conveyed to the hospital, where a pestilential fever prevailed, and where he would probably have perished. 'They said to me,' he writes, 'that, since I could do no more evil to their country, they considered me as one of their family, and, without losing a single moment, they took, during fifty days, all possible care of me.'

While he was yet disabled, the Spaniards attacked Ronda; and balls flew so near his chamber that the family were obliged to remove him to another part of the house. 'My host and hostess,' he continues, 'came to tell me, as calmly as possible, that the mountaineers were at the end of the street,

that they were gaining continually, and that by
the evening the city would be carried by assault.
They concealed in haste my arms and military
clothes, in order to prevent suspicion, and bore me,
by the aid of their domestics, to the highest story
of the house, where they placed me behind a little
chapel dedicated to the Virgin Mary, regarding
this consecrated place as an inviolable asylum.
They then hastened to bring two priests, who,
placing themselves near the door on the street,
could prevent its being entered.   The aged mother
of my hostess remained alone with me, repeating
prayers, counting the beads of her chaplet more
or less rapidly as the noise of the combat increased
or lessened.'   At last the assailants were repulsed
at all points, and he was saved.   His hosts re-
doubled their cares for him, passing many hours
daily with him, and singing their national airs,
accompanied by the guitar, for his diversion in
hours of pain.   One of their daughters, a nun in
a neighbouring convent, sent him daily perfumed
lint for his wounds.   The aged mother lavished
upon him the affection of a parent.   After nearly
three weeks of suffering, he was able to rise from
his bed.   He had to walk with crutches for a long
time.   ' I had totally lost,' he says, ' the use of one
leg.   I left Ronda in a waggon for Ossuna, taking
leave of my hosts with the same feelings with which
one departs for the first time from the parental
home.'   He was at last sent back to France,

'happy,' as he says, 'to escape, at whatever sacrifice, from an unjust and inglorious war, which my
best sentiments condemned.'

Rocca, officer of hussars and chevalier of the
order of the Legion of Honour, was a man of considerable culture. He became an author, and gave
to the world 'Memoirs of the War of the French
in Spain,' which passed through three editions, also
'The Campaign of Walcheren and Antwerp in 1809.'
He had nearly completed, at his premature death,
a novel which has never been published.

One of his very few personal friends who have
survived to our day says : ' He was the son of a
councillor of state, who was the issue of a noble
Italian family which had taken refuge in Geneva
for the faith. As a child he was distinguished by
marvellous address and intrepidity. He returned
from Spain with one leg broken, but not amputated,
and beautiful and interesting as it were well possible for a young man to be ; in a word, with all the
attractions suitable to inspire a new and *grande passion*. I have seen him on his superb black Anda-
lusian steed, having but one leg to sustain him,
descend, *au grand galop*, the stairs of the Burg de
Four, then in a straight line, and penetrate from
the Corraterie into the *allée* of the house where the
bank of Lombard, Odier, & Co. now stands, from
thence mount the ascent to the court, and clear the
stairs and slippery *allée* which ended on the Rue
de la Cité, and this extreme *tour de force*, all

prompted by the fact that in this house was Madame de Staël, with whom he became acquainted in the family of Argand-Picot. It is easy to conceive that the young man, so worthy of interest, presented by his cousin to the passionate Corinne, inspired her ardent and compassionate heart with a most lively and tender sympathy. The force of will, the energy of character, which he had so often displayed, triumphed in the fulfilment of his own prediction—that by the strength of his love ·he would compel her to marry him. The hungry heart of Madame de Staël could not have been taken in a nobler snare.'[8]

They were privately married in 1811, she being forty-five years old, he twenty-three. Not till the reading of her will was their secret revealed beyond a doubt; she authorised her children to make it public, and to recognise Louis Alphonse Rocca, her only child by this marriage.[9] There were obvious, if not sufficient, reasons for the concealment of the marriage : her literary works and fame were identified with her name, and she might reasonably wish to retain it unchanged ; a sincere but romantic

---

[8] Manuscript *Souvenirs* of Pictet de Sergy.

[9] Bonstetten says he had the splendid eyes of his mother. His infancy was spent, down to her death, in Longirod, at the foot of the Jura, near Nyon, under the care of Dr. Jurine. 'His teacher,' continues Bonstetten, 'tells me that he is full of mind.' Still later he writes : 'The young Rocca is a wonderful child : he studies little, but has the brightest child-mind that I have ever known. He is full of spirit and of heart. I could not keep my eyes off of him.'—*Briefe* &c. ii.

passion like this, however compatible with her own fervid nature, would hardly be pardoned by the world, especially in view of the great difference of the ages of the parties ; but, above all, she had good reason to apprehend that her merciless persecutor would interfere with their happiness by recalling Rocca as a French officer,—a fear which was partially realised, though their relation was unknown to Bonaparte.[1]

The guests of Coppet invariably speak well of Rocca. Baron Vohgt writes, about the time of the unknown marriage : ' Young Rocca is exceedingly lovable. He combines a gentle character, a delicate constitution, with bravery and courage. He is so slight that we can hardly conceive how all his wounds could find place upon him. He is fascinated by his relation with Madame de Staël, and the tears of his father cannot induce him to abandon it.' Neither his father nor Vohgt understood the real character of the relation.

---

[1] There is some probability that her marriage was revealed, at the time, to Madame Récamier, and there is an intimation of it in one of her letters to Annette Gérando. These were her two dearest feminine friends. To Madame Gérando she writes : ' No cloud has ever obscured our friendship. I prize your heart and your enlightened mind ; and when I come forth from the agitations of this great event in my life, of which I cannot feel sure that my saint in heaven [her father] can entirely approve, I will go to see you and converse much with you, if you will permit me.'

CHAPTER XXX.

INCREASED PERSECUTION.

Persecutions at Coppet — Schlegel exiled — Montmorency exiled—
Madame Récamier exiled—Madame de Staël's indignant Record
of the fact—Her Letters to Madame Récamier—Her Literary
Labours—She writes to the Duchess of Saxe Weimar—She prepares to escape.

SHELTERED again in the family mansion at Coppet,
with a new and romantic tie binding her to life, she
hoped to enjoy the remainder of her days in resignation and peace. In her 'Delphine' she had
made Mademoiselle d'Albémar say to her heroine,
in too unqualified language, 'We have frequently
said to one another, my friend, that society, perhaps
even Providence, have permitted but a single happiness to woman—love in marriage—and if this is
withheld from her it is as impossible to repair the
privation as it is to recover youth, beauty, life, all
the immediate gifts of nature, of which nature alone
disposes.' [1] Pictet de Sergy, who knew her inti-
mately, writes that, 'in proportion as she advanced
in age, she experienced more keenly the need of
sheltering, in conjugal love, the passions of a heart

---

[1] *Delphine,* iii. Letter X.

which was ever demanding affection ; and her religions sentiments proportionately grew in energy.'[2]
The happiness of wedded love, as we have seen,
was the dream of her life. She wished now to
realise it in tranquillity. But her persecutor was
relentless.

'I was then at last,' she says, 'resigned to life
in this château, no longer publishing anything ; but
it was necessary, in making this sacrifice of any
talents that I flattered myself I possessed, to find
happiness in my affections ; yet see in what manner
the authorities arranged my private life, after they
had deprived me of my literary existence. The
first order that the Prefect of Geneva received required that my sons should not be permitted to
re-enter France without a new permit from the
police. This was to be their punishment for attempting to speak to Bonaparte on behalf of their
mother. Shortly afterwards the prefect wrote me
a second letter, demanding, in the name of the
Minister of Police, the proof sheets of my book,
which were supposed to be still in my possession.
The Minister knew exactly the number of the proofs
which I had forwarded, and the number I had kept ;
his spies had served him well. In my reply I gave
him the satisfaction of knowing that they had reported to him rightly, but I assured him that my
copy was not in Switzerland, and that I neither
would nor could give it to him. I added, never-

[2] Unpublished *Etude de l'Allemagne* &c.

theless, that I would not attempt to publish the work on the continent—for what continental government could then permit the publication of a book interdicted by the Emperor?'[3]

A few days later the Prefect of Geneva, M. de Barante, her friend and, as we have seen, an occasional guest at the château,[4] was dismissed for having shown her too much courtesy, though he had never failed in his duties, and had scrupulously addressed to her the harshest orders of government. 'His removal,' she says, 'was generally regretted in the department, and from that time all who sought the favour of the government avoided my house as if they were flying from a contagious disease.' The successor of M. de Barante treated her with rigour, and persecuted her with solicitations to purchase the goodwill of the government by writing something in favour of the Emperor.

Soon after these events her youngest son was ordered by his physician to the baths of Aix in

---

[3] *Dix Années,* ii. 2.

[4] He was the author of an able criticism on La Rochefoucauld, in an edition of the *Maxims*; of an *Introduction to the Study of Languages*, and other works. His son, Prosper, was a still more frequent guest at Coppet, and Madame de Staël had much influence on his intellectual development; he became Ambassador and Peer of France, and historian of the Directory, of the Dukes of Burgundy, of La Vendée, &c. One of his most remarkable productions (anonymous) was an *Essay on French Literature in the Eighteenth Century*, a critical notice of which, prepared for the periodical press by Madame de Staël, was interdicted by the government.

Savoy, about twenty leagues from Coppet. She accompanied him thither, at a time of the year when the baths were usually deserted, made known the fact to the prefect, and quietly established herself in a village where she knew not a single person. Hardly ten days had passed when a courier from Geneva brought her an order to return. The Prefect of Mont Blanc, who had jurisdiction over Aix, was suspicious that she intended to escape to England, and there write against the government, and had sent out his gendarmes to forbid the villages to provide her with post-horses on the routes. 'I was tempted,' she writes, ' to smile at this prefectorial activity against a helpless woman, but at that time I had a mortal terror of the sight of a gendarme. I always feared that an exile so rigorous might soon terminate in a prison—a fate more terrible to me than death.' She returned to Geneva, where the prefect forbade her not only to enter under any pretext into any region annexed to France, but even to travel in Switzerland. He advised her never to venture farther than two leagues from Coppet. She protested, but in vain ; and on the next day learned that Schlegel was ordered to quit, not only Geneva but Coppet. He was accused of being ' anti-French, and of declaring in one of his publications that the Phædra of Euripides is superior to that of Racine ; but,' she adds, ' the true motive of his exile was his friendship for me, the fact that his conversation relieved my solitude ; they wished to imprison my soul, and to deprive me of all the pleasures of intellect and of friendship.'

She was the first woman that Bonaparte exiled ; but very soon afterwards a great number of her sex suffered in like manner for their opinions,— among them the Duchesse de Chevreuse, who died of a broken heart, and was denied permission to consult her physician at Paris in her last sickness.[5] It had now become obvious that the unsubdued authoress was dogged by the agents of the government, and was to be the victim of unintermitted surveillance and persecution. She determined to flee. But whither, and how ?—these were questions which required time. While she was pondering them, other and, if possible, severer blows fell upon her. Her venerable and steadfast friend, Mathieu de Montmorency, sent her word that he was about to visit her, though Napoleon had expressed his disapprobation of his design. She went to meet him on the way. From Orbe they journeyed leisurely to Fribourg, enjoying the scenery, and examining the convent of female Trappists in the Val-Sainte. They crossed the mountains to Vevey, where she proposed to her friend a farther excursion to the entrance of the Valais, for she was curious to see its cretins. About three leagues from Bex was a famous cascade ; they went to see it, returning before the dinner hour. The Valais

[5] *Considérations* &c. iv. 8.

was forbidden ground, for it had been annexed to France, and the cascade was within its boundary; she had forgotten that she was limited to the French territory between Geneva and Coppet. On reaching Coppet she was reprehended by the prefect for this slight trespass. She was evidently watched everywhere. 'These continual chicaneries on the least actions of my life,' she writes, 'rendered it odious to me. I felt daily that I must escape, and daily I seized on some pretext for delay. At last a terrible blow struck my soul; God knows how I suffered under it.' Four days after his arrival at Coppet, Montmorency received there a *lettre de cachet* exiling him for his attentions to his exiled friend. 'The Emperor,' she writes, 'would not have been contented if he had not received this letter under my roof, and if it had not contained an intimation from the Minister that I was the cause of his misfortunes. I uttered cries of anguish on learning the calamity which I had drawn down on the head of my generous friend, and never in all my prolonged sufferings have I been so near to utter despair. Montmorency, calm and religious, exhorted me to follow his example. I accused myself of his separation from his family. I prayed to God without ceasing, but my anguish allowed me no rest, and every instant of life sickened me.'

The blow was to be immediately repeated. While still in this deep distress, for the relief of which she resorted to the use of opium, she received a letter from Madame Récamier, stating that she was on her way to the baths of Aix for her health, and would be in Coppet in two days. 'I trembled,' she says, 'lest the fate of Montmorency should befall this beautiful being, who has received the homage of all Europe, and who has never deserted an unhappy friend. I sent a messenger to stop her, beseeching her not to approach Coppet. She would not yield to my supplications; she could not pass under my windows without remaining some hours with me; and it was with convulsions of grief, and tears, that I saw her enter the château where her arrival had always been a fête. She left the next day, but it was in vain; the government pursued her, and struck her with exile.' Madame Récamier, whose beauty and virtue were the wonder and pride of Paris, was not readmitted to that city till the downfall of Bonaparte. Years later, when the tyrant was on his solitary rock in the ocean, where alone the world could any longer tolerate him, Madame de Staël exclaims, with just indignation: 'Such was the fate that I had brought upon the most brilliant creature of her times; and the sovereign of the French—a people so famous for their gallantry—showed himself without respect for the loveliest woman of Paris. He struck, at the same time, at rank and virtue in Montmorency, at beauty in Madame Récamier, and, I venture to say, at some reputa--

tion for talent in myself. Perhaps he flattered himself that he struck also at the memory of my father in the person of his daughter, in order that it might be truly said that on this earth neither the dead nor the living, neither piety nor beauty, neither intellect nor celebrity, were of any account under his reign. Anyone rendered himself culpable if he was wanting in the delicate shades of flattery, or did not abandon the sufferer who was marked with the imperial disgrace. Bonaparte recognised only two classes of men—those who served him, and those who were content not to injure him, but to live silently shut up in themselves. He would not admit that, in all the world, from the details of a private family to the administration of empires, a single will should be exercised without exalting his own. He wished, in taking from me all that caused my happiness, to trouble me sufficiently to force me to write a flattering platitude in the hope that it might buy my restoration. It was necessary, in order to please our master, so able in the art of degrading the self-respect of proud souls, that I should dishonour myself in order to obtain my return to France, and thereby afford him an opportunity of chuckling over my complaisance. I refused him this truly refined pleasure ; this is the only merit I have had in the long war between his omnipotence and my feebleness.'

The Duchesse d'Abrantès, notwithstanding her almost fanatical admiration of Napoleon, writes with indignation of the proscription of Madame Récamier. 'In the number of persecuted women,' she says, 'there was one who interested me more than any other, in spite of the sad fate of the Duchesse de Chevreuse, who died at Lyons from the sufferings of her exile. Madame Récamier suffered as an angel struck with punishment, and knew no place of repose where she could weep in peace. Her friendship for Madame de Staël, paid for by exile, seemed to be a mockery of all that is most sacred on the earth. That which the classic nations would have deified, which they would have honoured, at least as a noble devotion of the heart, was in this case insulted by all that is most outraging and most painful in despotism, and most disgraceful to it; for the most exalted brow, were it circled with twenty crowns, ought to bow before the regard of such an innocent victim.'[6]

The first news of the proscription of Madame Récamier utterly overwhelmed Madame de Staël. She immediately wrote to her : 'I cannot speak to you ; I cast myself at your feet; I beseech you not to hate me. In the name of God be careful for yourself ; in order that I may live, try to extricate yourself from this evil. I long to see you happy. May your admirable generosity not have injured you. Alas ! alas ! I hardly retain my reason ; but, believe it, I adore you, and prove to me that you feel it by endeavouring to save yourself ; for I

[6] *Mémoires* &c. xvii. 5.

shall have no repose till you are delivered from this exile. Adieu! adieu! When shall I again see you? Not in this world. Adieu.'

They did meet, however, in a short time, and, after parting, at Ferney, Madame de Staël wrote: 'I am subject, at times, to such profound me-lancholy that I would accept death. A species of despair devours me; life to me is like a ball, the music of which has ceased, and all that remains appears without colour. There is a fatality in my condition. I am an obstacle to the well-being of my children and my friends. I have recourse, without ceasing, to prayer, and sometimes it seems to me that I fatigue God, and that the heaven is brass over my head. I am convinced that the best service I can do to you, to Montmorency, to all about me, is to flee away.'

She was now studying a plan of escape; for in these times, when Napoleon's power was compli-cated with nearly every other government of the continent, it was difficult to evade it. Meanwhile, she resumed, somewhat, her literary labours, as a means of relief to her troubled mind. 'I regret,' she writes to Madame Récamier, 'the disuse of my talents—perhaps with egotism; but I feel within me powers which have not yet been developed, and their defeat afflicts me. Dear angel, in your prayers entreat from God peace for my soul.' In the winter of 1811 and 1812 she composed, at Geneva, her 'Reflections on Suicide,' published the next winter in Sweden ; it was designed to qualify, or counteract, the apparent sanction which the death of Delphine had given to that pusillanimous crime. She also projected a poem on ' Richard Cœur de Lion,' to which she alludes in another letter to her exiled friend. ' If it is granted me,' she says, ' again to see you, Montmorency, and my country, some years before I die, I shall be content with my fate. I have attempted a labour which is necessary to me ; it has a future. I think I have told you that it is an historical poem on Richard Cœur de Lion ; the researches that it requires help me at this moment ; they will sustain me for some time yet. God always extends his hand in our times of distress.'

About the same time she wrote from Geneva to the Duchess of Saxe-Weimar : ' A painful malady, caused by my sorrows, has kept me nearly a month in bed, or I should have instantly answered your letter. Sismondi, whom your highness has deigned to recollect, is giving here a course of lectures on the Literature of the South, with great success. He proposes to give a course on that of the North next year ; and Weimar will certainly not be forgotten in the history of the progress of the human mind. Benjamin Constant is at Göttingen ; Schlegel, whom they separated from me, has found an asylum in Switzerland,[7] at no great distance, yet very much too far ; but from whom am

---

[7] At Berne.

I not separated ! I pray you present my homage to the Duke. You are about to be encompassed with storms; this crisis is the last of the continent; whether prostrate or erect, each power will, after this epoch, preserve its place. As for me, I desire only to traverse the sea; my future depends upon the alternative of fear or hope which may be allowed me in this respect. I have not yet been able to procure the new production of Goethe. The passage of books is hardly more free than that of persons. If ever I make a voluntary journey again on this earth, it will certainly lead me to your feet. M. de Saint Priest,[8] whom you know, I believe, has been banished, at seventy-eight years of age, from Geneva—from France, from Switzerland, and from Italy. He is going to wander in Germany. It appears that he has been guilty of having a son in the service of Russia. I venture to solicit, from time to time, some marks of the remembrance of your highness. I shall not cease to follow, from afar, your noble destinies, and, if darkness envelope us all, there will remain, at least, some treasures of memory for a better world.'

She had now devised her scheme of escape and travel. She had wished to reach England, but the blockade rendered this impossible; and an edict had denounced, with the penalty of imprisonment, all French subjects who should attempt, without special authority, to enter that country. Napoleon

---

[8] He had been a Minister of Louis XVI. and colleague of Necker.

controlled all the continent except Russia, and was
about to invade the latter.   Where could she find
refuge?   She determined to seek it in Sweden.
Her friend Bernadotte was there as Prince Royal,
and her children had claims on the protection of
the land of their father..   But by what route could
she reach it?   None other seemed practicable but
across Europe, through Russia, before the invader
could arrive there ; and thence by Riga and water
to Stockholm.   Her health had been shattered by
agitation· and by opium, ' of which,' says the adopted daughter of Madame Récamier, ' she made a
great abuse.' [9]   She needed change of place, and
there was no hope of escape but in immediate
flight.

[9] Madame Lenormant, *Coppet et Weimar*, vi.

CHAPTER XXXI.

FLIGHT FROM SWITZERLAND.

Preparations for her Departure—Her Dread of Imprisonment—Farewell Scenes—Mental Conflicts—Her Flight—An agreeable Surprise—Rocca as a French Courier—Arrival at Vienna.

ON May 23, 1812, Madame de Staël commenced her secret flight from Coppet, hoping to put herself finally beyond the power of her persecutor, by reaching Sweden and, at last, England. She has left us a minute and touching record of the attempt, and of the mental agitation—the womanly fears and hopes—with which she began it.[1] 'I had passed,' she says, 'eight months in a state that cannot be described, trying my courage each day, and each day becoming more feeble under the apprehension of imprisonment. Any one would surely dread it; but my imagination has a terror of solitude; my friends are so necessary for the support of my soul—to animate me, to give me new prospects when I succumb under the fixedness of a painful impression—that death itself has never appeared to me so cruel as a prison; the confine-

---

[1] *Dix Années,* ii. 5.

ment, the secresy, in which one may remain for years, without hearing a single friendly voice. I have been told that a Spaniard, who defended Saragossa with astonishing bravery, wailed, with outcries, while enclosed in the dungeon of Vincennes, so enervating to even courageous men is such frightful solitude! I am not courageous; I have boldness of imagination, but not of character; all kinds of perils present themselves to me as phantoms. The species of talent that I possess renders impressions, or images, so vivid that, if the beauties of nature gain by it, dangers become the more formidable. Nevertheless I continually felt the necessity of departing, and a sentiment of pride prompted me; but I could say with a well-known Frenchman, "I tremble at the perils to which my courage exposes me." In short, if anything can add to the gross barbarity of the persecution of women, it is the fact that their nature is such as to be at once sensitive and feeble; they suffer more acutely than men, and are less able to escape suffering.

'Another terror agitated me at this time. I feared that, if I escaped, the moment the Emperor knew it, he would have inserted in the Gazettes one of those articles which he knew so well how to dictate, and by which he inflicted moral assassination. A senator once said to me that Napoleon was the best journalist he knew. If the *Moniteur* accused anyone, no journal, French, German, or Italian, dared to correct it. It can be imagined what

·could be done by a man at the head of a million
·of troops, with a thousand millions of revenue,
disposing of all the prisons of Europe, with kings
for his jailors, and using the press, while the
·objects of his persecution could not avail, themselves of even the intimacy of friendship for their
vindication.   However independent one's spirit
might be, I do not believe that anyone could contemplate without trembling such dangers.'

In her work on the French Revolution she
speaks with indignant eloquence of Bonaparte's
abuse of the press at this period.   With a slight
·simulation of freedom, it was thoroughly enslaved.
' Of all the suffering which the slavery of the press
inflicts,' she says, ' the most bitter is that of seeing
what is most respected, what is most dear, insulted
in the public journals, without the possibility of
an answer in the Gazettes, which are necessarily
more popular than books can be.   What cowardice
in those who insult the tomb, when the friends of
the dead are not allowed to defend them !   What
baseness in journals which attack also the living,
inspired by authority at their backs, and which
become the advanced guard of the proscriptions
that irresponsible power can impose at the first
suspicion !   What style can that be which bears
·the seal of the police ?   By the side of this arro-
·gance, this baseness, when one reads the speeches
of American or English public men who seek, in
addressing other men, only to communicate their

earnest convictions—one feels moved as if the voice of a friend were suddenly heard by the desolate thinker who no longer knows where to look for a kindred mind.'—' But,' she exclaims in the same chapter, ' mankind are never willing to consecrate the memory of fallacies, and, happily for the dignity of literature, no permanent monument of this generous art can be elevated on a false basis. The accents of truth are necessary to eloquence ; just principles are necessary to reasoning, if it is in the end to be successful. Courage of soul is necessary for the triumphs of genius. Nothing of this sort, however, can exist in the productions of writers who follow, with every wind, the direction of power. Is it thus that men of letters, the magistrates of thought, ought to conduct themselves in the presence of posterity ? ' [2]

But to resume her narrative : ' My health,' she says, ' was cruelly changed ; and the energy of my character enfeebled by so many sufferings. I abused, during these times, the patience of my friends, in for ever recalling my projects for deliberation. I endeavoured a second time to obtain a passport for America, but I was kept waiting till midwinter for an answer ; and then it was a refusal. I offered to engage myself to print nothing on any subject whatever, provided they would permit me to live in Rome. In begging for this permission I had the self-love to allude to " Corinne."

[2] *Considérations* &c. iv. 16.

Without doubt the Minister of Police bethought
himself that a similar motive had never been inscribed on his registers ; and the South, the air of
which was so necessary for my health, was un-
pitiably denied me. They ceased not to declare
that my whole life would have to be passed within
the two leagues between Coppet and Geneva. If
I remained, it would be necessary to separate from
me my sons, who were of an age to seek a career;
I should impose on my daughter the saddest prospects, by allowing her to share my fate. Each day
the number of those in whom I could confide
diminished ; all my sentiments became a weight on
my soul, instead of being a source of life ; and this
weight pressed on my talents, my comfort, my
existence ; for it is frightful to be unable to use
them for the benefit of one's own children—only to
injure one's friends by them. At last the news
that I received from all parts informed me of the
formidable preparations of the Emperor : it was
clear that he wished to become master of all the
ports of the Baltic, and to crush Russia. The
last outlet from the continent might be closed at
any moment, and I might find myself unable to
escape.

'I then decided to go while a possibility of
reaching England still remained ; but this possibility
was only by making the entire circuit of Europe.
I fixed on the 15th of May for my departure; my
preparations had long since been made, with the

most absolute secresy; but, the evening before
that day, my strength utterly forsook me, and I
persuaded myself that such a terror as I felt could
only arise from an evil action. I consulted all
kinds of presages; I interrogated my friends and
my own conscience on the morality of my resolution. It would seem that the part of resignation,
in all things, is most due to religion, and I am
not astonished that pious men have often shrunk
before resolutions which have sprung from spon-
taneous volitions. Necessity seems to bear a divine character, while the determinations of the
human will may be imbued with pride. Nevertheless no one of our faculties is given us in vain, and
that of deciding for ourselves has its use. The
atmosphere around me seemed to counsel repose,
for during six months no new persecution had
occurred, and we are always inclined to think that
which is, is that which will be. I was, in these
circumstances, so oppressed in mind, that it was
necessary for me to make one of the strongest
determinations that could be made in the private
life of a woman. My people, with the exception
of two, who were perfectly trustworthy, knew
nothing of my secret; most of my visitors had no
suspicion of it; and I was about to change, by a
single action, my entire life and that of my family.
Agitated by uncertainty, I wandered about the
park of Coppet. I seated myself in all the places
where my father had been accustomed to rest, and

to contemplate nature; I saw again the same
beauties of water and verdure which we had frequently admired together. I bade them adieu,
while once more receiving their sweet influences.
The tomb which encloses the remains of my father
and mother, and in which, if God permit, mine
shall be deposited, was one of the principal causes
of my regret in departing; but I had found always,
in approaching it, a sort of strength which seemed
to come from on high. I passed an hour in prayer
before the iron door which protects the most
noble of human remains, and there my soul was
convinced that I ought to depart. I recalled
there those famous lines of Claudian in which he
expresses the species of doubt which rises in the
most religious soul when it beholds the earth
abandoned to the wicked, and the fate of mortals
floating, as it were, at hazard. I felt that I could
no longer sustain the enthusiasm which had developed all that was good in me; that it was
necessary for me to hear the speech of those who
thought as I did, in order to protect my faith, and
to preserve me in the worship with which my
father had inspired me. Many times during this
anxiety I invoked the memory of my father. I
went to his study where his arm-chair, his table
and his papers, were still in their old places; I
kissed each cherished trace of him. I took his
cloak that, till then, I had ordered to be left on
his chair, and bore it away with me, that I

might wrap myself in it at any moment in which death might approach me. These adieus ended, I avoided, as much as I could, others which might expose me too much. I wrote letters of farewell to my friends, taking the precaution not to have them sent till many days after I had departed.'

The sublime integrity of her conscience, amidst this agitation and anguish of her woman's heart, is proved by the fact that she could have saved herself at any moment, by compromising with Napoleon; for, as we shall hereafter see, Schlegel attested, after her death, that he (now in exile at Berne) 'received from a public functionary semi-official overtures to relieve her exile, on condition that she would write something in favour of Bonaparte's dynasty; but her soul revolted at the proposition.' 'She would not devote a line,' he adds, 'to the eulogy of tyranny; she resolved rather to seek refuge in England, across Russia and Sweden.'

The next day, at two o'clock in the afternoon, she entered her carriage, as if to take an airing, leaving her domestics with the impression that she would return for dinner. She took no package; she and her daughter had their fans in their hands, and endeavoured to disguise, as much as possible, their anxious emotions; her son and Rocca bore in their pockets money for the expenses of a few days. 'On ascending the avenue of Coppet,' she says, 'I nearly fainted at the thought of leaving this dear old home;' her son took her hand and restored her courage by reminding her of the safety she would enjoy in England. By the route she had laid down for herself she was nearly two thousand leagues from that refuge.

When they were some miles on the road she sent back a servant to report that they would not be at home before the next day, and the little party continued their way, with all possible speed, day and night, to a farm beyond Berne, where Schlegel joined them. Her eldest son left her there, and returned to take charge of her pecuniary interests and the deserted home. [3]

She was now again overtaken by one of those crises of doubt and despondency which had repeatedly delayed her departure. ' My courage abandoned me,' she writes; ' this Switzerland, still so calm and always so beautiful; these people, who knew how to be free by their virtues, though they had lost their political independence—all around me held me back, and seemed to reproach me for my flight. It was still possible to return; I had not yet taken an irreparable step. My imagination could hardly endure these thoughts. I know not what would have become of me if my suspense had con-

[3] The young Baron remarks, in a note to the *Dix Années*, ' I returned to Coppet to look after her property; and, some days later, my brother left us with her domestics and her travelling carriage, to join her at Vienna. But not till this second departure did the police become aware of what had happened.'

tinned, for my mind was giving way. My children decided me, particularly my daughter, then hardly fourteen years old. I committed myself to her as if the voice of God ought to speak to me by the mouth of a child. When my son disappeared I could say with Lord Russell, " the bitterness of death is past." I entered my carriage with my daughter, and, my uncertainty once gone, I collected all my forces, and found in acting what I could not find in deliberating. Thus, after ten years of ever-increasing persecution, at first banished from Paris, then forced into Switzerland, then confined in my château, then condemned to the grievous privation of seeing my friends no more, and to the anguish of having caused their exile, I was obliged to quit, as a fugitive, two countries, Switzerland and France, by the power of a man less French than myself; for I was born on the banks of the Seine, where his tyranny was only naturalised.'

She hastened onward, through the Tyrol, towards Austria. ' From Innsbruck,' she says, ' I had to pass through Salzburg to reach the Austrian frontier. It seemed that all my inquietudes would end if I could enter the territory of this monarchy, where I had before found so good a reception. But the moment that I most feared was that in which I must make the passage from Bavaria to Austria ; for it was there that a courier might have preceded me, to forbid the authorities to let

me pass. I nevertheless flattered myself that I
should arrive without obstacle, and already my
fears were giving way to assurance, as I approached
my object, when, on entering an inn, a man accosted Schlegel, and told him, in German, that a
French courier had been there to inquire for a carriage which ought to arrive from Innsbruck bearing
a lady and a young girl, and that he would return
to seek news of them. I lost not a word of this
conversation, and turned pale with terror. Schlegel
was as much alarmed as myself. He made further inquiries, which proved that this courier was
French, that he came from Munich, that he had been
to the Austrian boundary to await us, and, not
finding us, had returned to seek us. Nothing then
could appear more clear: it was what I feared
before leaving Coppet, and all along the route. I
could not escape, since, as they said at the post, the
courier would inevitably meet us. I resolved instantly to leave my carriage, with Schlegel and my
daughter, at the inn, and to go on foot into the
streets of the city, and enter at random into the
first house whose host or hostess should present
a favourable countenance. I wished to obtain an
asylum for a few days. During these days Schlegel
and my daughter could say that they were going
to rejoin me in Austria, and I would leave, later,
disguised as a female servant. There remained no
other resource, and I proposed with trepidation to
use it, when I saw the dreaded courier, who was none

other than M. Rocca himself, enter my chamber.
After having accompanied me the first day of my
journey, he had returned to Geneva to conclude
some affairs, and now he came to rejoin me, disguised as a French courier, in order to profit by the
terror which this name would inspire, above all
among the allies of France, and to obtain a quick
supply of horses. He had taken the route from
Munich, and had hastened to the Austrian frontier,
that he might ascertain whether any dangerous
person had preceded us. He now returned to assure me that I might proceed without fear. Thus
my painful apprehensions changed into a sweet
sense of security and gratitude. At last we entered Austria, where I had previously lived so
securely for four years.'

She was immediately struck by the changed
aspect of the country. Its industries were in confusion, its finances in disorder, and its people de-
moralised ; for paper money had become its currency. It was bound, hand and foot, to France ;
and, as usual with Napoleon's allies, it was sinking
exhausted under the weight of its taxation. ' He
had,' she writes, ' the art of rendering the situation
of countries, even in times of peace, so unhappy,
that any change would be welcome to their people,
and that, after being forced to yield men and money
to France, their sovereigns should become so un-
popular as to enable him to displace them for his
own favourites.'

As her youngest son had not yet arrived, with her domestics and baggage, she stopped, before entering Vienna, at the monastery of Melk, situated on a height where Napoleon had contemplated the windings of the Danube and admired the landscape which he devastated with his army. ' He often,' she says, ' amused himself with poetical fancies on the beauties of the scenes which he ravaged, and on the effects of the wars with which he oppressed the human race. I who, in sadness and solitude, followed his traces on the mountain terrace whence he saw the distant country, could not but admire its fertility, and was astonished to see how quickly the bounty of heaven repairs the disasters caused by man. It is only moral riches that never return again, or that are at least lost for centuries.'

Her youngest son having at last arrived with her baggage and her domestics, the little party entered Vienna on the 6th of June.

CHAPTER XXXII.

HER PASSAGE THROUGH AUSTRIA TO RUSSIA.

In Vienna—Under Surveillance there—Departs for Russia—Persecutions on the way—Rocca in danger—Condition of the Country—Letter to Madame Récamier—Castle of Lanzut—Enters Russia.

HER arrival at Vienna was opportune, for the Russian Ambassador, Count de Stackelberg, who treated her with 'noble delicacy,' was to despatch in two hours a courier to Wilna, where the Czar Alexander was then stopping ; a special letter was sent by this messenger requesting a passport, which the Count assured her would reach her at Vienna in three weeks.[1] Her old friends in the city believed that she could remain there unmolested during this time ; but the Court was at Dresden, where Napoleon was holding his 'grande réunion' of the German princes ; and, in the absence of Metternich, another functionary had charge of the foreign affairs, and soon showed the timid subservience to Bonaparte which then so generally degraded the German governments. During the first few days he did not disturb her tranquillity.

---

[1] *Dix Années,* ii. 7.

As she had formerly been treated by the Emperor, the Empress, and all the Court, with the utmost cordiality, it was difficult to say to her that this time she could not be received because of her disgrace with Bonaparte, especially as this disgrace was, in part, incurred by the eulogies of Germany contained in her book ; but it was still more difficult to show her favour, and thereby displease a power to which Austria had already succumbed. She believed, therefore, that more precise instructions would soon arrive, for the Chief of Police, regarding her. She was, in fact, quickly placed under surveillance ; spies were stationed at her door ; they followed her about on foot when her carriage went through the streets of the city ; but in cabriolets when she drove out to the country, in order not to lose sight of her. She became anxious at this new indication, and was alarmed by intimations that her passport would probably be delayed some months, in which case the impending war might render it useless. She entreated the Russian Ambassador to give her one by which she might go through Odessa to Constantinople ; but, Odessa being Russian, it was equally necessary that this document should come from St. Petersburg. There remained open one other route, that through Hungary and Turkey ; but this, extending along the confines of Servia, was exposed to a thousand dangers. She might, however, by passing through the interior of Greece, reach a port, and thence find her way, by water, to England; but this course would necessitate much riding on horseback—too much for her daughter, whom she would therefore have to leave behind, to be conveyed by some of her party to Denmark and to Sweden.

She actually engaged an Armenian to conduct her to Constantinople, proposing to go thence by Greece, Sicily, Cadiz, and Lisbon. She applied to the Bureau of Foreign Affairs for a passport, permitting her to leave Austria, either by Hungary or by Galicia, for Constantinople or St. Petersburg, as she might finally judge best. She was answered that a passport allowing her to depart by two different frontiers was impossible. It was necessary for her to decide at once for one or the other of the routes; for the war was imminent, and her way might be blockaded by armies. She chose the route through Galicia, and, engaging a friend to follow her with the expected passport as soon as it should arrive from St. Petersburg, she set out accompanied by her daughter and her youngest son. Schlegel was left behind to obtain and bring after them the necessary funds. Rocca had to precede her in disguise; for, though he was disabled for service by his wounds and had resigned his commission, Bonaparte, on hearing that he was with her, had sent an order for his arrest and return as a French officer. A description of his person was distributed on their route for this purpose.

The pursued and persecuted authoress did not escape the annoyances of the police by escaping from Vienna. She was dogged all along her route. At Brunn, in Moravia, her passport, regularly issued at Vienna, was disputed with vexatious suspicion by the authorities. To her prayer that her son might be allowed to return to Vienna and procure further guarantees from the higher authorities, the only response was that no one of her company should be permitted to go back a single league. She had formed an intimate friendship with the noble Polish family of Lubomirska, who were influential at the Austrian Court, and at whose castle of Lanzut, in Poland, she was now eagerly expected. She longed to reach it, that she might find rest from her intolerable grievances; but her way was still beset with difficulties. She was commanded to hasten through Galicia, and to stop at Lanzut but a single day. Her passport protected her only through Austria; the Russian passport had not arrived: what was to be her fate when she reached the frontier? She appealed to the Governor of Moravia. Brody, the last town of Austria, was a miserable place, its population being mostly oppressed Jews; she might be detained there indefinitely, hedged in by armies, for Napoleon's war for the restoration of Poland was beginning, as preliminary to his invasion of Russia. Her prospect was full of dismay. The Governor showed her no sympathy, but shrugged his shoulders, and

pointed to his instructions. He knew their importance, as virtually dictated by the great conqueror
who, while shaking Europe, did not disdain to
attempt to shake the soul of the helpless woman
who was now flying, with her children, before him.
She hastened in despair to Lanzut in Galicia.
Lanzut was now the estate of the Princess Lubomirska, sister of Prince Adam Czartarinski, who
was Marshal of the Polish Confederation. The
Princess was generally esteemed for her character
and, above all, for the beneficence with which
she used her fortune. Her loyalty to the House
of Austria was well known. Her nephew and
her niece, Prince Henry and Princess Theresa,
who were particular friends of Madame de Staël,
and had been with her in Switzerland, were, she
says, 'endued with the most brilliant and amiable
qualities.'[2] On her way towards them she was
struck by the universal desolation of the people.
'I was completely prostrate,' she says; 'the
phantom of tyranny pursued me everywhere.
The Germans, whom I had known as so honest,
seemed now depraved by their *mésalliance* with the
French, which appeared to have corrupted the blood
of both subjects and rulers. I despaired of finding
an asylum for my soul. We saw at every post of
Galicia but three classes of people crowding around
the carriages of travellers—Jewish traders, Polish
beggars, and German spies. The country seemed

[2] *Dix Années,* ii. 8.

to be inhabited by only these three classes. The beggars, with their long beards and ancient costumes, inspired pity. We met on the highways processions of men and women bearing the standard of the Cross and chanting psalms ; an expression of intense sadness marked their faces. I noticed that when we gave them, not money, but better food than they had been accustomed to, they looked heavenward with astonishment, as if they did not believe themselves made to enjoy such gifts. It is the usage of the common people in Poland to embrace the knees of their superiors when they meet in the streets ; we could not take a step in a village without being saluted in this manner by women, children, and old men. I do not believe that any country has ever been worse governed.'

In nearly every third village she found a functionary who demanded her passport, and, in the bureaus of police, in these villages, all along her route, she saw placards admonishing the officers to watch her sharply. 'A corporal or a commissioner, or both together,' she writes, 'came to inspect my carriage, smoking their pipes, and when they had walked round it, took their leave without pronouncing a word. I advanced slowly ; for I wished to await the arrival of my Russian passport, as the only means of my salvation in these circumstances. At last the messenger from Vienna reached me with it. I was overwhelmed with gratitude and joy ; I flattered myself that I was now safe from further apprehensions. I hoped to be able to follow my first project, and rest briefly in the Château of Lanzut, so famous in Poland as uniting all that taste and magnificence could bring together. I was delighted with the prospect of seeing the Prince, Henry Lubomirska, the society of whom, as well as of his charming wife, had afforded me, in their sojourn at Geneva, moments of the sweetest pleasure. I proposed to remain with them two days, and then hasten onward, for from all parts came the news that war had been declared between France and Russia.'

While pursuing this memorable journey, she received a letter from Madame Récamier—herself in exile—to which she replied : ' You can have no idea, my dear angel, of the emotion your letter has caused me. It is in the interior of Moravia, near the fortress of Olmütz, that your celestial words have reached me. I have wept tears of anguish and of tenderness, in hearing this voice in the desert, as Hagar heard that of the angel. Oh ! if they had not separated me from you, I should not be here. Schlegel remains in Vienna to provide funds for us. I am, therefore, alone with my son and daughter in a country which is the saddest on the earth, and where German seems like my mother-tongue, so strange is the Polish language. I have met, on the roads, the common people going to implore God's help in their miseries ; for they hope for nothing from men, and would fain look higher.   Already we feel that we have quitted civilised Europe.   Melancholy chants announce from time to time the complaints of suffering beings, who sigh even while they sing.   I have much difficulty in freeing my imagination from the impressions of this country.   But it is necessary to go on, since I have begun.   Let me not fail to receive a word from you from time to time; it will be to me, for the past, what prayer is for the future—a ray of light from another world.   Ah! dear friend, what sad sentiments I repress, in order to act.   I shall, indeed, never see you again.'[3]

Hastening towards her friends at Lanzut, she reached early in July the chief place of the 'circle' to which it pertained.   Her carriage stopped before the post station, and her son, as usual, went to get her passport *viséd*.   After a quarter of an hour she was astonished that he did not return, and entreated Schlegel (who had now rejoined them) to inquire the cause of the delay.   Both of them returned, ' accompanied,' she says, ' by a man whose face I shall never forget; a gracious smile, playing over stupid features, gave his countenance the most disagreeable expression.   My son, quite beside himself, said that the captain of the circle declared I could not remain at Lanzut more than eight hours, and had sent this repulsive agent to see that his order was not disregarded ; he was to accompany me to the château, stay with me there,

---

[3] *Coppet et Weimar*, vii.

and not leave till I left.   My son had informed the captain of my extreme fatigue and prostration, which rendered longer rest necessary, but received only a brutal reply.   The agent who was to watch me fatigued himself with abject bows to the very earth ; and then, mounting a calèche, the horses of which touched the wheels of my carriage, followed us to the château.   The thought of arriving thus at the house of a friend where I had expected to spend some days in rest and joy, was insupportable to me.'

Her son, the young Baron de Staël, tells us, in a note to her 'Ten Years of Exile,' a reason for her anxiety which she does not mention—namely, that her proscribed husband was already in the château awaiting her, and might there fall into the hands of the police agent.   She was so tortured by this apprehension that, as they were driving onward, she was seized with an uncontrollable nervous attack.   Schlegel and her children bore her from her carriage, and laid her on the border of the road.   The police agent, without leaving his own carriage, sent his servant to bring her some water.   She detested herself, she says, for a weakness which could touch such a man with compassion.   On recovering, she resumed her route, followed by the watchful agent as by a spectre. When they reached the château, Prince Henry came forth gaily to receive her ; but he quickly perceived that she was pale and alarmed, for Rocca was rushing out to greet her, full of joy and confidence, having no suspicion that she was accompanied by a representative of the police. ' She was frozen with terror,' says her son, ' at his danger, and made a sudden sign for him to return into the house ; but, without the presence of mind of a Polish gentleman who was at hand, and who forced him to escape, he would infallibly have been recognised and arrested by the agent.' She quickly enabled Prince Henry to comprehend the situation ; he did not for a moment lose his *sang-froid*, his firmness, or his cordiality for his friend ; he managed the agent adroitly, and she might probably even have had a few more hours at the château, but she left it at the appointed time—'left it,' she says, ' with bitter tears.' She could not endure the humiliating presence, in such a circle, of her impertinent, though obsequious, spy. His instructions required him to be constantly with her ; he even followed her to the table of her princely host. He whispered blandly to her son, that he had been commanded to guard her at night, within her chamber, in order that she could have no dangerous private conversation ; but that, out of regard for her sex, he would forego that delicate duty.' ' And you may add out of regard for yourself also,' replied the indignant youth ; ' for, if you place your foot in the chamber of my mother, I will pitch you out of the window.' ' Oh, Monsieur ! Monsieur ! ' responded the agent, bowing more abjectly than usual before the impetuous courage of the boy—a courage which was, in a few years more, to cost him his life, on a less worthy occasion.

She had still fifty leagues to pass over before she could escape from Austria. The police agent followed her faithfully to the limit of his 'circle.' Thence to Leopol, the capital of Galicia, she found grenadiers stationed, from post to post, to watch her movements. At the capital she was treated by the functionaries with some courtesy ; her way was no longer obstructed, and she entered Russia with a thankful heart.

'Such,' she says, 'was my passage through the Austrian monarchy, which I had before seen powerful and just and magnanimous. Its alliance with Napoleon had reduced it to the third rank among nations.' As she crossed the line, she was struck by what she considered a singular coincidence. It was on July 14, the anniversary of the first day of the Revolution. 'Thus,' she writes, ' closed for me that cycle of the history of France which commenced July 14, 1789.' Another coincidence, had she been able to anticipate it, would have increased her surprise : she was to die on July 14, 1817. ' What mind,' asks her devout son, ' is not seized with religious emotion in observing such mysterious coincidences in human destiny !'

She now made a solemn resolution, justified by her long sufferings. ' When the barrier which separates Austria from Russia opened to let me pass, I swore never to place my feet again in any country subject in any manner to the Emperor Napoleon. Will this oath permit me, ever again, to see beautiful France?'

Sismondi wrote (July 11, 1812) to the Countess of Albany : 'Her son (the Baron) is still shut up at Coppet—things seem now to be taking a favourable turn for her; but two months are still necessary before she can be in entire safety; and that safety must be across the sea, and in a foreign land, where she must live separated from all her friends, far from all her former haunts, from her native language, and the pleasure which her eloquence and her social power daily procured her. When we combine all these privations, and think that it is a woman who endures them—a woman who for a long time has been enfeebled by ill health, and who could avoid them all by an act of submission which so many men have conceded—when we think that her determination, far from being a momentary ebullition of temper, is a project declared eighteen months ago, and executed eight or ten months after her last vexations—it seems that no one can refuse her the admiration due to heroism, and that all elevated souls must accompany her with their prayers.'[4]

[4] *La Comtesse d'Albany.* By Saint-René Taillandier. Paris, 1862.

CHAPTER XXXIII.

IN RUSSIA.

Bonaparte's Invasion of Russia—Madame de Staël's Impressions of the Country—Kiew—Russian Scenery—Coachmen—Peasantry—Rustic Dances—Moscow—Patriotic Enthusiasm—Education—Russian Prospects.

On June 22, 1812, Bonaparte declared war against Russia, by the proclamation of Wilkowitz, and the French troops crossed the Niemen on the 23rd, precisely one month after Madame de Staël commenced her flight from Coppet. She was fleeing before her great adversary and his host of half a million men, and had no time to lose. Even on Russian territory she was, at last, unsafe. She hastened towards Moscow, whither the French army was making its way by forced marches; [1] it intercepted her more direct route to St. Petersburg.

Whatever hazards still beset her course, she was exhilarated by a sense of emancipation as soon as she crossed the Russian boundary; and, after the painful narration of her vexations and perils thus far, we are refreshed by the new tone with which she relates her remaining adventures, her

[1] *Coppet et Weimar,* vii.

descriptions of the country, her generous comments on Russian life and character, and the increased hopefulness with which she advances towards her final deliverance. The memory of the charities of her father had, as we have seen, touched the heart of the sanguinary Santerre, and led him to befriend her at the Hôtel de Ville. The first person who now accosted her on Russian soil was a Frenchman who had been in the service of Necker, and who spoke of him with grateful tears. ' This,' she says, ' seemed a good omen.'

Her observations on Russia have to us the special interest which arises from the comparison of the condition of that great empire, in her day, with what it is in ours.

' In this Russian Empire, so falsely called barbarous, I have experienced,' she writes, ' only agreeable and noble impressions. I entered it at a moment when the French army had already penetrated its territory ; but I met no persecution, no official annoyance arrested for an instant the foreign traveller. None of my company knew a word of Russian ; we spoke only French, the language of the enemy who was devastating the country. Without the aid of a German physician, Dr. Renner, who generously offered to be our interpreter as far as Moscow, we should have deserved the title of " deaf and dumb," which the Russians give to travellers who know not their language. We must necessarily go by way of Moscow, as the immediate route to St. Petersburg was already occupied by the armies. We must make a détour of three hundred leagues ; but we had already traversed fifteen hundred, and I was glad to have the opportunity of seeing Moscow.'[2]

She had been recommended to a nobleman of Volhynia, a part of Russian Poland ; but, on arriving at his château, she learned that the French were marching on that province, and she immediately hastened forward. 'This country,' she says, 'is, like Galicia, inundated with Jews, but much less miserable. I had already reason to fear that I might encounter the French on my way. Singular fate for me—that of fleeing, first at home, from the people among whom I was born, and who have carried my father in triumph, and now of fleeing before them to the confines of Asia. I apprehended that I might have to hasten on to Odessa, and thence to Constantinople and Greece ; but I' consoled myself under the prospect of this great journey with the thought that it would afford me aid in the composition of my projected poem on Richard Cœur de Lion. In this work I proposed to paint the manners of the East, and to commemorate a grand epoch of English history—that in which the enthusiasm of the Crusades gave place to the enthusiasm of liberty. But, as we can paint only what we have seen, and express only what we have felt, it was necessary that I should go to Con-

[2] *Dix Années,* &c. ii. 10.

stantinople, to Syria, to Sicily, and follow the foot-
steps of Richard. My companions, judging better
than myself of my strength, dissuaded me from this
enterprise, assuring me that I could press on, by
post, faster than an army.'

They hastened to Kiew, the principal city of
the Ukraine. 'It is a fertile, but not otherwise
an agreeable country,' she says ; ' you see immense
plains which seem to be cultivated by invisible
hands, the habitations are so rare. In approaching
almost any city of Russia, you do not see, as in the
West, increasing indications of population, and the
roads show no improvement. On arriving at Kiew
the first thing I saw was a cemetery. I thus perceived that I was near a place where men congre-
gate. Most of the houses resemble tents, and, at a
distance, the city looks like a camp ; it seems a
copy, in wood, of the abodes of the Tartars. A few
days suffice for their erection ; they are frequently
consumed by fire, and the people send to the forests
for new houses, as to the markets for their winter
provisions. In the midst of these cabins, however,
rise palaces, and, above all, churches, whose green
and gilded cupolas are exceedingly striking. In
the evening, when the rays of the setting sun flash
on the domes, one imagines an illumination for a
fête, rather than durable monuments.

' The Russians never pass a church without
making the sign of the cross, and their long beards
add to the religious expression of their physiognomy.

They wear an ample blue robe, girdled by a red belt; the dress of the women also looks Asiatic. You observe, everywhere, that taste for bright colours which appears natural to countries where the sun is beautiful. I soon became so interested in these Oriental habits that I no longer like to see Russians clothed like other Europeans.

'The Dnieper runs through Kiew. Rivers are the greatest beauties of Russia. Seldom do you see there small streams, so absorbent are the sands. There is no great variety of trees. The birch abounds everywhere in this monotonous region; one even longs to see stones; the eye is fatigued in beholding no new objects, neither hills nor valleys. The rivers relieve the imagination from the fatigue. The priests bless them. The Emperor, the Empress, and all the Court, assist at the benediction of the Neva, in the time of the greatest cold of winter.

'This people fears neither fatigue nor physical pain. Patience and activity, sadness and gaiety, characterise them. One sees in them the most striking contrasts; and this fact presages great things; for usually only superior beings possess such opposite qualities; the masses are, for the most part, of a uniform character.'

Her first experience of Russian hospitality was at Kiew, the governor of which, General Milora-dowitsch, 'overwhelmed me,' she writes, 'with kind attentions. He was an *aide-de-camp* of Suwarrow,

and as intrepid as he. He inspired me with a confidence which I had not yet felt in the military
success of the Russians. He invited me, the evening before my departure, to a ball at the house of
a Moldavian princess. I regretted that I could not
go. All these foreign names of peoples who are
not really Europeanized arouse the imagination
singularly. One feels in Russia that one is at
the door of another world, near the East, whence
have come forth so many religious faiths, and
which still encloses in its bosom incredible treasures.'

She had still nine hundred versts (600 miles) to
pass over before she could reach Moscow. 'My
Russian coachmen,' she writes, 'flew with me like
lightning, singing, meanwhile, airs which contained
compliments to their horses. " Forward ! " they
exclaimed ; " forward, my friends ! we understand
one another ; forward ! fly ! " I have seen nothing
barbarous in this people ; on the contrary, their
appearance has something gentle, and even elegant,
that we see nowhere else. A Russian coachman
never passes a woman, of whatever age or condition,
without saluting her ; and the women respond
with an inclination of the head, which is always
noble and gracious. An old man, who could not
make his speech intelligible to me, pointed first to
the earth and then to heaven, to indicate that the
one would soon be, for him, the way to the other.
I know it may be said that Russian history is full

of atrocities; but I would accuse the Boyards, depraved by despotism, rather than the nation itself. Political dissensions always impair national character; and nothing is more deplorable, in history, than the rise and fall of rulers by crime; but such is the fatal condition of absolute power on the earth. Civil functionaries of an inferior class —those who expect to make their fortunes by their suppleness or intrigues—resemble but little the people of a country, and I admit all the evil that is said, and ought to be said, against them; but it is necessary to study the real character of a military nation among its soldiers, and the class from which it draws its soldiers—the peasants.'

Though she was borne along with great rapidity, 'I hardly,' she says, 'seemed to advance, so monotonous is the country. Plains of sand, forests of birch, villages far apart, and built of wood on the same model, give you an impression like that of a dream, in which you believe yourself always moving, but never advancing. This country seems an image of infinite space, to traverse which requires eternity. Ever and anon couriers flit past you; nothing stops their little vehicles drawn by two horses. Their drivers are often jolted two feet above their seats, nevertheless they descend with astonishing adroitness, and hasten on shouting " Forward ! " with an energy like that of the French in the day of battle. The Sclavonian tongue is singularly resonant; it has a metallic ring, like the striking of brass—quite different from anything in our Western dialects.'

Half way between Kiew and Moscow she was not far from the armies, and became anxious for her safety. But she reached at last a part of the country where she was beyond the immediate theatre of the war. She arrived at the provinces of Orel and Toula. 'I was received,' she writes, 'in these solitary places (for the provincial towns appear solitary), with perfect hospitality. Many gentlemen of the neighbourhood came to our inn to compliment me on my writings; and I acknowledge that I was flattered to find that I had a literary reputation so far from my own country. The wife of the governor received me in the Asiatic style, with sherbet and roses. Her apartments were all elegantly ornamented with pictures and with musical instruments. The Russian common people are not miserable; and the higher classes, with much luxury, know how to endure privations and hardship. A mixture of privations and of the most refined enjoyments characterise this country. The nobles, whose houses combine luxuries from all parts of the world, can undergo, not only in war but in many circumstances of life, the greatest physical inconveniences. In travel they endure patiently worse accommodations than fall to the lot of our French peasants. The rigour of their climate, their deserts, their forests, place them at war with nature. They can relish luxury; but, when this is impossible, they can go without even what we consider the necessaries of life. The hardiness, the imagination of the Russians are without bounds. In all things they are characterised by somewhat that is gigantic; ordinary dimensions are not applicable to their country. With them all is colossal rather than proportioned, audacious rather than considerate; and if their object is not obtained, it is usually because it is surpassed.'

As she approaches Moscow, she can discover little or no change in the aspect of the country. The wooden villages are not less distant from one another; there is little or no movement on the vast plains; there is silence on the highways; the country mansions are not more numerous. 'There is so much space in Russia, that all things appear lost in it, even the châteaux and the population. You seem to be travelling over a country in which the nation has come and gone. The absence of birds deepens this solitude; cattle are rare, or at least are kept at a great distance from the high roads. The vast space makes all things disappear, except the space itself, the impression of which is like certain metaphysical ideas, which, once seized by the imagination, cannot be thrown off or defined.'

The evening before they arrived at Moscow they paused in a pleasant meadow, to repose after the travel and heat of the day. Some peasants, clothed in the picturesque costume of the country, appeared, returning from their labours, and singing the airs of the Ukraine, the words of which were in praise of love and liberty, and were tinged with a melancholy as of regretful memories. At her request they danced on the sward. 'I know nothing,' she says, 'more graceful than these dances of the country, which have all the originality that nature gives to the fine arts. A certain modest voluptuousness characterises them ; the Bayaderes of India must have something analogous to th mixture of indolence and vivacity, the charm of the Russian dance. These traits indicate imagination and passion, two elements of character that civilisation has yet neither formed nor subdued. I was struck by the sweet gaiety of the peasant girls, as I had been, with shades of difference, by that of most of the Russians whom I had met elsewhere.'

Confident of her present safety, she thus tranquilly, though rapidly, travels on, observing, with an artist's eye, everything interesting ; communicating her own relieved and generous feelings to all that she sees ; and seeing most things, perhaps, in a too favourable light ; for, though she notes the vices of the nation, she has always at hand some extenuations, some apologetic explanations for them.

At last Moscow bursts upon the prospect—a splendid, oriental, barbaric vision, and yet appearing more 'like a province than a city, with its mansions and cabins, its palaces and bazaars as in the East—its churches, public establishments, pieces of water, of woods, of parks.' The diversity of manners and of nations which compose Russia, she writes, 'are displayed in this vast city. Do you wish, I was asked, to purchase cashmere shawls in the Tartar quarter? Have you seen the Chinese city? Europe and Asia are here combined. The colossal fortunes of the great nobles are employed in forming collections of every kind; in great enterprises; in *fêtes*, the models of which are to be found in the " Thousand and One Nights." When I arrived, the only talk was about the war, and donations for it. A young Count Momanoff raised a regiment for the State, and was content to serve in it as sub-lieutenant; a Countess Orloff, amiable and Asiatically opulent, contributed a quarter of her income. As I passed palaces surrounded by gardens as spacious here in the city as elsewhere they are in the country, I was told that the possessor of this superb abode gave a thousand peasants; of another, two hundred. It was to me, at first, a strange phrase—this giving of men; but the serfs were equally patriotic, and offered themselves with ardour. When a Russian becomes a soldier, they cut his beard, and from that moment he becomes free.'

The churches bear the imprint of Asiatic taste. 'You see everywhere in them ornaments of gold, silver, rubies. This imaginative taste has not yet, however, manifested itself in the Fine Arts, or in poetry. It advances quickly to a certain point, but there it stops. Impulse makes the first step, but the second is dependent on reflection ; these people, so distinct from those of the North, are hardly yet capable of meditation. Many houses are painted with green, or yellow, or rose colours, and sculptured in detail, as with ornaments of the desert. Many of the palaces are built of wood, merely for festivals ; the riches expended upon them are wasted for the splendours of a day.'

Of course the Kremlin was a spectacle of special interest to her. She contemplated from one of its towers the outspread city. 'Though the exterior character of the edifices is,' she says, 'oriental, still the impression of Christianity is evident in the multitude of venerated churches which everywhere attract the eye. We recall Rome in Moscow—not assuredly that the monuments are of a similar style, but that the mixture of the solitude of the country with the magnificent palaces, the vastness of the city, and the infinite number of temples, give to the Asiatic Rome a sort of resemblance to the European Rome. The day was superb ; and the sun seemed to delight to pour his rays on the glittering cupolas. For a moment I thought that Napoleon might stand on the same tower from which I admired the city which his presence was destined to destroy ; for a moment I imagined that he might be proud to enthrone himself in the palace of the Czars ; but the heavens were so beautiful that I repelled the

thought.   A month later this magnificent city was
in ashes.   But the calamities of Moscow regenerated
the Empire ; this religious metropolis perished as
a martyr whose fate gives new courage and force
to all his surviving brethren.'

The Count Rastopschin, 'whose name filled the
bulletins of the Emperor,' called upon her.   His
wife was a literary lady, and presented to her a
book on religion, of which she was the author—
'very pure in its style and its moral teachings.'
She visited the Countess at her palace in the 'interior of Moscow.'   'I had,' she says, 'to pass
through a forest and over a lake.   It was this
mansion, one of the most agreeable abodes in
Russia, that the Count Rastopschin himself fired
at the approach of Napoleon.   Such an act may
well command the admiration even of enemies.'

She saw in Moscow men 'most enlightened in
letters and science ; ' but most of the professors
in the learned institutions were there, as in St.
Petersburg, Germans.   Education was hardly yet
appreciated by the Russians ; they nevertheless
had already begun to try their capacity for literature, and, contrary to the usual opinion of foreigners,
she thought their language especially adapted, ' by
its sweetness and resonance,' for music and poetry.
Peter the Great, by founding St. Petersburg, had
opened an inlet for European ideas and culture ;
and the mighty Empire was no longer destined
to be Asiatic, overshadowing Eastern Europe with

Oriental omens ; but to reverse its march, bearing European civilisation, surely, however slowly, over the vast expanse of Central and Northern Asia, and thus sharing in the great mission of the Teutonic race, which is extending that civilisation through Southern Asia, over the North American continent, and over the island world of the Southern hemisphere. Russia could already present, to the French authoress, illustrations of her theory of the progressive improvement and final perfectibility of the human race.

CHAPTER XXXIV.

IN ST. PETERSBURG.

Passage Northward—The Scenery—Appearance of St. Petersburg—
Splendid Houses of the Nobles—National Traits—The Churches—
Hospitality—The Court—Interview with the Empress—With the
Emperor—Character of Alexander—Stein's Notices of her in St.
Petersburg—A Scene at the Theatre—Institutions of Charity and
Instruction—Resumes her Flight.

BONAPARTE was marching towards Moscow; and
Madame de Staël left it with regret and hastened
northward. 'The eternal birches,' she writes,
'fatigue the eye on the route by their monotony;
it is said that even these become rare as you
approach Archangel. They are cared for there,
as we take care of the orange trees in France.
The country from Moscow to St. Petersburg is, at
first, a waste of sand and then of marsh. When
it rains, the soil becomes black, and it is difficult
to trace the roads. The houses of the peasants,
nevertheless, everywhere indicate ease; they are
ornamented with columns; arabesques, sculptures
in wood, relieve their windows. I felt menaced
with winter, which seemed to conceal itself behind
the clouds. The fruits we ate were harsh, as if

their maturity had been too much hastened; a rose caused in me emotions as a souvenir of our more beautiful country ; the flowers seemed to bear their heads with humility, as if the cold hand of the North was already about to seize them.' [1]

From Novgorod to St. Petersburg the country appeared to her an immense marsh, and the splendid metropolis of the North rose before her sight ' as by magic—one of the most beautiful cities of the world, where an enchanted hand had made to spring up, in the midst of deserts, all the marvels of Europe and Asia.' It was to her one of the grandest proofs of ' that power of the Russian will which knows no impossibility.' It is built on a swamp ; its superb masses of marble rest on piles. She marvelled at the miracle of so magnificent a city erected in so short a time. An imposing equestrian statue commemorates Peter the Great; but he needs no such memorial there ; the whole city is his monument. To the foreign visitor might be addressed the words inscribed in St. Paul's to the honour of its architect : ' If you ask for his monument, look around you.'

Her first sentiment, on arriving at St. Petersburg, was one of gratitude that she was on the margin of the sea. She exulted at the sight of the British flag floating on the Neva, after ten years exclusion from the continent. ' I feel,' she says, ' in confiding myself to the ocean, as if I passed

---

[1] *Dix Années,* ii. 15.

again under the immediate protection of the Deity. By an illusion, which we cannot banish, we believe ourselves more in the hands of God when we are in the power of the elements, than when we depend upon man—above all, the man who seems the incarnation of the evil principle in this world.'

Though the din of war filled the air, and the whole empire seemed tremulous under the tread of armies, and the grand crisis which was to startle Europe was impending at Moscow, she found the people, not excepting the higher classes or the Court itself, self-possessed, under the invincible national will, and ready to afford her all courteous attentions. Her own attention, meanwhile, was too much absorbed by the novel sights around her to allow her to be anxious for her safety. 'The edifices,' she writes, 'have yet a dazzling whiteness, and at night they stand out in the moonlight, like great, pale, immovable phantoms, looking down upon the Neva. I know not what is the peculiar beauty of this stream, but never have the waters of any other river appeared to me so limpid. Quays of granite, thirty versts (twenty miles) in extent, border its course, and this magnificence is worthy of the transparent waters which it decorates. The great nobles display the tastes of the people of the South. It is necessary if you would understand them, to see them in their grand houses, built on islands made by the Neva, within the limits of the city. Southern plants, the perfumes of the East, the divans of Asia, embellish their abodes. Immense greenhouses, where the fruits of all countries ripen, afford an artificial climate. The owners of these palaces would not lose a ray of the sun during his appearance upon their horizon ; they fête him as a friend who is soon to leave them, but whom they have before known in happier latitudes.'

The Genevan author, Galiffe (J. A.), who had resided in the city many years, in charge of the foreign correspondence of the banker of the Court, Baron de Rall, devoted himself assiduously to her, not only in her financial affairs, but as companion in the social circles of the capital. 'When,' says a good authority, 'she launched into conversation, he never failed to provide her beautiful hands, as she advanced, with those objects—flowers, leaves, pieces of paper—the manipulation of which was the unconscious but necessary accompaniment of her eloquence. Madame Necker de Saussure attributes this characteristic to her infantile habit of making paper kings and queens perform improvised tragedies. We believe rather that, at heart much more timid than is generally supposed, she was one of those persons who need to have the hands occupied in order to converse with ease and without distraction. Frequently she accepted these little attentions of her compatriot without perceiving them ; at other times they did not escape her notice, and she then would say, 'You tease me ; but I like very much to be thus teased, and you know it.'[2] He wrote to his family, at Geneva, 'I find her better than when I saw her twenty-one years ago. She is charming, and all the world here is enchanted by her.' In one of his works, years later, he speaks of her with enthusiasm. 'She was probably the most remarkable woman,' he says, 'that Europe has produced; the self-conceited of her own sex, and the pedants of ours, can alone refuse her their admiration—following in their judgments the petty rules imagined by their petty minds.'[3] In response to one of his eulogistic letters, Anna Galiffe writes from Geneva, 'I am not astonished that you find her very lovable; as for myself, I have always had a great fear of her; but I know not why, for she is very generous. Years ago I met her at Madame de Montolieu's house; she was delicious; her fascination was irresistible. Later, I have seen her play in tragedy and comedy. When I have seen her in soubrette rôles, I have been in despair that I was not a splendid young man, that I might address to her the most assiduous gallantries. We have had here the famous Talma, who, in speaking of the amiable fugitive, said that he could compare her condition, before she escaped, only to a most painful nightmare.' Galiffe became her confidential correspondent on military and political affairs in

[2] *D'un Siècle à l'autre,* &c. ii. 6, by J. B. G. Galiffe. Geneva, 1878.

[3] *Notices généalogiques sur les Familles Génevoises;* article *Necker,* vol. ii.

Russia, while she was in Sweden, and furnished her with information by which she effectively influenced the policy of Bernadotte. He was now almost daily with her, not only in society, but as her guide to places of interest in the capital.

Soon after her arrival she dined with one of the most esteemed merchants of the city, who maintained Russian hospitality; that is to say, he displayed from his roof a flag as a token that he dined there that day, and that all his friends were welcome to his table without further invitation. 'We dined,' she writes, 'in the open air; so much do they prize here these poor summer days, of which a few still remained, but such as we would hardly think worthy of the name in the south of Europe. The garden was very agreeable; trees and flowers adorned it; but at a few steps from the mansion commenced the desert or marsh. Nature, in the environs of St. Petersburg, has the aspect of an enemy who snatches back his rights the moment that man ceases to fight him.'

She went to the magnificent churches; but, though built of granite and marble, they had been erected too hastily, and failed to please her as works of art, particularly Notre Dame de Casan, which was built by Paul I. in imitation of St. Peter's at Rome. 'It differs the more from its model,' she finely remarks, 'because it is an imitation. We cannot do in ten years what has cost the best artists of the world a century. The Russians wish, by rapidity, to escape time and space; but time sanctions only that which it has itself founded; and the fine arts, though inspiration be their first source, are dependent upon reflection.'

Amidst the resplendent ornaments of these churches she looked in vain for befitting tombs, those grand monuments of the antique temples of western and southern Europe; and their absence suggests a subtle, though paradoxical, remark on the national character. 'The thought of death,' she says, ' produces little effect on the Russians; whether from courage or the inconstancy of their impressions, long regrets are not natural to their character. They are more capable of superstition than of emotion; superstition is related to this life, religion to the next; superstition is allied to fatality, religion to virtue; it is by the vivacity of earthly desires that we become superstitious; it is, on the contrary, by the sacrifice of these desires that we become religious.'

Romanzow, Minister of Foreign Affairs, paid her special attentions. Count Orloff invited her to spend a day at his palace on the most beautiful island of the Neva, where she again saw the splendour of Russian life and hospitality. ' Oaks, rare in this country, shade the island. The Count and Countess spend their fortune in receiving strangers. One is as much at ease there as in a country house, though enjoying all the luxuries of the city. The isle of Orloff is the centre of all those where the great nobles, and the Emperor and Empress themselves, have their summer abodes. Not far from it is the isle of Strogonoff, where the late opulent proprietor collected precious antiquities from Greece ; he kept open house all his days ; whoever had been present once, could return at any time ; he never invited anyone to dinner or supper a second time, the invitation being a standing one ; often he knew not half the persons who dined with him ; but this luxury of hospitality pleased him like all other magnificence. Many of the mansions of St. Petersburg display similar hospitality.'

She was received at Court with distinguished attentions ; first privately, by the Empress Elisabeth, ' who,' she says, ' appears as a guardian angel of Russia. Her manners are reserved, but what she says is full of vigour ; her sentiments and opinions have derived warmth and force from all generous thoughts. I was moved, in listening to her, by something indescribable which belonged not to her grandeur, but to the harmony of her soul. It was a long time since I had witnessed this union of power with virtue. While I was conversing with her a door opened, and the Emperor Alexander appeared. What struck me at first in him was an expression of benevolence and dignity, such that these two qualities seemed inseparable and to make but one. I was also touched by the noble candour with which he spoke of the great interests of Europe in the very first sentences which

he addressed to me. I have always considered as
a sign of mediocrity that fear or ambiguity with
which most European sovereigns treat serious questions; they hesitate to pronounce words which
have a real meaning. The Czar, on the contrary,
conversed with me as would English statesmen,
who find their force in themselves and not in circumstances. The Emperor, whom Napoleon tried
to disparage before Europe, is a man of real intellect and of great information. I do not believe
that he can find a minister equal to himself. He
regrets his mistaken favourable opinion of Napoleon,
but a noble soul cannot be deceived twice by the
same person. He expressed to me also his regret
that he is not a military genius. I responded to
this fine modesty, that a great sovereign is more
rare than a great captain; that, to sustain the
public spirit of his nation by his example, is to
gain the most important of battles. He spoke to
me with enthusiasm of his country and of what it
is capable of becoming. He wished that all the
world could know him, and the ameliorations which
he was attempting in the condition of his people.
" Sire," I replied, " your character is a constitution
for your Empire, and your conscience is its guarantee." " If this were the case," he rejoined, " I
should still be only a happy accident." Noble
words; the first, I believe, of the kind, pronounced
by an absolute monarch. How much virtue is
necessary in a despot in order that he may judge

despotism! He is more liberal than his great nobles. Accustomed to rule their serfs absolutely, they wish him, in his turn, to be all-powerful, in order to maintain the hierarchy of despotism. The middle class does not yet exist in Russia, but it is beginning to arise.'

From the Emperor she went to pay her respects to his mother, 'that Princess to whom calumny has never been able to impute a sentiment unfaithful to her husband, her children, or the family of the unfortunate of which she is the protectress. She conducts an Empire of Charity amidst the all-powerful empire of her son. One of the salons of her palace was built by the Prince Potemkin, and is of incomparable grandeur; a winter garden occupies a part of it, in which you see plants and trees through the colonnade that encircles the centre. All is colossal in this abode. The conceptions of the prince who erected it were strangely gigantic. He built cities in the Crimea merely that the Empress might see them in her passage. He ordered an assault on a fortress only to please a beautiful woman, the Princess Dolgorouki. One sees in the great men of Russia—the Menzikoffs, the Suwarrows, and, still earlier, in Ivan Basiliewitch —something fantastic and violent and ironical; this people still retain their Russian force and originality notwithstanding their external imitation of other nations. I passed a day with M. Narisch-kine, Grand Chamberlain of the Court, a clever and

accomplished man, but who does not know how to
live without continual *fêtes*. From him one gets
a true idea of that vivacity of taste which explains
the faults of the Russians. His house is always
open, and if he has less than twenty guests, he
becomes restless in this philosophic retreat. Ob-
liging to strangers, always in movement and, nevertheless, quite capable of reflection, it is necessary
for him to behave as if at Court ; eager for the
pleasures of the imagination, he discovers them in
things and not in books ; he is impatient everywhere except at Court ; intellectual, magnificent,
rather than ambitious ; seeking in all things a
certain grandeur in which fortune and rank are
exemplified, rather than the individual good of
anybody. His villa is as charming as it can be
rendered by the hand of man, though all around
it are wastes of sand and marshes. From its
terrace you see the Gulf of Finland and the palace
which Peter the Great built on its shores, but the
space between lies all uncultivated ; the Park of
Narischkine alone relieves the eye. We dined in
the Moldavian Hall—that is to say, in a *salon* con-
structed according to the taste of the Moldavians.
It was arranged as if protected against the sun, a
precaution useless in Russia ; nevertheless the imagination is so struck with the idea that you are
among a people who are only accidentally in the
north, that it seems natural to find here usages of
the south ; as if the Russians would, some day or

other, bring hither the climate of their ancient country. The table was covered with the fruits of all lands; according to the custom of the East, these adorned the board, while a crowd of servants handed the viands and vegetables to the guests. We were treated with that music of horns which is peculiar to Russia; some twenty musicians joined in the performance, each producing a single given note whenever it recurred in the piece. Each man bore the name of his note and is called the *sol,* the *mi* or the *re* of M. Narischkine. The horns are graduated in size, from rank to rank, and the orchestra has been called a living organ. Its effect is very fine at some distance, the justness and purity of the harmony producing the noblest impressions; but when you approach these poor musicians, each of whom serves as a single pipe, your interest cools; the mind refuses to see the fine arts converted into mechanism.'—A toast to the success of the combined arms of Russia and England was given at the table, and while it was shouted through the halls and saluted with artillery in the garden, Madame de Staël burst into tears, for, though she wished for the defeat of the invader, she knew it must be by the overthrow of her countrymen. There were some half-savage Calmucks in the palace,—a not unusual sight in the great houses of St. Petersburg. After dinner, long carriages, drawn by splendid horses, conveyed the company through the park. Though August still lingered, the atmosphere was chilly, and the vegetation was beginning to show the change of season; the birds were not heard. A band of music was stationed on the road, and the day ended with the gayest recreations; for these northern people are eager to enjoy their transient summer.

The celebrated German statesman, Baron Stein, the 'reorganizer of modern Germany,' was now in St. Petersburg, and met her frequently at the palace of Narischkine. On the 17th of August, 1812, he wrote to his wife, 'I have seen Madame de Staël; she has an appearance of goodness and simplicity, though she evidently takes no trouble to please ; a certain trustful carelessness, an extreme *abandon*, explain the numerous imprudencies of her language, excusable besides on account of her position in the midst of such a capital as Paris, and of a people perverted and excited by all the passions. She is accompanied by her daughter, who is excellent and without pretension. She proposes to accompany her son into Sweden, and will probably publish there her work on German literature. I do not think she will be appreciated here; for literary taste does not exist in Russia, and women are extraordinarily idle here.' On the last day of the month he again writes : 'I have passed a very agreeable day at Count Orloff's; we were a little intimate party on his island. After dinner Madame de Staël read to us some chapters of her book on

Germany; she saved a copy of it from the claws of Savary, and will print it in England.—She read the chapter on Enthusiasm, which was suppressed by the imperial censorship. It deeply moved me, as much by the profoundness and nobleness of its sentiments as by the elevation of its thoughts; which she expresses with an eloquence that goes to the heart. Perhaps I may be able to copy some passages and send them in this letter. You will be affected and instructed by them.'

Arndt, the friend of Stein, was also in St. Petersburg, and with him witnessed there a scene which he records, and which shows the resentful passions of the people at the time of the French invasion, while it illustrates the sensibility and loyalty of the French exile. Attended by her son and another companion, she went to the Théâtre Français to witness the representation of Racine's 'Phèdre.' They were hardly seated in their box, when the report spread among the spectators that they were French, on which the crowd in the *parterre* rose, and shouted furiously, 'Turn out the accursed French!' The performance was stopped, and the actors fled from the stage. Madame de Staël was led out, deeply grieved and indignant, and bathed in tears, exclaiming aloud, 'O the barbarians! the barbarians! O our Racine!' Arndt was struck by her eloquent and patriotic emotion. 'Would a German woman, or even a young German girl, thus pour out her tears; would she passionately sob if she heard a piece of Schiller or Goethe hissed in a London or Paris theatre ? Perhaps a little of this French and Russian passion would do us no harm.'[4] After this stormy night, the French theatre at St. Petersburg was never opened again till the end of the war.

Madame de Staël found better entertainment in visits to the public places of instruction or charity, which were under the patronage of the two beneficent Empresses. The Institution of St. Catherine, consisting of two edifices, sheltered some four hundred young girls, ' who were guarded with more care than a rich family could give to its daughters.' ' Order and elegance marked every detail of these establishments, and the purest sentiments of morality and religion presided over instruction in the fine arts.' The Russian women ' are naturally graceful,' and she was received with elegant courtesy. She was surprised, and deeply affected, by a recitation in French from her father's ' Cours de Morale Religieuse,' which the Empress herself had ordered. The young girls sung for her sacred chants in choirs. After a repast they gathered in a superb hall, and danced before her. ' The beauty of their features was not striking, but their grace was extraordinary. These were the daughters of the East, with all the decency which Christianity has introduced into the life of woman.' ' An Institution for the Deaf and Dumb, and

---

[4] *Coppet et Weimar*, vii.

another for the Blind, are under the care of the Empress. The Emperor also gives much attention to a school of cadets. All these establishments are truly useful, but are too splendid. If this nation could have peace, it would experience every kind of improvement under the beneficent reign of Alexander. Who knows, however, that the virtues developed by such a war as the present, may not be precisely those which regenerate nations ? The Russians are a military people ; in all other arts they are yet but imitators ; the art of printing has been introduced among them within a hundred and twenty years. The higher civilisation will appear when they put their natural energy into language and literature, as they now display it in action.'

She abandoned herself to the pleasure which the novelties that she saw each day afforded, and almost forgot the war upon which the fate of Europe was depending. 'It was so great a pleasure,' she says, ' to hear expressed, all around me, sentiments which I had long repressed in my soul, that it seemed there was nothing now to fear.' But the war was advancing. Disasters were falling on the country. A foreigner whispered to her that Smolensk was taken, and that Moscow was in great danger. She was again seized with discouragement. It seemed, she says, that the deplorable history of the peace with Austria and with Prussia, followed by the subjugation of their capitals, was about to be repeated. But the Russians, apparently impassive for a time, at last rise with invincible purpose and energy—'thenceforward they know no obstacle, fear no danger, but triumph over both man and the elements.' Still, the heroic deed by which they were to send the invader, reeling and ruined, out of their country—the voluntary destruction of their ancient capital—was inconceivable to her ; the surges of war seemed about to overwhelm the northern capital, and it was time for her to resume her flight.

CHAPTER XXXV.

IN SWEDEN.

Bernadotte—Alexander and Bernadotte at Abo—Madame de Staël's last Interviews at St. Petersburg—In Finland—Scenery—Abo—Letters to Madame Récamier—Dread of the Sea—Arrival at Stockholm—Publication of the 'Reflections on Suicide'—Its Dedication to Bernadotte—Its Character—Letter to Madame Récamier—Letters to the Duchess of Saxe Weimar—To Frederica Brun—Arrival in London.

MARSHAL BERNADOTTE had been chosen, by the Diet of Sweden, Prince Royal, or successor to the reigning sovereign, whose heir had died in 1810. Bernadotte had been a favourite guest of the *salons* of Madame Récamier and Madame de Staël. They were still his correspondents, and Madame de Staël could confide herself and her children to his protection, could she but safely reach his capital.

Before she left Russia the Czar went to Abo for consultation with Bernadotte respecting the war. The news of the fall of Smolensk was confirmed while they were together; they exchanged vows never to make peace with Napoleon—it was to be a war *à outrance.* 'Petersburg,' said Alexander, 'will be taken, but I shall retreat into

Siberia. We will there resume our ancient customs and, like our long-bearded ancestors, we will return to win the Empire again.' 'That resolution,' exclaimed Bernadotte, 'will save Europe.' 'The prediction,' adds Madame de Staël, 'soon began to be verified.'[1] Bernadotte had been one of the wisest of Napoleon's military counsellors. He now condemned, from a strategic point of view, the invasion of Russia as a fatal blunder. He saw in it the beginning of the end. When the news of the entrance of the French into Moscow reached him, and the foreign envoys at his Court had gathered around him in consternation, he said to the representative of Austria, whose troops were still in the French army, 'You may write to your Emperor that Napoleon is ruined, though this exploit seems the greatest in his career.'[2]

On the return of Alexander from Abo to St. Petersburg he conversed freely with Madame de Staël, who says that she was 'convinced of the firmness of his will, and that, in spite of the taking of Moscow, and all the noise which followed, he would never succumb.'

Towards the end of September, 1812, she left St. Petersburg, hoping to reach Sweden through Finland. Previous to her departure she received

---

[1] *Dix Années,* ii. 20.

[2] *Considérations* &c. v. 4. 'I was near him when he thus expressed himself, and I acknowledge that I could not entirely believe his prophecy; but his great knowledge of military science revealed to him this (to others) most unexpected event.'

distinguished farewell attentions from her 'new friends,' as she calls them ; those whom conformity of sentiments had gathered about her in the remote northern metropolis. It was a critical hour for them and for all the European world ; they were to remain and confront an unknown fate ; it was well for her, a woman, to escape, but she took leave of them with profound emotion :—' Sir Robert Wilson, who everywhere sought an occasion of fighting and of inspiring his friends with his own spirit ; M. de Stein, a man of antique character, who lived only in the hope of seeing his country delivered ; the envoy of Spain ; the Minister of England, Lord Tyrconnel ; the intellectual Admiral Bentinck ; Alexis de Noailles, the only French refugee from the imperial tyranny who, like myself, was there to witness for France ; Colonel Dornberg, the intrepid Hessian, whom nothing could turn from his object ; and many Russians whose names have since become celebrated by their exploits. Never was the fate of the world in greater danger ; no person dared to say so, but each knew it ; I alone, as a woman, was not imperilled ; but I could reckon for something that which I had already suffered. In bidding farewell to those worthy chevaliers of the human race, I knew not who among them I should ever see again.'

She has little to say of her passage from St. Petersburg to Stockholm, and we are turning over the last pages of her unfinished narrative of 'The Ten Years of Exile.' 'When one enters Finland,' she writes, ' all things indicate that one has passed into another country, and that one is among another than the Sclavonian race.' They are a simple and unsophisticated people ; there are no châteaux of nobles ; the parsonages of the pastors are the places of hospitality for strangers—the pastors are the great men of the country. 'The aspect of Finland is very different from that of Russia. Instead of the marshes and plains which surround St. Petersburg, you see rocks, mountains, forests ; but soon you perceive that these mountains are monotonous, that these forests are composed of the same trees, the fir and the birch. You see few cities, and these have few inhabitants. There are no centres, no emulation, nothing to say, hardly anything to do, in the northern provinces of Sweden or Russia ; during eight months of the year all living nature sleeps.'

She arrived at Abo, the capital of Finland. 'There is,' she writes, ' a university in this city, and they attempt, to a small extent, the culture of the mind ; but bears and wolves come so near to them in the winter, that all thought is absorbed by the necessity of securing a tolerable physical existence. The labours necessary for this, in the North, consume a good part of the time which is elsewhere devoted to the pleasures of social or intellectual life. It can be said, however, that the difficulties with which nature environs men give them firmness of character and save them from the disorders which attend idleness and ease. Still every moment I regretted the sunbeams of the south, which had penetrated into my very soul.'

She found the Prince Royal still at Abo; his new relations with Bonaparte, as well as his old relations with her and her friend Madame Récamier, disposed him to give her a hearty reception. She wrote from Abo to Madame Récamier on September 29 : 'You sent me long since a letter which I have just received here. You doubt my tenderness for you ; I cannot express to you the wrong this doubt does me ; there are blood and tears between us, and a sister could not be dearer to me than you are. I wrote you from Galicia, and since then I have written no more to you, or Mathieu,[3] or anyone. The place where I have kept this silence has pleased me much. I have thought at times of our design to go there together; would that we had followed that project! The person [4] whom I have sought here speaks of you most tenderly. I have reason to praise him, and I hope my son will profit by his good intentions. What are your plans? Alas! I have ruined your existence ; never shall I have peace while this situation continues. At this moment I

---

[3] Mathieu de Montmorency. She could not safely write from Russia.

[4] Bernadotte.

have no other project than to continue in Sweden. Letters reach me in about fifteen or twenty days. This country, it is true, offers me very few resources, and I am being frozen here already, but I am treated very kindly. My host pleases me, and I already owe him very much.'[5]

Except a few hours, in crossing the Channel, she had never been on the sea, where experience alone gives courage. The French have never been able to reconcile themselves to marine discomforts, and the ' mal de mer ' is to them an unendurable grievance. She dreaded, therefore, with a sort of childish timidity, a voyage on the Baltic, though it were only from Abo to Stockholm. We are struck with surprise at the reflections of so philosophic a mind on such a trivial occasion. She becomes again the sensitive, shrinking woman. ' Since I have been so cruelly persecuted,' she says, ' by Bonaparte, I have lost all confidence in fate ; I believe nevertheless in the protection of Providence, but it is not in the form of happiness in this world. Every need of resolution therefore frightens me, and nevertheless exile has frequently forced me to extreme determinations. I now feared the sea ; all who were about me said that everybody has made the passage, and without harm. Such remarks usually give confidence to voyagers, but my imagination could not be relieved by this kind of consolation ; and the abyss of the sea, from

[5] *Coppet et Weimar,* vi.

which so feeble a protection now separated me, tormented my thoughts. M. Schlegel, perceiving my anxiety, pointed, near Abo, to the prison in which one of the most unhappy Kings of Sweden, Eric XIV., had been incarcerated some time, before dying in another prison near Gripsolm. " If you were there," said he, " how you would long for this sea passage which you now dread." So just a reflection very soon gave a new direction to my thoughts, and the first days of our voyage were quite agreeable. We passed by several islands, and, though there is much more danger near the shore than in mid sea, one never feels there the anxiety that one experiences far out on the waste of waters which seem to touch the sky. I longed to see land on the horizon, however distant I might be from it. The infinite is as fearful to the sight as it is pleasing to the mind. Contrary winds compelled us to cast anchor on the coast of an island near Stockholm ; it was covered with rocks, intermingled with trees but little higher than the rocks from which they sprung ; we hastened to walk on this spot in order to feel the earth again under our feet.' Here closes her narrative, with the single additional but broken sentence, heretofore cited, on her mental sufferings.

She arrived in Stockholm after a voyage which was not without perils. Her health was impaired by her protracted banishment and anxieties ; and, as she had long designed to vindicate her father

by writing a history of the French Revolution, she
now dropped the record of her exile to compose,
as soon as some slighter tasks should be despatched,
her ' Considérations sur les principaux Evènements
de la Révolution Française.' [6] She remained in
Sweden some eight months, and revised there her
' Réflexions sur le Suicide,' which she had written,
as we have seen, in Switzerland in the present year.
It was published at Stockholm early in 1813 ; its
dedication to Bernadotte is dated in December 1812.
' I wrote,' she says to him, ' these reflections at a
time when I felt, in affliction, the necessity of for-
tifying my soul by meditation. It is under your
protection that my sufferings are assuaged. My
children and myself have done what the shepherds
of Arabia do when they see a storm approaching ;
they retreat for shelter under the laurel. I have
heretofore dedicated my works only to the memory
of my father ; I now ask liberty to render this
homage to you whose public life has been signalised
by all the virtues which merit the admiration of
thinkers. Pursue the career which offers you so
beautiful a future, and you will remind the world
again of the lesson which it has so entirely forgotten,
that the highest reason teaches morality, and that
truly magnanimous heroes, far from despising the
human race, believe themselves superior to other
men only by the sacrifices that they make for
them.'

[6] Note, by her son, at the end of her *Dix Années* &c.

In this essay she treats first of the action of suffering on the human soul ; secondly, of the laws which the Christian religion imposes relative to suicide; and thirdly, on the question, In what consists the greatest moral dignity of man on earth ? Goethe's romance of ' Werther' had led to not a few suicides in Germany, but the impassive sage of Weimar felt no responsibility for what he considered to be an abuse of his book. Madame de Staël's conscience shrunk from any such responsibility, direct or indirect. She wished to counteract, by this small but powerful treatise, any countenance given to suicide in her work on ' The Influence of the Passions,' and her ' Delphine.' Her cousin mentions,[7] as her immediate reason for writing it, a double voluntary murder, accompanied by romantic circumstances, which had excited in Germany a foolish enthusiasm among journalists and people of society. She saw in the late ' horrible scene ' an insensate vanity, a miserable melodrama, a sort of affectation in the victims who thus made their death a spectacle before the world. Treating the subject in a general way, she uses the utmost force of her talent to develop the resources which moral elevation and true religion afford to man in misfortune. She describes suffering as a means of discipline and regeneration in the hands of Providence. The study of the ethics and, above all, of the spirit of Christianity, demonstrates, as she shows, that it

---

[7] *Notice* &c. i.

condemns suicide . and places moral dignity in resignation and fortitude rather than in impatience
and revolt. In other works she has exalted Christianity as the consolation of the afflicted ; in this,
' the last on these matters that she wrote, she
places herself in the very centre of the system,
and she herself, so great a sufferer, adheres to the
single faith which saves from despair by consecrat-
ing sorrow.'

We have but slight intimations of her further
sojourn in Sweden.[8] On October 18 she again
writes to Madame Récamier from Stockholm : ' I
can at last, dear friend, write to you with a little
more freedom. Fourteen months have passed since
I saw you last, and before my great voyage I
postponed six months saying adieu to you. During
the four months I have been travelling, I have experienced so much agitation that I have been unable to feel the full pain of our separation till now,
when I am safe, or at least believe myself to be
safe, from all peril. From one end to the other of
my great tour I have been received as a princess.
I am treated with special kindness by our common
friend here. He offers for Auguste a career which
combines, as it seems to me, all possible advantages.

[8] Galiffe (J. B. G.) gives, in his *D'un Siècle à l'autre* (ii. 6)
numerous extracts from her letters at this time to her confidential
correspondent at St. Petersburg, J. A. Galiffe ; but they are mostly
brief notes of compliment or business. They add, however, as the
author says, to the proofs that ' it was she, certainly, who contributed
the most to decide Bernadotte to declare himself against Bonaparte.'

He will commence his diplomatic life in America, and from there he will go where circumstances may place me.'

Though she alludes in this letter to the greater safety of her correspondence, it still imperilled her friends. A few months after this date, Bonstetten wrote to Frederica Brun : 'Have you heard of the misfortune of M. de Sabran, whom you have seen at Coppet ? A letter from Madame de Staël, which he answered, has placed him in the prison at Vincennes, perhaps for life.'[9]

On January 13, 1813, she wrote to the Duchess of Saxe Weimar : 'I know not that the souvenir which I sent you from Russia has reached you, but I cannot find myself again in a tranquil situation without feeling the need of expressing my gratitude for your kindness to me. Circumstances have been more propitious to me than they could have been had I left earlier. It is not the first time that the sufferer who has confided himself to God has been conducted to happiness through trials. I am as well situated here as one can be in these times. The Prince Royal is the true hero of our age, for he joins virtue to genius, a union which seemed to be dissolved. My younger son has entered the Swedish army, and I think he will have occasion to exercise his taste for war. What astonishing events have we seen ! A single conversation with you

[9] Bonstetten's *Briefe an Friederike Brun,* &c. ii. Frankfurt a. M. 1829.

and the Duke would be precious to me. I wish I
could transport you both hither in a magic cloud ;
perhaps you would be better off for the change.
The only inconvenience of my abode here is the
climate. In a still ruder climate I have seen your
illustrious niece,[1] who has inspired me with the
profoundest interest. I had a most flattering reception from her august husband, and saw in his
manner a presage of his course. Here the Prince
of Sweden often speaks to me with admiration of
the conduct of your Highness ; he witnessed it, and
wishes me to offer you his homage. He has
singularly flattered me in saying that, at the time,
you' spoke to him of me with kindness. The con-
ference at Abo has inseparably bound the three
Powers, and the Emperor Alexander has spoken
to me of the Prince of Sweden with the highest
esteem,' &c. She again writes to the Duchess :
' We have often spoken of you here at our fireside,
so necessary in the climate of Stockholm. I take
the liberty of sending you an essay that the sad
meditations of my exile have inspired. The dedication, at least, will interest you ; it contains nothing which is not profoundly true. I expect to
be in London in about a month. I hope that, as
letters circulate more readily, I shall not there be
separated from the world, but shall have the advantage of receiving a word from you through
our Minister, M. de Jacobi. Have the kindness to

---

[1] The Czarina.

speak of me to Goethe, and to Madame de Shardt. Would that I could revisit Weimar! Has Schlegel's work on the Continental System reached you? It seems to me that it ought to interest you.' Though this essay bore Schlegel's name, Pluchart, a Brunswick publisher, catalogued it as a work of Madame de Staël. It is not improbable that she influenced its composition.

On March 30, 1813, she wrote to Frederica Brun: 'You are kind in offering me your house at Copenhagen. I should be happy to see you there; but I fear Mons. Alguier, not personally, but as Ambassador of France. And besides, while the Continental system is still unchanged, could I venture from Sweden among the Danes [2]—I who am so much attached to the Prince Royal? I should feel as if I had re-entered my country could I again fold you in my arms, and your beautiful Ida, so charming an image of Italy!

---

[2] 'Yes! she would have been received with enthusiasm before the publication of the pamphlet on the *Continental System* which was attributed to her! She was far from having written it.'—Madame Brun's note to this letter. Madame de Staël herself wrote from Stockholm, May 7: 'Where have you learned that I am the author of the *Continental System*? Schlegel wrote it. I do not thus intermeddle with politics. If I ever publish anything on the subject, it will be from the philosophic standpoint.'—Galiffe's *D'un Siècle à l'autre* &c. ii. (2 vols.). Geneva, 1878. A translation was nevertheless immediately issued in England, entitled 'An Appeal to the Nations of Europe against the Continental System. Published at Stockholm, by authority of Bernadotte, in March 1813. By Madame de Staël-Holstein. London: Printed for J. M. Richardson, No. 23 Cornhill, 1813.'

You can understand the mixture of sentiments.
with which my heart has been seized in reading
of the expulsion of the French from Hamburgh.
They were not made to be thus detested; and
were it not for the Corsican, they would remain
what they were created to be, the delight of the
world.   But they have brought Europe to behold,.
in the Calmucks, liberators! What singular representatives of liberal ideas—the Cossacks! But
they will be welcome if they render to each nation,.
as to each man, its natural individuality. The
Prince Royal soon leaves Stockholm, and it will
then become cruelly tiresome to me. Would that
I could be near you! I suffer from the malady of
ennui, but, as I have often said, I have never
experienced it in any place where you were. You
enable the soul to live in an atmosphere which
is never penetrated by this villanous disease; you
sustain, you animate one's talents; and I, more
than any other person, need you, for I know not
how to subsist by myself.'[3]

Having spent the winter in Stockholm, she
departed for England about the end of May. The
ensuing four months were spent mostly in society
(where her reception was an incessant ovation) and
in preparing for the publication of her ' Allemagne,'
which appeared in October, and produced a profound and universal sensation in the literary and
fashionable worlds.

[3] Bonstetten's *Briefe an Friederike Brun* &c. ii.

CHAPTER XXXVI.

IN ENGLAND.

Arrival in England—First Impressions—Condition of England—Her Reception there—Her Opinion of London Society—Conversation—. Byron's Allusions to her—Mackintosh—Wilberforce—Fanny Burney again—Death of Albert de Staël—A Severe Letter to him.

ABOUT twenty years had passed since Madame de Staël's first visit to England—years of agitation, of anguish. She came now in better mood to observe and enjoy English scenery and life—so comparatively tranquil and secure, girdled by the defences of the seas. She not only felt personally safe, but she shared the presentiment, which was everywhere rife, that a fatal crisis in Napoleon's destiny was now impending, for the avenging Nemesis had been outlined on the clouds which had gathered, in the far East, over his doomed host of nearly half a million men. The season was also propitious with genial weather and the promise of the fields. 'The waves,' she says, ' of the North Sea, which bore me from Sweden, still inspired me with fear, when I perceived afar the verdant island which alone had escaped the subjugation of Europe. We landed there in the month of June 1813.

From Harwich to London we passed over a grand road, nearly seventy miles long, which was bordered, at short intervals, with country mansions, on the right and on the left ; a series of habitations ornamented with gardens and interspersed with villages. The common people were well clothed ; there were no ruined cottages. Even the cattle had an air of peace and prosperity, as if there were rights for them as well as for man in this great structure of social order.'[1]

In spite of the restrictions which Napoleon's policy had imposed on British commerce, and serious derangements of the currency, England had not ceased to advance. Capital had been productively invested in agricultural improvements ; ' the number of houses had increased everywhere, and the growth of London within a few years was incredible.' But above all she found there liberty protected by law, so long an unknown blessing on the Continent. She wrote to the proscribed General Moreau : ' Let us not be distrustful of principles because of their misfortunes. Truth, and, by consequence, liberty, will always be the chief power of honest men. The country that I now inhabit is indeed a splendid proof of the value, the glory, of limited, representative government ; personal merit prevails here above all things, and can do all things.'[2]

Her reception in the society of the English

---

[1] *Considérations* &c. vi. 3.   [2] *Coppet et Weimar,* vii.

metropolis was enthusiastic. She was recognised there as the chief of her sex in literature; and the British hostility to Napoleon procured for her universal sympathy as one of the chief victims of his power. The great houses in which she was received were crowded by the nobility and people of culture ; and such was their eagerness to see her, that the ‘ ordinary restraints of high society ’ were, we are told, quite disregarded. At the house of Lord Lansdowne, and other similar places, the first ladies in the kingdom mounted on chairs and tables to catch a glimpse of her.[3] A lady who herself ornamented some of the best circles of London, records that ‘ she was received with all the honours due to her genius, sought for in every society. The Prince Regent, with more taste than he now often displays, went to Lady Heathcote’s one evening, purposely that she might be presented to him previously to her appearance at his fête, where she could not have gone without having been introduced before it.’ ‘ She has received 1,500*l.* for her work on Germany.’ [4]

She records high opinions of English society ; but misjudged it somewhat, from the throngs and enthusiasm with which she was almost suffocated in the selectest circles.[5] ‘ Though this country,’ she says, ‘ includes the most interesting men and

---

[3] Norris’s *Madame de Staël*, xlviii.

[4] *Remains of the late Mrs. Richard Trench*, edited by her son, the Dean of Westminster. London, 1862.

[5] *Considérations* &c. vi. *passim*.

the most splendid women, the real enjoyments of
society are rarely found here. If the foreigner
understands the language and is admitted to the
less crowded companies, he enjoys the noblest
pleasures that the intercourse of thinking beings
can afford ; but it is not of such intellectual fêtes
that English society consists. One is every day
invited in London to immense assemblies, where
they elbow one another as in the pit of the theatre.
The women are a majority there ; and ordinarily
the throng is so great that their beauty even has not
sufficient space for its display ; and of course there
is no opportunity for the play of talent. Considerable physical force is necessary in order to make
your way through the salons without suffocation,
or to get again into your carriage without accident ;
hardly any other superiority can be necessary in
such routs. The more serious men abandon them
as soon as possible to the *grand monde*, as it is called,
and it is, one must needs say, the most arbitrary
combination that can be found of elements so distinguished. These reunions arise from the necessity
of admitting a great number of persons into the
circle of one's acquaintance. The list of visitors
that an English lady receives sometimes com-
prises twelve hundred persons. French society is
infinitely more exclusive ; the aristocratic spirit
which presides over the formation of circles among
us is favourable to elegance and amusement, but
accords little with a free state.' ' In France, under

the old régime, conversation led everything; in England this talent is appreciated, but it is useful in nothing pertaining to the ambition of those who possess it; it is consequently neglected by public men. The national character of the English being inclined to reserve and timidity, a powerful motive is necessary to prompt them, and such a motive is found only in the importance of public discussions.'

She was oppressed by the *éclat*, the hurry, the crowds, with which she was received at the great houses of the metropolis. Among her hosts, or guests, were Lords Lansdowne, Holland, Grey, Jersey, Harrowby, Erskine, Byron. All party repugnances gave way before her brilliant presence, and men of the most opposite public positions united in paying homage to her genius. 'I can never forget,' she says, 'the society of Lord Grey, of Lord Lansdowne, and of Lord Harrowby. I name these because they belong to different parties, or sections of parties, which represent nearly all the shades of English political opinion. There are others that I recall with great pleasure.' She proceeds to record her impressions of their personal traits, their domestic life, and the thorough courtesy of their social intercourse. At Lord Lansdowne's country house, Bowood, 'I have seen,' she writes, 'the most splendid gathering of cultivated men that England, and consequently the world, could present. Sir James Mackintosh, the historian of the constitutional liberty of England, a man so

universal in his knowledge and so brilliant in his
conversation, that the English cite him with pride
to foreigners, to prove that in these respects also
they can be among the first ; Sir Samuel Romilly,
a light and honour of that English jurisprudence
which commands the respect of the world ; and ·
poets, and other men of letters, not less remarkable
in their career than the statesmen in theirs, each
contributing to the splendour of such a society
and of the illustrious host who presided over it,
for in England intellectual and moral culture
are united.'[6]   To her this blending, in social life,
of distinguished men of all political sentiments,
seemed a moral superiority over French society.
At Lord Harrowby's house she found 'the most
perfect example of what a conversation can be, by
turns literary and political, and in which the two
subjects are treated with equal ease.'

Though she admired the elegance of English
society, her more liberal, not to say republican
sentiments were shown in the less fastidious composition of her own parties at her residence, 30
Argyll Place, Regent Street.   'Her drawing-room
was,' it is said, 'the rendezvous of all the rank and
fashion of the town ;'[7] she was 'the lion of the
season and, according to an aristocratic witness,

[6] In the company at Bowood were (besides herself, her son and
daughter): Romilly ; Dumont, the friend of Mirabeau and Bentham ;
Count Parmela ; Mackintosh ; poet Rogers ; Ward, afterwards Earl
of Dudley, &c.—Romilly's *Memoirs*, vol. iii.   London, 1840.

[7] Norris's *Madame de Staël*, xlviii.

spoiled the campaign of Dr. and Miss Edgeworth, who had been the fashion during the earlier part of the year.' In her evening receptions were mingled all classes; she required only personal merit, in genius, literature, or any other good distinction, or promise of distinction, for admission; and her own hearty and facile manners enabled her to harmonise the contrasted elements thus brought together in reunions so contrary to the predilections of English society. By the side of the representative of the highest 'West-end' aristocratic life, was often seen a humble but hopeful representative of 'Grub Street.' Byron expresses his astonishment at the mixed, un-English scene; it reminded him, he says, of 'the grave where all distinctions are levelled.' The young poet, now rapidly ascending to the zenith of his fame, saw her frequently in the London circles, and has left us numerous allusions to her which betray his cynical temper, his contemptuous distrust of all feminine literary pretensions, and yet show that even he was at last completely conquered by her indisputable power, though she was not afraid to rebuke severely his moral defects.

It is not uninteresting to read the impromptu judgments of such a man on the character of such a woman—judgments given in familiar letters, or jotted down in a private journal. 'Rogers,' he writes, 'is out of town with Madame de Staël, who hath published an essay against Suicide, which,

I presume, will make somebody shoot himself.'
'The Staël attacked me most furiously—said that
I had no right to make love—that I had treated
. . . barbarously—that I had no feeling, and was
totally insensible to *la belle passion,* and had been
all my life. I am very glad to hear it, but I did
not know it before.' The news of the deplorable
death of her son Albert reached London, where-
upon the reckless poet writes : 'Madame de Staël
has lost one of her young Barons, who has been
carbonaded by a vile Teutonic adjutant—kilt and
killed in a coffee-house at Scrawsenhawsen. Corinne
is, of course, what all mothers must be, but will,
I venture to prophesy, do what few mothers could
—write an essay upon it. She cannot exist without a grievance, and somebody to see or read how
much grief becomes her. I have not seen her
since the event, but judge (not very charitably)
from prior observation.' There was some truth in
this judgment, for she had some of the 'infirmities
of genius,' but Byron never uttered a judgment
more completely copied from himself. Again :
'To-day received Lord Jersey's invitation to Middleton—to travel sixty miles to meet Madame . . .!
I once travelled three thousand to get among silent
people ; and this same lady writes octavos and
talks folios. I have read all her books. I like
most of them and delight in the last ;[8] so I
won't hear as well as read.' Again : 'At Lord

8 The 'Germany' had now appeared in London.

Holland's I was trying to recollect a *quotation* (as I think) of Staël's, from some Teutonic sophist, about architecture. " Architecture reminds me of frozen music," says this macaronico Tedescho. It is somewhere, but where? The demon of perplexity must know, and won't tell. I asked M——, and he said it was not hers, but P——r said it must be *hers,* it was so *like.*' The phrase is really Goethe's (*eine erstarrte Musik*), and was cited by Madame de Staël in her 'Allemagne.' Byron was doubtless hunting it up as a vindication of a similar metaphor in his ' Bride of Abydos.' In the sixth note to that poem, an edition of which was now issued by Murray, he quotes her in self-defence against his critics, and adds an opinion of her intellectual rank which may be set off against all his cynical allusions. ' She is,' he says, ' the first female writer of this, perhaps of any age.' But, to resume these allusions, he writes still later : ' Received a very pretty billet from Madame la Baronne de Staël-Holstein. She is pleased to be much pleased with my mention of her last work in my notes. I spoke as I thought. Her works are my delight, and so is she herself for half an hour. She is a woman by herself, and has done more than all the rest of them together intellectually. She ought to have been a man. She *flatters* me very prettily in her note, but I *know* it. The reason why adulation is not displeasing is that, though untrue, it shows one to be of consequence enough, in one way or another, to induce people to

lie, to make us their friends ; that is their concern.'
Again: 'Asked for Wednesday to dine at Lord
Holland's and meet the Staël.   Asked particularly,
I believe, out of mischief, to see the first interview
after my answer to her note, with which Corinne
professes herself to be so much taken.   I don't
much like it—she always talks of *myself* or *herself*,
and I am not (except in soliloquy as now) much
enamoured of either subject—especially one's works.
What the —— shall I say about " Germany!" I
like it prodigiously.   I read her again and again,
and there can be no affectation in this ; but, unless
I can twist my admiration into some fantastical
expression, she won't believe me ; and I know, by
experience, I shall be overwhelmed with fine things
about rhyme,' &c.   Again : ' Dined at Lord Holland's on Wednesday.   The Staël was at the other
end of the table, and less loquacious than heretofore.   We are now very good friends, though she
asked Lady Melbourne whether I really had any
bonhomie.   She might as well have asked that
question before she told C. L., " C'est un démon."
True enough, but rather premature, for *she* could
not have found it out.'   ' I do not love Madame de
Staël,' he writes to Murray, ' but depend upon it
she beats all your natives hollow as an authoress ;
and I would not say this if I could help it.'   Again,
in the Journal : ' More notes from Madame de
Staël—unanswered, and so they shall remain.   I
admire her abilities, but really her society is over-

whelming—an avalanche that buries one in glittering nonsense—all snow and sophistry.' 'Dined with Rogers, Madame de Staël, Mackintosh, Sheridan, Erskine, &c. Sheridan told a very good story of himself and Madame Récamier's handkerchief. *She* says she is going to write a big book about England; I believe her. We got up from table too soon after the women; and Mrs. Corinne always lingers so long after dinner that we wish her in—the drawing-room.' The 'big book' was probably her 'Considérations sur la Révolution Française,' which she had now begun, and which, though designed to be a vindication of her father's political life, is largely a discussion of English institutions and politics. Again, writes Byron: 'The Staël outtalked Whitbread, was *ironed* by Sheridan, confounded Sir Humphry, and utterly perplexed your slave. The rest (great names in the Red Book nevertheless) were mere segments of the circle. Mademoiselle de Staël danced a Russ saraband with great vigour, grace, and expression.'

Byron makes one allusion to Rocca : 'Asked for Wednesday to dine and meet the Staël. The lover, Mr. ——, was there to-night, and C. said it was the only proof *he* had seen of her good taste. Monsieur l'Amant is remarkably handsome, but I don't think him more so than her book.'[9] Her marriage with Rocca being still a secret, Byron's mistake about him was natural, though quite characteristic.

---

[9] Moore's *Byron*, vol. ii. *passim.*

Sir James Mackintosh was her ardent admirer,
and was now almost daily associated with her at
dinner parties, where he shone with hardly less
brilliancy than herself as a talker—'the brightest
constellation of the North,' as Byron called him.
'On my return,' he writes, 'I found the whole fashionable and literary world occupied with Madame
de Staël, the most celebrated woman of this, or
perhaps any age. She has long been persecuted
by Bonaparte with the meanest rancour for the
freedom of her sentiments. She treats me as the
person she most delights to honour. I am generally
ordered with her to dinner, as one orders beans
and bacon. I have in consequence dined with her
at the houses of almost all the Cabinet Ministers.
She is one of the few persons who surpass expectation. She has every sort of talent, and would be
universally popular if, in society, she were to con-
fine herself to her inferior talents—pleasantry, anecdote, and literature, which are so much more suited
to conversation than her eloquence and genius.' 'I
saw Lord Wellesley fight a very good battle with
her,' remarks Mackintosh, on another occasion, 'at
Holland House, on the Swedish treaty ; indeed
he had the advantage of her, by the politeness,
vivacity, and grace with which he parried her eloquent declamations and unseasonable discussions.
I could tell you a great number of good sayings
and stories if I had strength and spirits, but I must

reserve them for a season of more vigour.'[1] Mackintosh's great conversational powers, distinguished
by a sort of French vivacity, sustained her own in
English society.   Alluding to a dinner party where
he had failed to meet her, she writes to him : ' We
have dined with Ward, but you shone there as the
images of Brutus and Cassius ; there is no society
here without you. Ward was amiable enough, but
he preached in the desert.' ' It is very irksome to
dine without you, and company flags when you are
not here. I nevertheless have Sheridan, but in
English I have only ideas, not words.' She maintained through the remainder of her life a familiar
correspondence with him, and translated his celebrated speech for Peltier.

' She was,' says another authority,[2] ' the most
popular guest at Lansdowne House and Holland
House. Lords Grey, Harrowby, Erskine, and Jersey
were alternately her hosts and guests. At Rogers'
literary dinners she always had her seat, and Byron
and Mackintosh, nay, all the leading men of the
day in politics or literature, were her intimates.'
Even Madame d'Arblay (Fanny Burney), who, after
her friendship at Mickleham, had disowned her
at Paris, in deference to Napoleon, now relented.
' I am truly glad,' she wrote, ' that you had a gra-

---

[1] *Memoirs of the Life of the Right Honourable Sir James Mackintosh*, edited by his Son, 2nd edit. vol. ii. chap. iv.   London, 1836.

[2] Wharton's *Queens of Society.*

tification you so earnestly coveted—that of seeing Madame de Staël. Your account of her was extremely interesting to me. As for myself, I have not seen her at all. Various causes have kept me in utter retirement; and in truth, in respect to Madame de Staël, my situation is truly embarrassing. I do not recollect if I communicated to you our original acquaintance, which at first was intimate. I shall always, internally, be grateful for the partiality with which she sought me out upon her arrival in this country before my marriage; and still, and far more, if she can forgive my dropping her. She is now received by all mankind, but that indeed she always was (all womankind I should say) with distinction and pleasure.' This looks somewhat like late repentance. The English authoress had mellowed a little by years and suffering, and had acquired some of the amiability of her French friend. She was now reading the ' Allemagne.' She writes again: ' I am only advanced to about a third of the first volume; I perpetually long to write to her, but imperious obstacles are in the way; and next, to you, to tell you, as the person most likely to sympathise with me sincerely, the pleasure, the transport rather, with which I read nearly every phrase. Such acuteness of thought, such vivacity of ideas, and such brilliancy of expression, I know not where I have met with before. I often lay the book down to enjoy for a considerable time a single sentence.

I have rarely, in the course of my whole life, read anything with so glowing a fulness of applause. But there! I now stop.'[3]

She met Wilberforce occasionally, but the good man's notions of piety rendered repugnant to him these scenes of colloquial wit and gaiety. An eloquent talker himself, he enjoyed her conversation, but his journal abounds in intimations about his temptations to accept, and his religious scruples against accepting, invitations to the ever-recurring dinner parties in which she was the idol. He mentions, however, with pride her presence at one of his Anti-Slavery meetings, at which the Duke of York presided, supported by the Duke of Sussex, two Archbishops, the Chancellor of the Exchequer, &c. Wilberforce was applauded to the echo ; he was not insensible to such demonstrations ; but in alluding to them he mentions the fact of her presence, evidently as one of the most grateful flatteries of the occasion. She was in hearty sympathy with his philanthropic schemes, and endeavoured to promote them on the Continent, as we shall soon see. In her 'Considerations on the French Revolution,' she alludes to this meeting and says : ' The man the most beloved and the most esteemed in all England, Wilberforce, could hardly make himself heard ; the applause of the people drowned his voice.' Her political liberalism and her womanly sympathies interested her profoundly in the man

[3] *Diary and Letters*, v.

as well as the cause he represented. 'Romilly,' he writes, 'told me aloud that Madame de Staël assured him she wished more to be acquainted with me than any other person. The Duke of Gloucester made me, by her express desire, fix a day for meeting her at dinner. She told the Duke that I did not think how really religious she is.' He dined with her at last at the Duke of Gloucester's. 'Madame de Staël, her son and daughter, the Duke, two aides-de-camp, Vansittart, Lord Erskine, poet Rogers, and others present. Madame de Staël quite like her book, though less hopeful, complimenting me highly on Abolition. "All Europe," &c. But I must not spend time in writing this.'

He again dines with her, and 'her son and daughter, and two other foreigners, Lord Harrowby, Lord and Lady Lansdowne, Sir James Mackintosh. She asked me to name the party. A cheerful pleasant dinner. She talking of the final cause of creation—not utility but beauty. Did not like Paley. Wrote about Rousseau at fifteen, and thought differently at fifty. Evening, assembly, but I came away at half-past eleven—a brilliant assemblage of rank and talent.' 'The whole scene,' he writes the next day, 'was intoxicating even to me. The fever arising from it is not yet gone off (half-past eight A.M.), though opposed by the most serious motives and considerations both last night and this morning.' 'Wilberforce,' said Madame de Staël to Mackintosh, 'is the best talker I have

met with in this country; I have always heard
that he was the most religious, but I now find that
he is the wittiest man in England.'[4] She later
corresponded with him, and, at the Duke of Wellington's request, translated his 'Letter to his Yorkshire Constituents.'

Her oldest son, Auguste, had joined the family
in London, and was her best comforter under the
terrible news, so heartlessly mentioned by Byron,
of the death of Albert. This unfortunate youth
was 'endowed,' says his sister, the Duchesse de
Broglie,[5] 'with much personal beauty and a mind
full of grace and originality.' He accompanied his
mother, as we have seen, to Russia and thence
to Stockholm, where, under the auspices of Bernadotte, he entered the army of Sweden with brilliant prospects. 'During the few weeks which
he had passed in the service,' continues his sister,
'he displayed an excess of bravery which men
habituated to courage, in a time when it was so
common, witnessed with astonishment. He seemed
to live at ease only in danger; he sought it with
passion on occasions when there was no utility in
exposing himself, and against the remonstrances
of those around him. War had always been the
single object of his ambition; a sedentary existence was intolerable to him, and, from his infancy,

---

[4] *Life of Wilberforce,* iv.

[5] *Notice* &c. introductory to the *Œuvres diverses d' Auguste de
Staël,* i. Paris, 1829.

he often perilled his life in his sports. In taking leave of his mother, he said, " I will cover myself with glory, or return no more." He perished when not twenty years old. Albert and Auguste were affectionately attached to each other, in spite of the contrasts of their characters. The same warmth of soul, the same natural generosity, characterised them ; but with the elder brother these qualities were kept under a grave self-control, with the younger they were impetuous and irregular. Auguste joined to the tenderness of a brother the solicitude of a father for Albert ; he watched over him and feared the dangers which beset a nature so headstrong and ardent. He wept for Albert as for a brother and a son ; and devoted himself more than ever to his mother, in order to soften an affliction so cruel.' Such is the too partial account of the case from a sister's pen.

It would have been a relief to the mother's grief had the youth perished in battle, but he fell ignobly in a duel—a consequence of his impetuous temper and heedless courage. One of his earliest play-mates, who still survives, says : ' He led an irregular life, and met a deplorable death at Doberan, a small city of the Duchy of Mecklenburg-Schwerin, on the coast of the Baltic Sea, a favourite resort in summer for bathing, gambling, &c. Some officers of the état-major of Bernadotte had gone to try their luck in this place of play and pleasure. They quarrelled over some louis, and a duel immediately ensued. I well remember that the Grand Duke Paul of Mecklenburg-Schwerin told me he was there at the time, and, while walking with his tutors in the park, suddenly heard the clinking of swords in a neighbouring thicket. They ran to the place, and reached it just in time to see the head of Albert fall, cleft by one of those long and formidable sabres which were carried by the Prussian cavalry.'[6] He was characteristically reckless. We have seen a good example of his spirit in his defiance of the police officer who insulted his mother at Lanzut, Poland. He had occasioned his family continual anxiety, and the severest document that remains from his mother's pen is a letter to him, in his eighteenth year, in which she was constrained to rebuke his indiscretions with bitter anguish and indignant reproaches. It may well be cited as an example of maternal faithfulness towards a perverse child, whose conduct added to the afflictions of one of the darkest periods of her life, for it was written about the time when she was preparing for her flight to Russia. 'I believe it to be my duty,' she says, ' to write you, Albert, though a sentiment of pride would deter me from doing so to any other person than my son. Look at the picture of your conduct. You have insulted, in the grossest manner, a woman who has here neither brother nor husband; whom I alone protect; and who, in her noble country, could not encounter a single man

[6] M. Pictet de Sergy's unpublished *Souvenirs.*

capable of outraging a woman, and, above all,
of outraging her without the least danger. Your
conduct unites feebleness of soul with hardness of
heart. After two days you have not made to her
the least apology, nor to me either, and you live in
my house, under the shelter of my home and of my
fortune, without deigning to show me any regard.
It is on your account that this conduct afflicts me,
for you ought to understand that I can dispense
with your homage, and you are not in a state to
know the mother that you have. You should
know that it is to my name, or rather to that of
my father, that you owe all that is agreeable to you
in the world. And on what, I ask you, is your
arrogance founded? Is it on your past life? You
know what I know of it. Is it on the knowledge
you have acquired—the consideration which you
enjoy? The most indulgent say for you, " He is
foolish, but this will pass off." I see no great reason
for pride in such praise. Meanwhile life advances,
and you alienate from you your mother, your
brother, your sister. Except the miserable attach-
ments which a fine face can procure, I know not
a single tie that you have. M. de Montmorency is
here; you stand aloof from him. Nothing pleases
you but vulgar habits, the pipe, &c. Neither the
intellect of your mother, nor the dignified manners of your brother, nor the charm of your
sister, nor the talents of M. Schlegel, attract you.
No idea of religion occupies you. Obedience, and

respect for your mother, which God commands, appear to you only a burden of which you must relieve yourself as soon as possible. In short, what good, what duty do you accomplish throughout the day? And, if I should die to-morrow, what memory could satisfy you as regards your relations with me from the day that you came into the world? You believe that life consists in pleasure; it is quite otherwise. I am neither severe nor cold; pleasures, those at least which captivate the imagination, have also had too much influence over me; but, God be thanked, I should not sleep in peace did I believe that I had wounded an unhappy being, and I could not endure for one hour the idea of having wronged my father. Albert, you are preparing for yourself a deplorable life; not that I will charge myself with the punishment you deserve. I will follow towards you what I conceive to be the line of duty. You imagine that it is admirable to be eighteen years old, and to be five feet and six inches high; there are, nevertheless, other examples of these distinctions. You suppose, in addition to this idea, that bravery is perfection; it is a beautiful thing, but you have still a misfortune. It is that even in this quality you are wanting in that generosity towards the feeble, in that respect for woman, which alone makes bravery chivalric. John can brave death as well as you, and even with more presence of mind. Of what service, then, is it to you that you are the grandson of

Necker? And do you never think that this title, which now protects you, will very soon be your accusation?'[7]

The fate of such a character could hardly be doubtful. Madame Necker de Saussure, who knew him well, agrees with his sister, however, in allowing him some redeeming qualities. 'His impetuous disposition,' she says, ' had always occasioned much anxiety to his family, but his noble and tender sentiments were worthy of the tears he caused them.'[8]

---

[7] *Revue Rétrospective,* First Series, tome iii. There are a few other letters of Madame de Staël, and also of Necker, in this valuable periodical, in both the first and the second series. (20 vols.) Paris, 1833–38.

[8] *Notice* &c. i.

CHAPTER XXXVII.

IN ENGLAND—THE 'ALLEMAGNE.'

Publication of the 'Allemagne'—Its History and Plan—Byron's Opinion
of it—Mackintosh reviews it in the ' Edinburgh Review '—Its early
Editions—Criticism on it—Its Standpoint—The Romantic School
—Sainte-Beuve's Opinion of the ' Allemagne '—Villemain's Opinion
—Lamartine's—Vinet's Criticism—Goethe's Opinion—It discloses
German Literature to the World—Maturity of her Genius and Fame
at this time—Napoleon's Downfall.

THE interest excited in England by the brilliant
social qualities, the literary fame, and the persecutions of Madame de Staël was suddenly and im-
measurably enhanced by the publication of her
' Germany,' in London, in the autumn of 1813. It
proved to the sober, practical English mind that
the dazzling talker was also a profound thinker.
No work from a feminine hand had ever equalled
it in masculine vigour, and depth of thought as well
as of sentiment.

We have seen how the precious manuscript
escaped the hands of the Government, at Paris, by
the forethought of her son, and afterwards by her
own evasion of the police at Coppet. Secretly carried through all her flight over Germany, Poland,
Russia, the Baltic Sea, and Sweden, it was now

secured to the world for ever by the press of England, and all intelligent Frenchmen have since been proud of it as one of the monuments of their national literature.

In her preface she told the British public the story of its misfortunes, inserting the insulting letter of Savary, the Duke de Rovigo, already noticed. 'At the moment,' she said, ' when this work was about to appear, and when ten thousand copies had already been printed, the Minister of Police, known by the name of General Savary, sent his gendarmes to the publisher, with orders to cut into pieces the whole edition. Sentinels were stationed at the different outlets of the building, to prevent the escape of a single copy of so dangerous a book. A commissioner of police was charged to superintend this expedition. General Savary obtained an easy victory, but the poor commissioner died, I am told, from his anxious labours to make sure, in detail, of the destruction of so many volumes, or rather of their transformation into perfectly white pasteboard, upon which no trace of human reason should remain. The intrinsic value of this cardboard, estimated at twenty louis, was the only indemnity that the publisher obtained from the Minister.[1] At the moment that my book was destroyed in Paris I received an order, in the country, to surrender the copy from

---

[1] She, however, sent the publisher 15,000 francs. See her Letters to Camille Jordan, in Sainte-Beuve's *Nouveaux Lundis*, **xii.** p. 314.

which it had been printed, and to leave France in
twenty-four hours.' Such a statement could not fail
to excite the wonder of England. Such a petty, per-
secuting policy, on the part of Napoleon, was inconceivable to the British mind, accustomed to the
utmost liberty of thought and speech, and almost
as unrestricted liberty of the press. The incredible
history of the work now gave it incredible success.

She appended to her preface a brief outline of
its design and plan. 'I have thought,' she says,
'that it would be beneficial to make known the
country of Europe in which study and meditation
have been carried so far that we may consider it
the land of thought. The reflections which the
country and its books have suggested to me may
be divided into four sections. The first will treat
of Germany and the manners of the Germans; the
second, of literature and art; the third, of philosophy and morals; the fourth, of religion and enthusiasm.'

The 'Allemagne' could not, like 'Delphine' and
'Corinne,' appeal to popular readers, the readers
of 'light literature;' but it commanded immediately and universally the interest of the enlightened classes. We have noticed how Byron
admired it, in spite of his cynical dislike of her
conversation and her person. 'I delight in it,' he
wrote. 'I like it prodigiously. I read her again and
again.' Mackintosh immediately reviewed it in the
'Edinburgh Review.' 'The voice of Europe,' he said,

'has already applauded the genius of a national painter in the author of " Corinne." But it was there aided by the power of a pathetic fiction, by the vanity and opposition of national character, and by the charm of a country which unites beauty to renown. In the work before us she has thrown off the aid of fiction. She delineates a less poetical character and a country more interesting by expectation than by recollection. But it is not the less certain that it is the most vigorous effort of her genius, and probably the most elaborate and masculine production of the faculties of woman.' Those chapters which treat of Society and Conversation, he remarks, are the most perfect, and 'exhibit an unparalleled union of graceful vivacity with philosophical ingenuity.' The chapter on Taste, he says, is 'exquisite,' 'balancing with a skilful and impartial hand the literary opinions of nations.' The third part, which treats of Metaphysical Systems, is, he adds, 'a novelty in the history of the human mind, and, whatever may be thought of its success in some of the parts, it must be regarded, on the whole, as the boldest effort of the female intellect.' The concluding portions of the work, on Enthusiasm, he pronounces the most eloquent, 'if we except the incomparable chapter on Conjugal Love.' 'Thus,' he says, after a long citation, 'terminates a work which for variety of knowledge, flexibility of power, elevation of view, and comprehension of mind, is unequalled among the works of women, and which, in the union of the graces of society and literature with the genius of philosophy, is not surpassed by many among those of men.' [2]

The London edition was issued by Murray in three vols. 12mo. In the following year it was reproduced at Paris and Geneva, and in an Italian version at Milan. The next year another edition appeared in Paris in 4 vols. 12mo. and in 3 vols. 8vo. In less than two years later a revised edition was issued in Paris in 2 vols. 8vo. Editions and translations followed in all the principal tongues of Europe. [3]

So imposing a work could not fail to provoke criticism ; besides innumerable ' periodical' reviews, no less than six publications, discussing its merits and demerits, appeared in less than a year, in the German, French, and English languages, from the presses of Heidelberg, Hanover, Bremen, Paris, London, and Edinburgh.

It is from the standpoint of the Romantic School that Madame de Staël considers Germany. The two Schlegels, Ludwig Tieck, Goerres, Brentano, Arnim, Kleist, were then the representatives of that school, and Goethe was hailed as their chieftain, though the universality of his genius rendered him superior to the limitations of any literary sect. These writers endeavoured to be national by reproducing the spirit of the elder German literature

---

[2] *Edinburgh Review,* Oct. 1813.
[3] Querard's *La France Littéraire,* ix.

and legends—the idiosyncrasies of the Northern
mind.   They succeeded to some extent in their
somewhat exclusive aim, in spite of the claims of
culture on all the other possibilities of literature
and art.   Madame de Staël wrote under their
inspiration, and thereby painted a more genuine
picture of intellectual and social Germany than she
could otherwise have produced.   An able German
critic remarks that it is important her readers
should bear in mind this standpoint of her 'remarkable work.'[4]   She took it spontaneously, though
influenced by her favourite German authors; her
previous work on 'Literature' showed her predilections for the Romantic School; it is pervaded by the ideas of that school, and she was
among the first of its founders in France.   She
gives in the 'Allemagne' a fine chapter, discri-
minating the two schools.   'The songs of the
Troubadours, born of Chivalry and Christianity,'
originated, she says, ' the poetry of the Romantic
School.   If we do not admit that paganism and
Christianity, the north and the south, antiquity and
the middle age, chivalry and the Greek and Roman
institutions, divide the empire of literature, we
shall never be able to judge, from a philosophic
standpoint, ancient and modern taste.   Classic
poetry is simple and salient, like external objects;
Christian poetry has need of all the colours of the

----

[4] See the article of Spazier on Tieck, in the *Revue du Nord,*
March 1835.

rainbow. But the question for us is not between the Classic and Romantic poetry, but between the imitation of the one and the inspiration of the other. The literature of the ancients is, with the moderns, a transplanted literature ; the Romantic literature is with us indigenous ; it is the product of our religion and our institutions.'[5]

The fact that she was the principal founder of the Romantic school, in France, shows the salient energy of her genius. Romanticism is legitimate in its own sphere. Its chief fault was its exclusiveness ; for the capabilities of art are as manifold as the needs of culture. While vindicating the Romantic school, Madame de Staël did not exclude Classicism. The partisan spirit provoked by its theorists was irrelevant. Lerminier remarks that ' one party repeated, with Madame de Staël and the Schlegels, that Romanticism was the product of Christianity and chivalry ; another, with some English critics and poets, that its origin was in Saxon and Norman traditions. There were still others, more refined, more metaphysical, who saw in Romanticism the expression of the most profound sentiments of the soul, and an indefinable ideal. There was a resonant shock of systems and theories.'[6] Romanticism, which produced, besides Madame de Staël, such writers as Chateaubriand and Lamartine, and culminated, in our day, in the

---

[5] *Allemagne,* ii. 11.
[6] *De la Littérature Révolutionnaire,* chap. iii. Paris, 1850.

genius of Victor Hugo, has enriched the literature of the modern, without impairing the literary claims of the ancient, world. Lerminier affirms a truth, though not without a spice of malice, when he says that 'Hugo, wishing to establish his title as chief of the Romantic school, its Aristotle, has appropriated the ideas long since put in circulation by Madame de Staël, the Schlegels, Sismondi, and Benjamin Constant, and driven them to an extreme.' The Romantic school has seen the end of its day as an exclusive sect; it will never see the end of its day as a legitimate and brilliant school by the side of Classicism. It is as legitimate there as Gothic architecture is by the side of Greek.

Considered as the initiative of foreign criticism on German literature, Sainte-Beuve esteems the 'Allemagne' a work which 'no other person could have produced at that period.'[7] Madame de Staël was the first writer who effectively disclosed, not only to France, but to Europe generally, the rich mines of the German intellect.

Villemain says : 'We admire the penetrating glance which it casts on all the literature of a nation : its profound intelligence, the vivid sensibility which gives to the analysis all the interest of passion and all the novelty of inspiration. This book—this enthusiasm of literary independence, this apotheosis of duty, this ardour of spiritualism—was in reality an indirect and continual pro-

[7] *Critiques et Portraits Littéraires*, iii.

test against the system of government which then dominated France.' 'The work of Madame de Staël, all animated as it is with a sort of moral independence, breathing hatred of personal interest, enthusiasm for noble sacrifice, for liberty, the liberty of the soul subjected to the single law of duty, shocked the political maxims of the conqueror. The passion which reigns in the book, and which animates it with a single spirit in all the diversity of its subjects and forms—it is moral sentiment.'[8]

Lamartine speaks of the 'Allemagne' with his usual poetic ardour: 'It is a book through which she has poured, and as it were filtrated, all the resources of her soul, of her imagination, of her religion. Appearing about the same time in England and France, it became the subject of the conversation of Europe. Her style, without losing any of its youthful vigour and splendour, seemed now to be illuminated with more lofty and eternal lights as she approached the evening of life and the diviner mysteries of thought. This style no longer paints, no longer chants, it adores. One respires the incense of a soul over its pages. It is Corinne become a priestess, and seeing, from the border of life, the unknown God beyond the horizons of humanity.'[9]

Vinet says that 'its appreciation of authors

[8] *Cours de Littérature Française*, iv.
[9] *Histoire de la Restauration*, ii. 15. Paris, 1852.

and of works is spirited and delicate, and shows rare penetration ; its analyses are full of movement and life, and the cited passages are translated with great talent ; respect for genius, and the sense of the beautiful, illuminate every step of the writer.' Vinet, like Sainte-Beuve, claims for the work a high moral and political purport. ' It was,' he says, ' an enterprise of reaction against the triple despotism of a man in Politics, a sect in Philosophy, and a tradition in Literature. It was one of those life-boats which, in the stress of the storm, is employed courageously for the salvation of a ship in distress. The ship was France, all the liberties of which were, in the opinion of Madame de Staël, perishing at the time. Persuaded that nations are called upon to help one another, she went this time to demand from Germany, humiliated and conquered Germany, the salvation of France. There is more patriotism than national egotism in the work.' ' It inaugurated in literature a new era. For good or for evil its influence was paramount. It put an end to the isolation of two great neighbouring nations. It revealed Germany to France for the first time. All Germany does not appreciate this fact, but hear what Goethe wrote in his old age : ' This book,' he said, ' ought to be considered as a powerful engine which made a wide breach in that Chinese wall of antiquated prejudice which divided the two countries, so that beyond the Rhine, and afterward beyond the Channel, we became better known, a fact that could not fail to procure for us a great influence over all Western Europe.' Vinet thinks that the 'Allemagne' marks the point of maturity of thought and of talent in Madame de Staël—that in style it is the richest, and in moral sentiment the most advanced, of all her works. 'It is in the "Allemagne," if I am not deceived, and particularly in the last part of it, that she shows herself a poet. In approaching the regions of supreme truth, and, by consequence, of repose, she has felt that harmonious concert of sensibility and imagination, which is properly poetry, commence in her soul. Without making use, as in "Corinne," of poetical phraseology, without deviating from the movement of prose, she, perhaps, for the first time sings.'[1]

The 'Allemagne,' as Goethe admits, breached the wall that had barricaded German literature. It did so for England as well as for France, and, finally, for the whole exterior intellectual world. Some twenty years earlier Scott, influenced chiefly by Lewis (author of the 'Monk,' and a thorough German scholar) had given intimations of the wealth of German thought, and made some translations from Bürger and, later, from Goethe, but lost money by their publication. Thirteen years before the appearance of the 'Allemagne,' Coleridge published his translation of Schiller's 'Wallenstein,' and began to talk German philosophy among his friends; but Englishmen continued to

---

[1] *Littérature Française* &c. i.

think the language inexorable, if not barbarous,
and the originality of the German mind fantastic,
and incompatible with British ' common sense.'
The ' Allemagne ' dispelled this prejudice, and, revealing the abundant treasures of German genius
and learning, opened the way for that influx of
German thought which, principally by the subsequent labours of Coleridge and Carlyle, has, for
good or evil, been flooding the English mind and
transforming English scholarship, criticism, and
speculation.

'The " Allemagne " was all a revelation,' says
Philarète Chasles, and what a success ! And how
it has maintained that success ! ' ' Her style,' he
adds, ' shows the influence of German thought on
French literature. She opened the way for that
influence, and was its first example.'

Her ' Corinne ' disproved, as has been remarked, the charge of some of her earlier critics,
that she was insensible to the best impressions
of the fine arts; the ' Allemagne ' presented a
splendid refutation of her alleged incapacity to
appreciate poetry. We have seen Schiller's premature judgment of her in this respect. No
critic has better estimated his own poetic genius.
And where, in all the range of literary criticism,
can be found more poetic as well as more philosophic appreciation of poetry than in the second
part of the ' Allemagne ' ? ' That which is truly
divine in the heart of man cannot,' she says, ' be

defined; if there are words for particular traits. there are none for the *ensemble,* above all for the truly beautiful of all kinds. It is difficult to say what is not poetry; but if we would comprehend what it is, it is necessary to call to our aid the impressions produced by a beautiful landscape, harmonious music, the aspect of a cherished object, above all that sentiment of religion by which we feel the presence of the Divinity. Poetry is the natural language of all religions. The Bible is full of poetry; Homer is full of religion. It is not because there are fictions in the Bible, nor dogmas in Homer, but enthusiasm gathers in one centre divers sentiments; enthusiasm is the incense of earth ascending to heaven; it unites the one to the other. The gift of revealing by words what is felt in the depths of the soul is very rare; there is poetry, nevertheless, in all beings capable of vivid and profound affections; the expression of it is wanting to those who have not endeavoured to discover it. The poet strives to liberate, if we may so speak, the thought, the sentiment imprisoned in his inmost being. Poetic genius is an interior disposition of the same nature as that which renders us capable of a generous sacrifice; the composition of a beautiful ode is a reverie of heroism. If poetic talent were not unstable it would inspire beautiful deeds as often as touching words; for they both equally proceed from the consciousness of the beautiful, felt in ourselves.—Prose is factitious; poetry is natural. The least civilised nations express themselves at first in poetry, and from the moment that a strong passion agitates the soul, the most vulgar spontaneously use images and metaphors; they call to their help external nature for the expression of what is within them inexpressible. Common people are much more poetical than men formed by artificial society; because *convenance* and *persiflage* serve only as limitations, they cannot inspire.' Again: 'Lyric poetry expresses itself in the name of the author himself; he does not transfer himself into a personage, a character; it is in himself that he finds the movements which animate his muse.—Beautiful verses are not poetry; inspiration in the arts is an inexhaustible fountain which vivifies from the first to the last word. Love, patriotism, faith, all ought to be deified in the ode; it is the apotheosis of sentiment. It is necessary, in order to conceive the true grandeur of lyric poetry, to wander, in imagination, in ethereal regions, to forget the noise of the world while listening to celestial harmonies, to consider the entire universe as a symbol of the emotions of the soul.—The enigma of human destiny is nothing to many men; it is always present to the imagination of the poet. The idea of death, which discourages vulgar minds, renders genius more audacious, and the mingling of the beauties of nature and the terrors of destruction excites an indefinable delirium of joy as well as of fear, without which one can neither comprehend nor describe the spectacle of this world. Lyric poetry recounts nothing, restricts itself in nothing to the succession of time or the limitations of places; it soars over countries and over ages; it gives duration to the sublime moment during which the soul rises above the pleasures and pains of life. It feels, in the midst of the marvels of the world, as a being at once creator and created, which must die and yet not cease to be; whose heart, at once trembling and strong, is proud of itself and prostrates itself before God.'

This is poetry as well as poetic criticism. She fails not to avow her favourite 'Romantic' theory of the art. 'The moderns,' she says, 'cannot escape, in poetry, a certain profoundness of ideas to which they have been habituated by a spiritualistic religion. It is necessary that nature assume ideal grandeur, to the eyes of man, in order that it may serve as the emblem of his thoughts. The groves, the flowers, the streams, sufficed to the poet of paganism; the solitude of the forests, the boundless ocean, the starry heavens, can hardly express the conceptions of the infinite and the eternal which fill the Christian imagination.' Such are but detached passages of a single chapter;[2] they are worthy of citation, and are relevant here not only as refutations of the charge against

[2] *Allemagne,* ii. 11.

her poetic taste, but still more as revelations of
both her heart. and head, and prophecies of the
highest tendencies of poetry since her day.

It was her good fortune to write the 'Allemagne' at a time when the German intellect was
at its zenith, culminating in Goethe, and illustrated
by a splendid array of other lights—by Klopstock,
Schiller, Wieland, Winkelmann, Lessing, Herder,
Tieck, Richter, the Schlegels, Werner, Wolf,
Jacobi, Kant, Fichte, Schelling,[3] and almost
innumerable others—most of them still living
when she last visited Germany. The enduring
products of the German mind have since multi-
plied vastly in every department, but its splendour
at the epoch of the 'Allemagne' has never been
surpassed, and probably never will be. Yet the
book has, by the lapse of time alone, become deficient as a survey of German life and literature.
It abounds also in special faults; its critical estimates are sometimes inadequate, at others exaggerated.[4] But works of genius are essentially
immortal. It is the distinction of genius that it
imparts somewhat of its own personality to its

[3] Hegel, whose later influence on German thought was so important, is not mentioned by her, though he began his first lectures at
Jena in 1801, two years before her arrival in Weimar, and published
his work on Fichte and Schelling in the same year, and his *Pheno-
menology of the Soul* in 1807.

[4] The Germans themselves have most complained of it, par-
ticularly Richter. See *Heidelberger Jahrbücher der Literatur*, 1815.
Richter could hardly fail to resent her criticism of his writings.
(*Allemagne*, ii. 28.)

productions. 'Style is the man,' and style, of both thought and expression—the individuality of the artist—is the everlasting charm of classic works. The touch of genius thus gives enduring life to even obsolete facts. It is like the word of the prophet in the 'valley of vision,' the dry bones rise up at its bidding, embodied and armed. The fragments of the Parthenon sculptures are precious, not because of their mythologic fictions, but because, in their very ruins, they still glow with the genius of Phidias. The 'Allemagne' is imbued with the richest genius of its author,—with exalted sentiment, with profound thought, with grand moral truth, with the eloquence of style, with the power, the essence of a great soul. There is scarcely a page of it which does not present something that the world can never willingly let die. As a monument of intellect, especially of a woman's intellect, it is classic and immortal.

It would betray an unpardonable lack of sensibility were we to feel no profounder sentiment than mere satisfaction with this signal literary triumph. In its peculiar circumstances it is a spectacle for generous, for enthusiastic admiration. It is the vindication of the supremacy of the human intellect ; of that sovereignty of mind which, from the prisons of Boethius, Tasso, Cervantes, and Bunyan ; from the exile of Ovid, Martial, Dante, and Spinoza ; and from the humiliation of the old age and poverty of Milton, have sent forth,

through all the world and all time, proofs, if not
of the invulnerability, yet of the invincibility of
genius, irradiating their names with honour when
the sword or the sceptre which oppressed them
has sunk into oblivion or ignominy. Throughout
her prolonged sufferings the intellect of this persecuted woman has been ever in the ascendant.
Each of its new productions has been superior to
its preceding one. The victory of the pen over
the sceptre is now, in her case, incontestable.
Corinne is crowned anew in the land of constitutional liberty with laurels gathered in 'the land
of thought.' Meanwhile the crown is falling from
the brow of her imperial persecutor. She has
fled over Europe with her proscribed manuscript
before his armed hosts ; he knew that she was
fleeing in his front, as we have seen by his
attempts to embarrass her flight and to seize
Rocca. His hosts have been rolled back, in disastrous overthrow, from the ruins of the ancient
capital of the land which then gave her shelter,
leaving in their retreat more than 250,000 dead
men, victims of the sword or the climate.[5] His
unparalleled energies rallied again, and he triumphed at Lutzen, at Bautzen, at Wurtchen, at
Dresden. But in the very month in which the
'Allemagne' issued from the London press, was
fought the great 'battle of the nations,' as it has
been called ; Germany, united, rose with overwhelm-

---

[5] Scott's *Napoleon,* vii. 14.

ing resentment, and on the battle-field of Leipsic broke for ever the domination of the tyrant. The 'Edinburgh Review' appeared with Mackintosh's superb criticism on the 'Allemagne' amidst the acclamations of England over the great victory—the resurrection of the people whose intellectual claims it had vindicated. In less than six months Napoleon abdicated, and the authoress, now the most distinguished woman of Europe, re-entered the French capital. Her 'Corinne' had been the apotheosis of Italy; her 'Allemagne,' delayed by her persecutor till the resurrection of Germany and his own downfall, was now her own apotheosis.[6]

[6] She indulges, in the *Allemagne,* that disposition to commemorate, in either the text or notes, the names of her personal friends, which we have noticed in her other works. Besides those of them whose names, as authors, more legitimately belong to her pages, such as Goethe, Schiller, Wieland, Werner, Müller, the Schlegels, &c., we find there those of the philanthropists Vohgt, Fellenberg, and Pestalozzi, with whom she maintained intimate relations, and those of Sabran, Constant, Lemercier, Lacretelle, Oehlenschlaeger, Sismondi, Dumont, Davy, Madame Necker de Saussure, Frederica and Ida Brun, Prevost, Chateaubriand, and, of course, her father.

CHAPTER XXXVIII.

LITERARY AND OTHER HABITS.

Her Habits of Composition—Self-control of her Faculties—Her laborious Revisions—Her Moral Courage—Exemption from Physical Drawbacks—Indifference to Hostile Criticism—Her Letters—The Duc de Broglie's Estimate of her—Scherer's Estimate—Her Business Capacity—Her Hospitality—Her Conversational Talent—Music—The Dance—Dramatic Talent—Her Religious Character—Her Politics—Napoleon's Dread of her Power—Her Generosity.

WE have already paused at several points in our narrative to consider, more or less, the characteristics of Madame de Staël as they have revealed themselves in particular periods of her development. She had now attained the richest maturity of her intellectual life and her literary fame. This is a convenient moment for another pause for the rehearsal of some of those peculiar or familiar habits which are always interesting in the history of distinguished characters, and are often their best illustration.

She usually premeditated her subject a considerable time before writing, though in a casual way. Having once designed its outlines, she wrote out an ample sketch 'without retracing her steps, without interrupting the course of her thoughts,

·except for necessary researches.'[1] This first composition she transcribed entirely with her own
hand, carefully modifying her ideas and often
·classifying them anew, but giving no attention
whatever to the correction of her style. Her
transcript, with its emendations, was then copied
by her secretary, and it was on this copy, but more
frequently on the printed proofs, that she laboured
to perfect her diction. As with most superior
writers, her proofs were a terror to the printers.
And yet her critical readers are aware that she
frequently allowed verbal defects to escape her
attention, for she was intent on transmitting the
delicate lights and shades of her thoughts and
·emotions, rather than on the mechanical niceties of
style. Though, by her vivid temperament and the
affluence of her thoughts, she was nearly always
in writing mood, the claims of hospitality and her
insatiable love of society and conversation, almost
daily interrupted her studies and labours. 'She
had no pedantry,' says her cousin, 'in her pursuits
as an author; study and composition were for her
·a necessary resource, a means at once of tran-
quillising her agitated soul, and of maintaining her
mind at its true height. The route and the object
agreed equally with her nature. Meanwhile her
friends too often interrupted her, because they were
always welcomed. Except in moments of her very
highest inspiration, she seemed delighted to see

---

[1] 'Avis des Editeurs,' prefixed to her *Considérations* etc.

them enter her house.' There were such moments, however, such as Carl Ritter has described on a preceding page, when her intellect seemed on fire ; at these times she continued her work, but kept her doors open for her guests, leaving them for the time to entertain one another.

From her youth she had cultivated the generous habit of ' accepting interruptions with gaiety.' As Necker had dissuaded his wife from composition because he did not like to interrupt her on entering her study, his daughter, who wished not to draw on herself such a prohibition, ' had accustomed herself to write, if we may so say, on the wing, and her father, seeing her always erect or leaning against an angle of the chimney, could not imagine that he was interrupting a serious labour.' She so much respected this weakness of Necker, that not till long after she lost him did she have in her chamber the least permanent provision for writing. At last, when ' Corinne ' had made a great noise in the world, she said, ' I have long wished to have a large table, it seems to me that I now have a right to one.'

Her cousin remarks that it was impossible to find out how or where she meditated her works ; her life appeared so broken and versatile that no time seemed devoted to preparatory reflection. ' She always developed to me the plan of her next writing, and we discussed it together. Once, at Geneva, I said to her, " You sleep all night and act or talk all day: when do you study your plots?" "In my palanquin," she replied, smiling. Now, she was never but a few moments at a time in her palanquin, nevertheless she had in this instance determined there the title and all the chapters.'

The self-command and vitality of her faculties enabled her promptly to resume any given course of thought, and we seldom detect traces of inter-missions.

Though incessantly interrupted by others, she hardly ever had to suspend her labours through indisposition, whether physical or mental; her fa-culties dominated her pains, and, as there often existed a relation between what she wrote and the cause of her sufferings, she could still compose, when reading could no longer afford her sufficient distraction. 'I comprehend nothing that I read,' she would say; 'I must turn to my writing.'

She was in no haste to publish; leisure for reviewing, as well as the quick and accurate insight of her genius, compensated therefore for her fervid haste and habitual interruptions in composition. Her manuscript works were, as we have seen, read and discussed in her literary circles at Coppet, Geneva, and Paris,—an inestimable advantage to any author however accomplished. After her ample studies and notes on Italy, she spent one year in writing 'Corinne' in Switzerland, besides a large part of another in finishing it in France. She was occupied about six years on her 'Germany,' and devoted at least two years to the labour of its composition, aided by the criticisms of Schlegel, Vohgt, Werner, Sismondi, and many others. A whole year was given to the revision of the first two volumes, and a part of the third, of her 'Considerations on the French Revolution,' and this able work (an indispensable authority for any writer of modern French history) was still reserved for further elaboration, and did not appear till after her death. She spent several years in writing her other principal posthumous work, the 'Ten Years of Exile ;' it was interrupted by the hardest trials and travels of her banishment, and was never completed.

The facility and freshness with which she could resume work, in almost any circumstances, made up for that incapacity for long sustained attention to any one subject to which allusion has been made in an early part of our record, and which her cousin attributed to the effect, on her mental health, of her mother's rigorous system of education, before her emancipation at St. Ouen by the advice of Tronchin. Genius can never despise labour, but it does often despise mechanical methods of labour ; it is apt to create methods of its own, methods which, though real to itself, only appear defiance of method to superficial observers. It is difficult to account for the sustained vigour and continuity of Madame de Staël's chief writings, when we consider her habits of literary labour. She seems, as has been remarked, to pass through elaborate trains of thought, to reach lofty and difficult acclivities, by the mere alertness, the flight of her genius. Her mind did not need to delay to construct bridges over broad chasms, but leaped them, in a direct, fair, and triumphant passage, and held on its swift and splendid way. Her thoughts on the profoundest subjects were intuitions, and her intuitions were demonstrations. Pindar has said that ' he is gifted with genius who knoweth much by natural talent,' and the converse of his saying is equally true.

For many years she had no assigned hours for work. Not till she was compelled to live in retreat at Coppet did she see the importance of system in her life, and then it was adopted not so much as an aid to labour as a means of relief to her sufferings; for, as we have repeatedly seen, absorbing occupation was with her, as it is with all energetic minds, a necessary condition of contentment and of mental health. ' I see,' she says, ' that time divided is never long, and that regularity abridges all things.' She was never willing, however, to become the slave of any system, and could readily sacrifice her plans and hours of work for her friends. Notwithstanding the extreme susceptibility of her temperament and a constitutional tendency to sadness—a tendency which, she insisted, is inherent in the Northern literature, is a necessary attribute of the Romantic school, and equally so of the Christian religion itself[2]—she bravely maintained her will in the control of both her inward and outward life, excepting only her affections, which she delighted to surrender to their own instincts. Her invincible firmness against Bonaparte ; her heroism in behalf of her friends, amidst the perils of the Revolution ; the determined courage with which she undertook great literary projects in times of almost hopeless persecution and distraction, and thereby vindicated her claims to the attention of Europe in spite of the machinations of the government, are proofs of her indomitable nature. She professed to have no ' animal courage,' but she had superlative moral courage. Very rarely did she experience that physical depression or irritability which so often afflicts her sex. ' Never,' says her cousin, ' has the mechanism of the human organisation had less effect than with her ; no blind power controlled her ; at any hour that occasion required she could change her manner of life. Experiencing but few material needs, not knowing languor or discouragement, she was never tired of acting or thinking. Cold, heat, the changes of the seasons, had no influence upon her. If she had great need of moral movement, yet physical exercise seemed never necessary. She believed but little in " weakness of the nerves," and rather despised minute cares about health. " I should be sick like others," she remarked one day, " if I had not conquered

[2] *De la Littérature* &c. *passim.*

physical nature." But alas!' adds her less robust and almost equally endowed cousin, 'but alas! one never has the last word with this physical nature.' Madame de Staël suffered at times intensely from her affections, but there is only one recorded instance in which she succumbed entirely to 'nervous agitation,' and then, as we have seen, only momentarily, while fleeing towards Russia, under the most intolerable grievances of her exile. She was heartily indignant at herself for this weakness.

She would never overwork her mind after the adoption of method in her life. The morning was devoted to business affairs and to literary labour, the afternoon exclusively to society and correspondence. Though she laboured hard and long in revising her works before publishing them, she never liked to recur to them after they had once been before the public. 'When my work is printed,' she used to say, 'I wish to have nothing more to do with it; it must then make its own way whether for better or for worse.' Madame Necker de Saussure says that, with the exception of 'Delphine,' respecting the moral effect of which the critics had disturbed her mind, 'I believe that she never re-read her own books; she thought so little about them as to forget them all successively. If we cited to her a particular phrase from any of them, she was astonished, and rejoined: 'Did I indeed write that? I am charmed by it; it is,

marvellously well expressed.' One day two of her
friends rearranged the chapter on Love, in her
essay on ' The Influence of the Passions,' by sub-
stituting divine for earthly love ; when they read
it to her, she listened, to the end, with the greatest
attention, quite enchanted, and impatient to know
the name of the author.'

She seldom replied to criticisms on her works ;
a forbearance which has been attributed to her
magnanimity, but which was mostly attributable
to her reluctance to return to old ideas, to work
which had been once completed—a feeling which
is common, perhaps, to most authors. ' Had her
enemies threatened,' says her cousin, ' to destroy
all her published works, they could hardly have
much alarmed her. The oracle once delivered, she
was willing, like the Sibyl, to leave the oak leaves
to the winds. She felt more the necessity of
writing than of publishing ; she bore patiently the
suppression of her " Germany," and when she was
told that General Savary would convert the whole
edition into pasteboard, she replied carelessly, " I
wish he would only send me the pasteboard for
my bonnets." Never has an author been less dependent upon reputation ; never has one been less
intoxicated by success. There was always with
her some sad return from the pleasures of self-love
to thoughts of what destiny might yet have in reserve for her, and she seemed to say of such
pleasures, " Is this then all ? " '

Her cousin, while denying that she was vain, admits that she was not deficient in pride. While apparently so indifferent about the criticism of others, her own critical estimates of her books or her talents were never tinged by affected or 'voluntary humility.' She believed in her genius, and avowed that belief with perfect frankness; for what egotism she had sprung more from self-knowledge than from self-love. She would speak freely of 'my talent,' 'my success,' 'my reputation.' She did not hesitate to say of a critical opponent, 'He is not my equal; if I were to return his blows he would go limping out of the combat.' She was not so indifferent to favourable as to hostile criticism; as the latter is usually more or less malicious, it was morally repugnant to her fine nature, for though she was capable of honest and indignant resentment, she was incapable of malice, and she seemed never to have known ungenerous envy. She often said that critical eulogies afforded her more pleasure than hostile criticism gave her pain, and therefore she never regretted her choice of a literary career. While she was but little anxious for reputation, her womanly heart was always eager for affection, and the esteem or admiration which is inseparable from it. Only a woman could say, as she did, that she would sacrifice all her talents and fame for the personal loveliness of Madame Récamier and the universal regard which it attracted.

Few of her letters have been published, but her correspondents praise them as superior to her books. Bonstetten, who was in the confidence of the family at Coppet, deplores the destruction of those written, almost daily, to her father; he says they showed more talent, as well as more heart, than her best publications. If she had not, like Madame de Sévigné, a special talent for epistolary composition, ' a gift which,' remarks her cousin, ' appears to be independent of the faculties of the writer,' still her letters were transcripts of herself; her intellectual insight, her clear discrimination of characters and events, and, above all, her overflowing heart, with its unreserved confidence, its utter ' abandon,' characterise them. It is probable that their very genuineness, as utterances of her passionate and trustful soul, is the reason why they have not been more abundantly given to the world. The world could hardly understand how so much heart could consist with so much intellect, such moral womanhood with such mental manhood. For her nature seemed double, though harmonious, and this was its characteristic peculiarity—her chief distinction and supremacy among literary women. Some of the few of her letters which have almost if not quite accidentally been published, cannot be fairly construed without an intimate knowledge of her character.[3] Turn from

---

[3] See particularly those written to Camille Jordan, and first published by Sainte-Beuve in his *Nouveaux Lundis,* xii.

them to a page of the 'Germany,' or of the essay
on 'Literature,' and, in spite of their talent, you
doubt that both could have proceeded from the
same pen. In her correspondence she writes with
the open-heartedness, the ardour, the heedlessness,
of a child towards its parents, its sisters and its
brothers. But genius ever baffles, by transcending,
our mechanical canons of criticism; its rights are
imprescriptible, its prerogative is in its being a
law unto itself. Probably no woman of her day
had a larger circle of friendship than Madame de
Staël, and certainly none had more accomplished,
more astute, more intellectually varied friends; yet
no woman was ever more esteemed, more revered,
or more loved, than she was by the selectest minds
of her circle of correspondents—by the veteran
Bonstetten, who declared, as we have seen, that his
intellectual being was irreparably maimed by her
death; by the sober-minded and philosophic Sismondi, whom we shall see weeping at her grave
under the consciousness that all life is thenceforward changed and saddened for him; by the
critical Schlegel, whose admiration, through years
spent in her household, knew no limits; by the
powerful-minded, but morally weak, Benjamin
Constant; by the sentimental Chateaubriand, who,
from being her literary rival, if not her literary
adversary, became her enthusiastic, though always
capricious, friend; by the mystically devout Mathieu de Montmorency, who loved her and suffered

for her as a father ; by the graceful and guileless Juliette Récamier ; by the pure and strong-minded Madame Necker de Saussure ; and almost innumerable others, who read her more in her letters than in her books, and more in her life than either in her books or in her letters. Her most intimate friends formed an inner, a kind of esoteric circle around her ; they used only their Christian names in their conversations and correspondence ; they were an intellectual household, relieving their sufferings, from the terrible troubles of the times, by a sympathy and confidence sacred as the affections of home. Madame Necker de Saussure says that 'her long correspondence with me is a treasure of friendship, of confidence, a source of tears and yet of happiness, for the rest of my life. She was prodigiously powerful in the letters she wrote in moments of inquietude, of suffering, or indignation. Then, borne on by an overpowering sentiment, she almost unconsciously covered many pages, all brilliant with the most admirable eloquence. She used to say that when the pen was in her hand her brain became uncontrollable ; and she told me that at the age of fourteen, being required to write to an old friend of the family, she used expressions so vivid and passionate that her mother compelled her to recommence the letter three times before its style was calm enough to allow it to be sent to its destination.'

Her son-in-law, the Duc de Broglie, has accurately defined the qualities, the contrasts, which distinguished her peculiar temperament, and occasioned most of her sufferings. 'That,' he says, 'which characterised her before all, above all, was, on the one hand, impetuous, imperious activity, irresistible to herself, and, on the other, inexorable good sense. In all the transactions of life, public or private, all the preoccupations of intelligence, study, or meditation, composition or conversation, her genius transported her to the end at once, by sudden leaps, daring all hazards, and disposing her, in some measure, to attempt at times to surpass the actual, the possible. But she was the first to perceive any such error. Her admirable discernment of truth and reality quickly corrected it, and led to reactions which she was too candid to disguise, and thereby exposed her to the criticism of envious or malicious mediocrity. I am firmly convinced that all the faults, real or supposed (and mostly supposed) which have been imputed to her, arose from this combat between two qualities which dominated her by turns instead of limiting and tempering one another.' This is the just solution of the problem of her character—her noble though faulty individuality. She had the double nature which she attributes to Goethe, but it was without that admirable balance which was the perfection of his character. In other words, she was a woman. The Duke ascribes to this unharmonised contrast the 'ardour and the passionateness, the

storminess and the tumult of her life,' and even
' the destruction of her health and her premature
death, in spite of her natural vigour.'[4]

One of the best of living French critics, a
worthy successor to Sainte-Beuve, characterises her
with much candour and more enthusiasm.   After
alluding to the diminished recognition of her writings among her later countrymen, Edmond Scherer exclaims : ' What an expressive and attractive
physiognomy is hers !   How initiative her talent !
What fascination in her character !   The history of
this woman, at once so masculine and so tender,
is unique in literature.   Madame de Staël is above
all things a soul.   She is all passion, *élan*, enthusiasm.   She has immense need of being loved,
but still more of loving, of attaching herself, of
being compassionate.   She overflows with generous
sympathies.   And with this tenderness she has an
ardour for all great things, for truth, liberty, and
glory.   Never has a mind elevated itself more
naturally to the ideal.   Hence her genius : it is
identical with her vivid aspirations, her loving and
impetuous nature.   It was from her generosity
that her eloquence flowed.   She would touch, con-
vince, actuate, and therefore her talent is a sort of
oratory.   It is too much so, perhaps.   Her style
is nervous, intense, but not plastic ; her phrases
have light rather than colour, movement rather
than form.   She presents less of those fine utter-

---

[4] *Le Duc de Broglie,* by Guizot.   Paris, 1872.

ances which come from the imagination, than of
those great utterances which come from the heart.
She attains the sublime, but not perfection. She
is a thinker rather than an artist; and in reading
her, one follows her with admiration full of sympathy, but without the repose, the enjoyment of
fully satisfied taste.'[5] This fine criticism needs
some qualification. The critic is swayed too much
by the French characteristic love of antithesis.
Her style is indeed nervous and sometimes compli-
cated; her phrases, though they 'have light,' are
sometimes obscure; yet they do especially present
'colour'—colour being but refracted light, analysed light. She does present 'those great utterances which come from the heart,' for her pages
abound in great thoughts; and an astute French
thinker (Vauvenargues) remarks that 'great
thoughts come from the heart.' But she is rich
also in 'those fine utterances which come from
the imagination;' these especially characterise her
writings; no French writer has more of them. As
to 'the repose' of 'fully satisfied taste,' it is a true
remark, nobly true, that we do not find it in her
writings. There could hardly be a better tribute
to her genius. No great thought, no great object,
satisfies the mind at first view—nor at the last. No
such 'repose' was ever experienced, by a large
mind, at the sight of St. Peter's or the Colosseum,
Mont Blanc or Chimborazo, Niagara or Yosemite.

[5] Scherer's *Nouvelles Etudes* &c. Paris, 1865.

Themes or sights, of illimitable suggestion, dilate
and agitate the illimitable mind ; and, when it has
comprehended them, it demands still more, for the
soul transcends all things at last. We read the
works of this great woman with a continual consciousness of her reserved power. We follow her
splendid generalisations with such restless eagerness
that we wonder that she does not break through
all limitations and give us the full freedom of the
intellectual universe. Especially is this the case in
her highest, her moral generalisations, where the
heart as well as the mind speaks—those ' general
ideas, those universal sentiments which,' as she
says in ' Corinne,' ' appeal to the hearts of all men.'[6]
In the charmingly colloquial discussions of art in
her ' Corinne,' or of literary or social topics in her
' Allemagne,' we follow her with a tranquillity akin
to the ' repose' of ' satisfied taste ; ' but, at the
close of each chapter, we importunately, restlessly
demand more. ' Avouez cependant,' says Corinne
to Oswald, ' que le génie, et le génie de l'âme, sait
triompher de tout,'—genius conquers all things.[7]
Why then, we ask, does not she, who possesses it
in such abundance, lead us on to the final conquest? Why lead us so far, and yet not farther?
' The arts,' she says in the same chapter, ' are
limited in their means, but unlimited in their
effects. Genius seeks not to attack that which is
in the essence of things ; its superiority consists

[6] *Corinne,* xviii. 4.   [7] *Ibid.* viii. 3.

rather in its power to divine it'—in its power to compel the reader or the spectator to divine it by the exertion of his own awakened faculties. Exertion is not mental repose, but nevertheless it is the very joy of the mind. The great mind is the mind that arouses our faculties, that gives us impulse and bids us advance. In the contemplation of great objects, or great subjects, the intellect, encompassing and then dismissing them, for ever asks for something still greater. It is the highest function of genius to excite this never-satisfied demand. Genius is always more suggestive than expressive. Nevertheless, with some such qualifications, Scherer's characterisation is as accurate as it is eloquent.

Frenchwomen generally and justly pride themselves on their capacity for business, and the fortunes of many a household have been saved by their economical superiority over their husbands. But, down to the death of her father, Madame de Staël had no experience whatever in financial affairs. At that time she despaired of ever being able to manage her property, and dreamed only of impending ruin. But she soon overcame all difficulties of the emergency, and proved that she possessed fully the national competence of her sex for such exigencies. She came at last to despise the affectation, usual among men of genius, of such superiority in better things as necessitates inferiority in pecuniary affairs. She would not admit the ordinary, self-complacent apologies for this sort of incapacity ; to her it was not so much an excusable infirmity of genius as an inexcusable weakness of will, and therefore of character. The plea of indifference was less excusable to her than the plea of incapacity. Though literary history is full of examples of this supposed incapacity, she knew that they have been mostly among second-rate men, whose intellectual superiority has not been sufficient to justify them in the sufferings which their culpable negligence has brought upon their families as well as themselves. The higher classes, the highest class, of men of letters have afforded sufficient contrary examples to refute the pretension. Shakespeare, Goethe, Voltaire, Gibbon, Pope, Wordsworth, Macaulay, Scott, Dickens, were too great to be either indifferent or incapable in pecuniary matters. Notwithstanding the liberality and elegant luxury of Madame de Staël, her cousin assures us that the greatest order prevailed in the management of her household, so much so that her fortune was always accumulating. She was 'singularly impatient' when hearing of men of talent who inflicted suffering upon honest and industrious working people by failing to pay their debts; and she would have considered the failure to maintain her patrimony an impeachment of her understanding. She keenly dreaded financial misfortunes, and in the confusion of all things during the Revolution she suffered not a little from the 'fear of being ruined.' She then determined to maintain her children by her literary labours, and 'made precise calculations for this purpose.' She subsequently trained her eldest son to manage well the fortune of the family, but taught him, meanwhile, the lessons of a truly Christian philosophy regarding it. 'Do not torment yourself,' she wrote him, 'if misfortunes come ; only do your best come what may ; all that does not touch the heart leaves the life free.'

Though an economical calculator, she was not avaricious. Her cousin says, 'A Minister of Bonaparte assured her that the Emperor would pay her claim' of two million livres against the government, 'if she would only love him.' 'I know well enough,' she responded, 'that to receive one's dues from the government a certificate of life is requisite, but I never knew that a declaration of love is necessary.' During almost any moment of her long exile she could have obtained a settlement of that claim, if she would but succumb to the government ; but she had more regard for her conscience than for money. 'The essential thing with Madame de Staël, in the affairs of fortune,' continues her cousin, 'was to be without self-reproach. By consequence superfluous expenses displeased her, and though she would expend freely for real comforts, she allowed nothing for vanity.' They reproached her, one day, because her chamber at Coppet retained traces of the rude taste of the antique times when the château was erected—because it had no ceiling, and its huge beams were visible. 'Have you seen the beams?' she asked; 'I have not noticed them; but excuse me for this year, in which there is so much suffering. I can survive fancies which make so little impression on me.' The chief luxury upon which she delighted to spend her money was hospitality —to be able to lodge her friends, and give good dinners to persons whose acquaintance she desired. 'I have engaged,' she said, 'a cook whose heels are winged; is not this what is necessary to dine all Europe impromptu?' Voltaire had said that his house, at Ferney, was an inn for all Europe; compared with the château of Coppet, it was but a village cabaret compared with a city hotel.

She loved hospitality because she loved society; the two were identical with her. Society, as has been remarked, was indispensable to her being; she found in it a salutary, a necessary stimulant for her faculties; they were probably more developed by conversation with men of culture than by any other exercise. The *salon* was to her an arena of intellectual athletics, as well as a school of the best sentiments and manners. She discussed there the profoundest questions of life, of politics, of literature, of morals, of religion, and especially the subjects of her writings, with the highest ·minds. As her emotions were a dominant element of her genius and her works, she found in the excitement of conversation the best preparation for the more private studies of her literary projects. ' I have seen,' says M. de Barante, the historian, ' many of her works from the beginning ; for example, " Corinne " passed before me,' in the château at Coppet. Chénedollé, a guest there in 1798, writes : ' She was occupied with her essay on Literature, and wrote a chapter every morning. She brought under discussion at dinner, or in the *salon* each evening, the argument of the next chapter, and provoked discussion upon it ; she herself talked it over in a rapid improvisation, and the next day the chapter was written. It was· thus that the whole book was composed. The subjects that she treated while I was there were the " Influence of Christianity on Literature ;" the " Influence of Ossian on the Poetry of the North ;" " Poetry thoughtful at the North, sensational at the South," &c. Her impromptu discussions were much more brilliant than her chapters ; her writings are, comparatively speaking, but splendid blots.'[8] ' I have passed fifteen years with her,' wrote Sismondi to Madame Hortense Allert (author of ' Letters on the Works of Madame de Staël '), ' in an intimacy which afforded intellectual

[8] *Chateaubriand et son Groupe Littéraire sous l'Empire,* by Sainte-Beuve, i. 2. (2 vols.) Paris, 1861. Sainte-Beuve finely qualifies Chénedollé's last sentence : ' What was said of another woman can well be said of her : " You consider that she writes well ; if you heard her converse, you would think that she writes poorly." '

pleasures that nothing can restore. I have witnessed the birth of those works which you analyse with so much heart and talent. I have frequently heard the ideas, which they contain, developed in those eloquent conversations which all who were with her justly consider superior to her writings; for inspiration was with her instantaneous; a complete order of ideas presented itself at once to her mind, and labour added nothing to it.'

This intellectual need of society was one of the chief reasons of her love of Paris and her horror of exile. 'Show me the Rue du Bac,' she exclaimed to her friends at Coppet who pointed to the resplendent beauties of Lake Leman; 'I would gladly live at Paris on a hundred francs a year, lodged in the fourth story.'[9] Coppet and Geneva were tolerable to her only so far as she could reproduce Paris in them, by gathering around her brilliant minds.

Much has heretofore been said, in these pages, of her extraordinary success in conversation. It is the concurrent testimony of all witnesses who have left us their opinion on the subject, that no man or woman in Europe excelled her, that none could excel her, in this felicitous art. Lacretelle, who met her often, in Paris and at Coppet, remarks that, 'It was given, I believe, to Madame de Staël alone, among all admired authors, to surpass in conversation the most beautiful effects of her

[9] Madame Necker de Saussure, *Notice* &c.

written style. It was with her a lyre tuned for
every key. Art could go no farther; but she was
never artificial. Her sincere heart gave to all her
sentiments the ardour of passion. She was now
an inspired poet, now a transcendent philosopher,
now an orator, cogent in argument and full of
the finest movements of the soul. Corinne, her
own Corinne, would have appeared monotonous
by the side of Madame de Staël.'[1] Ticknor, who
heard her latest conversations, says, 'She was,
perhaps, the most remarkable person for talents
in conversation that ever lived.'[2] It was to her
the finest of the fine arts; not merely one of the
best means of self-culture, but of the improvement
of others. 'Her conversation, especially when *tête-
à-tête*, was,' says her cousin, ' something marvellous. No one could fully know her without it.
Her most beautiful pages are far from equalling it.
Then her great intellect spread its wings, took its
flight freely; then, no longer mistress of her inspiration, she exercised a preternatural power, and by
it subdued herself while subduing others.' ' In
the midst of her habitual circle she was full of
charm; she had a simplicity of manners, and even
an air of carelessness, which placed all who were
around her at ease. There was never any con-
straint about her; though always observing, she
never seemed to be examining; and as her attention appeared to be concentrated on the subject

---

[1] *Testament* &c. ii. 19.   [2] *Life* &c. i. 6.

discussed, rather than on the manner of the speakers, no one believed himself in the presence of a judge. Her superiority weighed upon no one.'

But with all her kindliness and forbearance, she could endure neither platitudes nor extravagance, much less affectation, in conversation; it was to her a gracious ministry of social life, and, however gay or sentimental, it must be instructive, and invigorating, and sincere. Sismondi wrote: 'Suffering is the surest means of making us truthful to ourselves; Madame de Staël always wished to pinch affected persons to see if they would cry naturally.' 'Absurdities,' says her cousin, 'made her impatient; extravagance fatigued her. The happy mean between imagination and good sense was always sought by her. "Insanity," she would say, " can be poetical, but nonsense never." ' In her own most excited conversation she never appeared absurd, though often paradoxical; however questionable might be her theories, her individual thoughts were always striking and brilliant, her running sentences were lines of inextinguishable Greek fire.

It was in colloquial disputation that she was most extraordinary, most dazzling; but 'her most impetuous vehemence was never accompanied by bitterness or contemptuousness.' No arrogance, and seldom any irony or sarcasm (as in the case of Fichte, heretofore related) marred her speech. There was a sort of flattery of her antagonist in the manner in which she overwhelmed him. And when the question was exhausted, and the conversation began to drag, she would collect all her forces, condense into a brief and luminous *résumé* the arguments of the debate, and give it a splendid and victorious finale which rendered its conclusion more interesting than its beginning. The brilliancy of the combat made even the defeated feel proud of it. 'Coppet,' says her cousin, 'was like that hall of Odin, in the Scandinavian paradise, where the slain warriors arose on their feet, able and courageous to fight again.'

Though no one ever had a greater temptation to talk merely for the display of talent in talking, she was noted for the conscientiousness of her colloquial discussions. She was intent on the truth; exaggeration, whether of thought or feeling, immediately repelled her. 'When one places a hundred for ten,' she said, 'the interest of such talk is gone. All natural sentiments have their proper modesty.' One was forced to speak the truth with Madame de Staël, because the contrary was too insipid. She wished, above all, to be instructed. She thought that a sure sign of decay, of either mind or character, is a repugnance to learn the truth. 'I knew,' she said, 'that Bonaparte would fall, when I discovered that he no longer cared to know the foundation of things.' She was sometimes even too emphatic in asserting her convictions of the truth. 'She once wrote to her daughter about some question or other : " I have injured it by maintaining the truth too passionately, but the truth always masters me." She always adhered to the simple side, the positive side, of any question. You could amuse her by whimsical theses, but she herself always took the part of common sense. Besides the fact that she could only speak from her convictions, she believed that more real intellect could be displayed in the cause of truth than in that of error, because it is not absolutely necessary to defend what is reasonable by trivialities.'

With all her consciousness of colloquial superiority, her compassionate heart never allowed her to oppress or embarrass a sincere though bungling interlocutor. She expressed a characteristic feeling of her own soul, in the admonition of Corinne to Lucile, not to permit her superiority to show itself in ' pride or coldness.' ' If such pride were unfounded, it would,' says Corinne, ' be perhaps less wounding ; for to use our rights chills the hearts of others more than unjust pretensions. True sentiment delights, above all things, in giving that which is not due.' [3] Nevertheless she elsewhere says, that ' It is wrong to fear superiority of mind or heart : it is very moral, this superiority ; for to comprehend, renders one very indulgent ; and to feel profoundly, inspires great kindness.' [4]

Allusion has already been made to her religious tendency.[5] It is acknowledged by her best friends

---

[3] *Corinne,* **xx.** 3.   [4] *Ibid.* xviii. 5.   [5] Chap. iv.

that she suffered, in her earlier years, from the vitiating, anti-religious sentiments which infected the moral atmosphere of all Europe at the epoch of the Revolution and under the First Empire. But whatever may have been the errors of her life, she never accepted the sceptical philosophy of those times. Her education, and especially the influence of her father, protected her against it. Her writings show a constant combat, in her mind, between the moral tendencies of the age and the better tendencies of her own soul. ' Alas ! ' she exclaims, in her ' Corinne,' ' what a conflict goes on in souls susceptible at once of passion and of conscience.'[6] The latter at last triumphed, and we have seen how profoundly the discipline of affliction influenced her moral nature, leading her to the consolations of Christian faith. ' A single resource,' says the dying Corinne, ' remains for me in the depth of the soul. God has accepted me. To prepare for immortality is, I believe, the sole end of existence. Happiness, suffering, all things, are means for this end. Be happy, but be so by piety. A secret communion with God seems to place in ourselves a twofold existence, the being who confides in Him

---

[6] Her alleged relations with Narbonne have already been noticed. Readers who have a taste for such gossip and scandal can consult, on her relations with Benjamin Constant and her supposed identity with the Elenore of his *Adolphe,* Sainte-Beuve, *Portraits Littéraires,* (tome iii.), and *Causeries de Lundi* (tome vii.), qualified by his essay, *Sur l'Adolphe de Benjamin Constant* (*Causeries,* xi.) ; Taillandier, *Lettres inédites de Sismondi,* and Lady Blessington, *Conversations &c. with Byron* (vii.).

and His responsive presence : it makes two friends
of a single soul.   Pray, as I do ; pray, and let our
thoughts meet and mingle in the skies.'[7]   Vinet
sees in the ' Allemagne ' a great advance of her
religious ideas.   ' In it,' he says, ' she declares that
all the qualities of the world are as nothing by the
side of the Christian virtues.'   ' Whatever devia-
tions we may make, we are compelled,' she affirms,
' to return to the recognition of religion as the
true foundation of morality.   It is the object, felt
and real within us, that can alone turn our regards
from external objects.   If piety cause not over-
mastering emotions, who would sacrifice even
pleasures, however vulgar, to the frigid dignity of
morality?'   Schlegel says that she was an habitual
reader of the writings of Fénelon.[8]   She spent a
part of her Sundays, at Coppet, in the instruction
of her children from the religious writings of her
father ; and she was to die at last pondering over
the devoutest of human books, the ' Imitation of
Christ,' by Thomas à Kempis.

The range of her knowledge was astonishingly
large and various.   It is seen in her early essay on
' Fictions ; ' in her treatises on the ' Passions ' and
on ' Literature ; ' in her ' Allemagne,' and her historical ' Considerations on the French Revolution.'

[7] *Corinne,* viii. 1, and xx. 3.
[8] See a remarkable letter of Schlegel to Mathieu de Montmorency,
written from Berne after his banishment, and first published in *Coppet
et Weimar,* vi.   ' Madame de Staël sent beaucoup d'attrait pour les
œuvres de Fénelon et les lit constamment.'

Her conversation abounded in learned allusions. 'She was acquainted,' says her cousin, 'with the greater part of European literature. She read rapidly and yet not superficially. She would never lose anything interesting, but would never give a moment to anything useless. She judged by her genius: an unerring instinct indicated to her immediately the intellect, the character, the intent of a writer, and she judged his work by this insight. No merit of execution could reconcile her to a design, or to sentiments, morally equivocal; and it was always by their qualities, as men, that she estimated writers.' As she considered style to be the most genuine indication of the individuality of an author, she always read foreign books in the original; and she had the courage to acquire in her advanced life the languages which had been neglected in her early education. She attached great importance to linguistic studies, for she found that the mind discovers new routes in the differences of idioms, and one of the best means of knowing the character of a people is a knowledge of their language. She cited with pleasure the remark of the poet Ennius, who said that 'he had three souls, because he could speak three languages.'

When asked what one author she would prefer, were she denied all but one, she replied, after excepting the Bible and her father's 'Cours de Morale Religieuse,' that she would choose Bacon, for he seemed to her the most inexhaustible of writers.

It was not, however, the mastery of difficult subjects that charmed her; Bacon's clear wisdom, fine wit, and rich imagination, were his chief attractions for her. As with Bacon, so with her, insight, imagination, taste, emotion, blended in all her mental processes. It was not so much the profundity as the vitality of a thought that she valued; she was more interested in the soul of a writer than in his subject. 'There were emotion and, if I may so speak, genius,' says her cousin, 'in all that she experienced. A piece of music, a dance, struck her; a poor organ in the streets delighted her. Once, when she saw Mademoiselle Bigottine dance a minuet, she was in ecstasies, and exclaimed, "For the moment I could almost wish for the re-establishment of the *ancien régime*."' She never tired of the graceful dancing of Madame Récamier, and commemorated it in a beautiful scene of her 'Corinne,' as she had earlier that of Madame de Krüdner in the 'shawl dance' of 'Delphine.' Music, as has already been remarked, was the most powerful of the arts with her; from it she derived inspiration and tranquillity, oblivion of trouble, and a presentiment of another existence. It had for her a charm which nothing could replace. Nevertheless, all kinds of music did not please her; only the airs in which the rhythm and the melody were well marked, impressed her. She cared little for elaborate music, and when her cousin said to her that certain passages, full of piquancy and originality, such as abound in the compositions of Haydn, produce an effect quite analogous to profound thought, she replied, ' I prefer to have any such thought spoken.' She was impatient of anything in music which did not affect her feelings, impatient as of a disappointed hope; she sometimes experienced indescribable excitement while listening to choice pieces, and would melt into tears.

She alludes to it constantly in her writings. ' Among all the arts, music alone,' she says in ' Corinne,' ' can be purely religious.' ' Of all the fine arts it is that which acts the most immediately on the soul. The others direct us to this or that idea ; this alone addresses itself to the intimate source of existence, and changes the whole interior disposition.' ' It has a happy incapacity to express any base sentiment, any artifice, any falsehood. Suffering, even, is in the language of music without bitterness, without irritation.' ' No words can express the impression caused by music ; for words limp after primary impressions, as translators in prose after the footprints of poets.' To her the gayest music had always an undertone of sadness ; but this was one of its sweetest charms. ' Music,' she said, ' is so fleeting a pleasure, one feels so much that it is escaping while we are enjoying it, that a sentiment of sadness mingles with the gaiety it causes ; but even when it expresses suffering, it gives rise to sweet emotions.' ' Nothing else retraces the past so much as music ; music more than

retraces it; when evoked by music, it appears
like the shades of those who were dear to us clothed
in mysterious veils.'[9]

Allusion has repeatedly been made to her passion for dramatic art. 'It was the most vivid of
all social amusements to her,' but it was more than
an amusement; she esteemed it one of the highest means of æsthetic entertainment and culture.
While despising most of the contemporary French
dramatic writers, she considered it an invaluable
privilege to study the great masters of the art in
their scenic representation, to witness a tragedy of
Corneille, Racine, Voltaire, or a comedy of Molière.
It was one of the attractions of Paris, which rendered her banishment intolerable, and she mentioned it as such in her letter to Bonaparte, at the
time of the suppression of her 'Allemagne.' Talma
was among her intimate friends, and we have seen
her seeking relief, in the worst period of her exile,
by spending weeks at Lyons to hear him in tragedy.
The domestic theatre at Coppet seemed indispensable to her; she habitually shared in its performances, and 'produced grand effects; the enthusiasm
with which she was inspired gave to her countenance a remarkably elevated and striking expression; the splendid whiteness of her arms; her
noble and graceful gestures; her effective attitudes:
her look—above all, her look—by turns sombre,
penetrating, intense, but always natural, gave to

9 *Corinne* viii. 3; ix. 2; xiv. 3.

her whole bearing a sort of artistic beauty which the tragic poet would have chosen. Her sonorous and modulated voice filled the hall, and no one has ever more completely commanded the attention of the spectators.' Her pathos often melted them into tears. Her animation inspired her friends who assisted in the performance ; ' and, as in conversation she made all interlocutors seem people of intellect, so in her little theatre she changed them into heroes.'

The seven small dramas which she composed for her domestic stage are unpretentious, but abound nevertheless in some of the best qualities of her genius. The comedies are her only writings which decidedly show her humour. ' Captain Kernadec,' or ' Seven Years in a Day,' is especially a proof that she possessed superior comic power. In ' Hagar in the Desert,' and in the ' Shunamite,' she successfully attempted, after the example of Racine, to reproduce Biblical scenes in dramatic forms. Her cousin remarks that ' the pathetic beauty of her language, the grandeur and the sincerity of her sentiments, were quite necessary, to give a religious disposition to an assembly met only for pleasure, and whose indifference or scruples were to be overcome ; nevertheless she always triumphed.'

Her political opinions have already been frequently indicated. Not the administrative form of government, but its fundamental principles ; not so much questions about Monarchy, Aristocracy or Democracy, as about the indefeasible rights of humanity, were essential in her political philosophy. But if the administrative form is inseparable from the doctrinal integrity of government, then without dispute she must be classed among Republicans. Her hypothesis of the perfectibility of the race, as presented in her essay on 'The Influence of Literature,' is based, as we have seen, on the theory of Republicanism; but the substance, the core of her political philosophy is the doctrine of popular sovereignty, that is to say, representative government, proceeding from, and amenable to the governed classes, whether its administrative forms be those of the Swiss or American Republic, or those of the British Constitution. Liberty was with her the fundamental interest of the world, the reason and the object of all legitimate government: justice itself but the assertion and protection of liberty by laws.

Her interest in politics grew with her advancing years. Schlegel complained bitterly of this fact; she was too liberal for his aristocratic prejudices. She believed politics to be sacred, next to religion itself; her 'Corinne' is her only book which does not, more or less, treat of them. 'Being profoundly convinced,' says her cousin, 'that institutions form human character, all that is beautiful and good appeared to her dependent on a right social organisation. To be occupied with politics, she said, "is religion, morality, and piety,

all together."' Her sympathies were with the
common people; they are the nations, they the
world. The divine government must be for them,
and human governments should be equally so.
Such was her political creed. 'The worship that
she rendered to liberty was at once Roman and
Christian. She had that passionate pride, that
hatred of tyranny, which characterised the ancients; and she felt quite an evangelic compassion
for the suffering lower classes; she wished not only
to relieve, but to lift up the self-respect, of those
who were most depressed in our social organisa-
tions. It is not therefore astonishing that liberal
ideas had passed, so to speak, into her very blood.
—Bonaparte did not deceive himself; he felt, as
by instinct, that all the words of Madame de Staël
must injure him. " They pretend," he said, " that
she speaks neither of politics, nor of me; but how
then does it come to pass that all who see her
like me less?" "She turns all heads in a sense
not convenient for me."'

Napoleon, without moral sense himself, had
nevertheless the sagacity to see its force in such
a nature as hers; he knew that she knew, and
could not but know, the inherent selfishness and
turpitude of his designs, and could never fail to
expose them by whatever power he left in her
possession. 'She carries a quiver,' he said, ' full
of arrows, that would hit a man were he seated
on a rainbow.' Coppet he affirmed was an arsenal

whence munitions were sent forth against him all over Europe. There has been no higher acknowledgment of her talents. 'Napoleon considered her,' says Lamartine, 'more dangerous than Lafayette to his tyranny.' 'She combined in herself Rousseau and Mirabeau.' 'Superior in talent, more generous in soul, than Madame Roland, she was a great man with the passions of a woman. But these tender and strong passions gave to her talent the qualities of her soul, the accent, the ardour, the heroism of sentiment.' 'This woman,' he continues, 'was the last of the Romans under this Cæsar, who dared not to destroy her, and could not abase her.' 'In her, Genius had two sexes—one for thought, the other for love. Her name will live as long as literature, as long as the history of her country.'[1]

Madame de Staël detested the excesses of the Revolution as degrading and destructive to liberty; she would trust so sacred an interest only to the highest agency of intelligence and morality, of patriotism and philanthropy. But the barbarities of the French struggle could never blind her view of the importance and dignity of freedom. Its image, however marred, ever stood out before her, amidst those scenes of darkness and blood, a benign, a divine vision. She saw in the condition of the French people, which produced such horrors, but stronger reasons for a better social organisation.

[1] *Histoire de la Restauration,* ii. 15. (8 vols.) Paris, 1851.

Her liberal opinions strengthened with the maturity of her life. ' She was convinced, to her heart's
core, of the fundamental equality of all men, children of God. She could not endure the claims of
distinguished people for those Eleusinian mysteries,
those initiations into pretended truths, that they
think it useful to conceal from the vulgar.' With
Lessing she believed, as we have seen, that no truth
is hurtful.

In her ' Considerations on the French Revolution' she shows very advanced opinions for the
Europe of that day. She denounces religious in-
tolerance. She favours the ' Voluntary Principle'
by pronouncing against the support of the Church
by the State, and the interference of the clergy with
State affairs. ' Christian morality is diffused through
that book,' says her cousin, ' and this is the first
time that it was applied to the politics of the age.'

Though strong in her opinions, she was superior
to the usual acrimony of party politics and literary
sectarianism. ' She so little imagined that she
could be hated for opinions, that she responded
to the most violent attacks, without suspecting a
hostile intention. But if she suddenly happened
to detect real malevolence, she, who was so prompt
at repartee, was entirely disconcerted, and was no
longer herself. In her youth she burst into tears
at the discovery of malignity; and, if her pride
could sustain her, hatred, nevertheless, produced
in her astonishment and a species of stupefaction.

The woman was always revealed in her conduct, by
the necessity that she had for affection.' When she
crossed the Rhine, for the first time in her exile
(1803), she wrote, in lines not designed for publication : ' I have thought of my friends in passing
the Rhine, but I know not that the thought of my
enemies has once occurred to me. I have always
regarded hatred, when I have been its victim, as a
sort of extraordinary and passing accident. I can
be convinced of it only by its effects ; so little do I
understand it. When I encounter an enemy I am
tempted to ask him, " Is it seriously true that you
hate me ? Know you not that I have not a bitter
sentiment in my heart ? " ' In her essay on Literature there is an eloquent chapter on ' Women who
cultivate Letters,' showing the peculiar disadvantages of the sex in literary life, their peculiar ex-
posure to criticism, their peculiar helplessness before it. The chivalric respect which is accorded
to woman by all manly minds, in her other pursuits,
was denied her in this her noblest aspiration. If
professional critics were not, in Madame de Staël's
opinion, usually a class of writers who, failing in
literature themselves, avenge their defeat by trying
to defeat worthier minds, she despised, nevertheless,
their affectation of superior acuteness, of smartness
and dictation, and especially their reckless severity
in the treatment of works which they themselves
could not produce. The Hallams and Sainte-Beuves,
the Scherers and Matthew Arnolds, who have

given judicial candour and conscientiousness to·
criticism, and have exalted it to the dignity of a
high literary profession, had not yet appeared.
Though remarkably insensible to hostile criticism
herself, she saw its formidableness to her sex generally. With touching eloquence she says, 'The
aspect of malevolence makes women tremble, however distinguished they may be. Courageous in
misfortune, they are timid before enmity. Thought
exalts them, but their nature remains weak and
sensitive. Most women, in whom superior faculties
have inspired the desire of fame, resemble Herminia
clothed in armour. The combatants see the helmet, the lance, the dazzling plumes; they believe
they are about to encounter strength ; they attack
with violence, and, with their first blow, wound a
heart.' While she was in Sweden, Galiffe, her St.
Petersburg correspondent, became embroiled with
a French nobleman there, who had ungenerously
criticised her writings.. She wrote to him, ' Our
best course with such persons is to forget their
resentment towards us. The more I advance in
life, the more I believe that the Gospel is the best
code of conduct in this world, in regard to both
wit and wisdom,' as well as morals.

Though she was indignant at the crimes of the
Revolution, she clung, nevertheless, as we have seen,
to its essential liberal principles ; and she owed the
Court no gratitude, for it had treated both herself
and her father with persistent disparagement ; yet.

in 1792 she devised a plan for the rescue of the Royal family, which she submitted to the Minister Montmarin, and according to which her friend Narbonne was to conduct the King, Queen, and Dauphin to the coast of Normandy, and thence to England. They distrusted Narbonne's ability to carry it out, or they might have been saved. She was incapable of revenge.

The most bitter words she ever publicly uttered were against her great persecutor, and they were wrung from her by intolerable grievances. She never failed, however, to acknowledge her admiration of his genius; and, in his misfortunes, offered her services, as we have shown, to rescue him from secret perils. He never relented. But her deliverance from his power is at hand, and we are soon to accompany her again to her native, her beloved Paris.

CHAPTER XXXIX.

HER RETURN TO FRANCE.

Her Literary Rank at this period—Compared with the Writers of the Revolution—Of the First Empire—Chateaubriand—Her relations to the Revolution—Her Fidelity to Liberty — The Uprising of Europe against Bonaparte—Goëthe, Fichte, Koerner—Madame de Staël returns to Paris—Sights and Impressions on the way—The Theatres—The King at Saint Ouen—Return of her Friends—Villemain's Account of her.

MEANWHILE, in resuming the narrative, can either the writer or the reader resist the temptation to pause yet a few moments, and contemplate its heroine in her present imposing attitude?

Have we not now reached a point in her history where it may be assumed that the highest claims made for her, in the outset, are vindicated?

We have traced her through most of her intimate personal life, and have found her to be a genuine woman, with the best qualities of her sex, though with its frailties as well.

We have seen her more than feminine genius, marvellous in childhood, rising, through the hardly paralleled trials of her womanhood, to continually greater ascendancy; the promise of the 'Letters on Rousseau' more than fulfilled in the treatise on Literature, 'Corinne,' and the 'Allemagne.'

Through the more than quarter of a century of the Revolution and the First Empire, she is incomparably the foremost character of French literature, the greatest of French writers, as Jeffrey, of the 'Edinburgh Review,' said, since the time of Voltaire and Rousseau. If we except some of the authors of the preceding period, who lingered into that of the Revolution, and a few of them into that of the Empire—Delille, André Chénier, Beaumarchais, Florian, Marmontel, La Harpe, St. Pierre—there was not one of the Revolutionary epoch who could approach her in genius or fame. The period of the First Empire produced no author who can be compared to her, if we except Chateaubriand.[1] Science flourished under the labours of Lacépède, Lagrange, Laplace, Cuvier; philosophy under those of De Gérando, Destutt de Tracy, Royer Collard, Bonald, Say; history had some conspicuous writers; Béranger, Delavigne, and Saumet had only begun to sing. Among the *romanciers*, Madame de Genlis, Madame Cottin, and Madame Flahaut-Souza, still survived from the ante-Revolutionary times. Chateaubriand and Madame de Staël are the two authors of the period best recog-

---

[1] Chateaubriand published his first work (the essay on Revolutions) in London, in 1797, but he belongs to the Napoleonic period by the writings which gave him a literary position.

nised by the literary world. She can advantage-
ously be compared with the splendid rhapsodist of
the ʻMartyrsʼ and the ʻGenius of Christianity,ʼ a
man of undoubted talent, but the enfeebled victim
of the traditional prejudices of his class.[2] If not
equal to him as a rhetorician, she was altogether
superioɾ to him as a thinker. French critics have
usually agreed to recognise him as the representative French author of his times, but the highest
of such authorities admits that this opinion does
not ʻestablish a rank,ʼ nor ʻfix the value of works,ʼ
but only ʻmeasures apparent relations.ʼ[3] These
ʻapparent relationsʼ arise from the coincidence
of his book, on Christianity, with a reaction of the
national mind from the materialistic scepticism of
the Revolution—a reaction which his book doubtless aided among a limited class, but which arose
from antecedent causes, and was essentially a
tendency of the political reaction of the period.
This fortunate coincidence has rendered historical,

[2] Macaulay's opinion of the *Génie du Christianisme* is too severe:
ʻ I am astonished at the utter worthlessness of the book, both in matter
and in manner. As to substance, it is beneath criticism; yet I have
heard men, of ten times Chateaubriand's powers, talk of him as the
first of French writers. He was simply a great humbug.ʼ *Life* by
Trevelyan, iv. 14. See Sainte-Beuve's opinion of the man as well as
of his works, *Causeries* &c. i. and x. These later criticisms qualify
Sainte-Beuve's earlier and exaggerated opinions of Chateaubriand as
expressed in his *Chateaubriand et son Groupe Littéraire sous l'Empire*
(2 vols.), Paris, 1861; which is his *cours* of lectures delivered at
Liége in 1848–1849. Scherer estimates Chateaubriand.with as much
justice as eloquence: *Études Critiques*, Paris, 1863.

[3] Sainte-Beuve's *Chateaubriand et son Groupe* &c. i. 1.

if not immortal, a work the false erudition and
falser logic of which have been redeemed from
critical contempt only by its surpassing rhetoric,
and its art, never surpassed, in the painting of
natural scenes.[4]　The 'Génie du Christianisme'
has no longer any rank among Christian 'Apolo-
getics.'　'It is,' says Vinet, 'too much for a simple
poem, too little for an apology.　The theologian
and the painter mutually embarrass themselves in
it; they exchange and confound their arguments.'
It was a plea for Christianism, more than for
Christianity; it aided Napoleon in restoring the
mediæval ecclesiasticism of France, but did little for
the rational spiritualism which alone can be enduring, and of which Madame de Staël was pre-emi-
nently a representative writer.　Lacretelle, who
passed through all the stages of the Revolution, and
was himself a representative, in the Academy and
in literature, of Christian spiritualism, says that
'Madame de Staël, born in the midst of the
philosophic circles of the times, but instructed by
a father and a mother always faithful to their

---

[4] He omitted in later editions some of his earlier subjects, such
as Celebrated Celibates &c.　Madame de Staël heartily encouraged
Chateaubriand, but had painful misgivings respecting the *Génie*.
Sainte-Beuve says that the chapter entitled 'Examen de la Virginité
sous ses rapports poétiques,' particularly startled her.　'Madame Récamier found her one morning with a volume of the work in her hand,
just received.　"I am quite miserable," she exclaimed; "poor Chateaubriand will be covered with ridicule; his book will fail."'　She soon
discovered, however, that it had charms enough to redeem its absurdities.　*Chateaubriand et son Groupe*, chap. vii.

religious sentiments, was inclined by the elevation of her soul, as well as the precocious power of her genius, to Spiritualism, and was the first who made us comprehend the necessity of returning to this high philosophy.'[5]   Sainte-Beuve places her by the side of Chateaubriand under the Consulate and the Empire : ' the two great names, then rivals, but since united in a common admiration.'   He admits that, though Chateaubriand was superior to her as a painter, she was superior to him in ' ideas.'   We hazard little in affirming that any one volume of the didactic works of Madame de Staël contains more original and profound ideas than can be gathered from all the writings of Chateaubriand.

She stands before us then not only superior to the feminine writers of any preceding age, but supreme among French writers, of either sex, in her own age.

We have followed her through the events of the Revolution and the First Empire,—the era of modern European history, and the most fruitful of social and political results in modern civilisation, unless we must except the great epoch which initiated it, the Revolution of North America. We have seen her active in these events, heroic in their perils, influencing them by her pen and

---

[5] *Testament Philosophique et Littéraire,* i. 15. (2 vols.) Paris, 1840. In the second volume (chap. xix.) he records, as we have seen, a conversation with her at Coppet, on spiritualism and optimism, the fullest example of her conversational eloquence that remains.

her *salon*—the most representative woman, as Sainte-Beuve has affirmed, of those marvellous times.

She has passed through the terrors of the Revolution and the reactionary period of the Empire without swerving from her liberal principles. She is almost the only important French writer who remained loyal to liberty ; and almost the only conspicuous French character, except her friend Lafayette, who was not recreant. Amidst the despair of French Liberals and the success of the Napoleonic reaction, she persists in asserting to her countrymen and to all Europe, in her treatise on ' Literature,' that the perfectibility of humanity is the order of God, and that it can be achieved only by the enlightenment, the emancipation, and the enfranchisement of the people. While statesmen, soldiers, authors, all around her, succumb to the conqueror and accept his bribes, she, a solitary woman, but invincible in her conscience and her genius, refuses all compromise with him, though pursued with a jealousy, and with cruel persecutions, such as he judged unnecessary towards any of his crowned opponents. She is faithful to her convictions, till her imperial persecutor is cast down from his throne, and cast out of Europe.

Thus embodying in her own person the history of her epoch—its best genius, its best opinions, its best social and political traits, she now rises before us a splendid representative character of her times,

a superb historic apparition, and the more imposing for being a superb woman.

A few years of life remain for her—less eventful than those we have been reviewing; but we
shall follow her through them with undiminished
interest.

The great event which was to emancipate the
Continent—'the Battle of the Nations'—was at
hand. The allies of Napoléon rapidly fell away
from him. All Teutonic and Slavonic Europe was
rising, in arms, and throwing itself against the one
hitherto all-victorious nation of the Latin race.
Kings, nobles, scholars, and the common people,
crowded to the field. The universities, the profes-
sions, the homes of Eastern and Central Europe, were
emptied for the contest. It was a *Dies Iræ*. There
could now hardly be a doubt of its result. Madame
de Staël had strong personal reasons for sympathy
with the Allies. They were marching against her
greatest personal enemy, the hitherto invincible antagonist of her most sacred political convictions;
many of her personal friends were prominent
in the sublime movement—Alexander of Russia;
Bernadotte of Sweden ; Prince Augustus of Prussia,
her guest at Coppet ; the Duke of Saxe Weimar,
her correspondent; besides many of her own
countrymen, some of whom she had saved from
the guillotine. Goethe had accompanied the
Duke of Weimar in the invasion of Champagne,
some time before—a thoughtful observer at least—

but his world was apart from the stormy scenes around him, and he was not now in the field; he was tranquilly recording the 'Truth and Poetry' of his early life. Fichte, though not there, had aroused his countrymen by his published 'Discourses to the German Nation,' delivered in the Berlin University, where the sound of the French drums blended with his voice; he offered his services in the army, but died of the plague, produced by the war, at the time that his countrymen were marching triumphantly on Paris. Koerner, 'the Tyrtæus of Germany,' had kindled their ardour by his songs, and had fallen in battle the next day after writing his Schwertlied, 'the Marseillaise of Germany.' Kotzebue was in the train of Alexander of Russia, writing his manifestoes and proclamations, documents which resounded over Europe. Woe unto all their class if the tyrant should again overwhelm their country, for most of its studious youth and scholarly men were under arms.

Genius is clairvoyant. 'I knew that Napoleon would ultimately fail,' said Madame de Staël, 'when I discovered that he cared not to know the foundation of things'—the fundamental truth of things. Being destitute of the moral sense, or ignoring it, at least, in his public conduct, he was at last to be confounded. The historian never prostitutes his function more than when he teaches that great men may successfully meet great emergencies by great crimes, or can ever successfully ignore the moral laws of the universe. Apparent success in such cases can never be ultimately real; for the moral, like physical, laws are independent of all our speculative theories, whether theistic or atheistic. They are founded in, and evolved from, the very nature of things. If there be no God, the universe becomes a God unto itself—an invincible God in defence of its own laws. If there be a God, then both He and all his universe must, at last, be overwhelmingly against the evil-doer. But the preachments of the Moralists are not necessary on such a truth; history itself forever teaches it. Napoleon scorned the advice of Necker to become the Washington of Europe; and writers who have glorified him have taught that an unscrupulous ruler alone could rescue Europe in his time. The fallacy is atrocious at any time, but it was especially so at his. The reaction in favour of order had commenced before his accession to power. France had learned the terrible retributive lesson of her errors. A great and conscientious man of genius could have led her as he wished. It was the opportunity for a European Washington: Napoleon saw in it only an opportunity for the aggrandisement of his family—of himself at the head of his family. Madame de Staël had understood from the beginning, as we have seen, his real character. She detected his supreme egotism—an egotism made up as much of

vanity as of pride. Its two elements qualified one
another somewhat for a time ; but these vices were
now to be his ruin. He had done some good and
great things for France, for they added to his glory
and aided his ambition ; but they could be easily
done by a ruler who commanded millions of men,
and robbed the treasuries of Europe. At last
his vanity, his love of applause, was defeated.
He had decimated all France, and devastated all
Europe ; there was hardly a family in the remotest
French village that was not in mourning for its
dead, sacrificed by his ambition. Benjamin Constant said publicly: 'Under Bonaparte we have a
government of Mamelukes : his sword alone governs.
He is Attila—he is Genghis Khan, more terrible and
more odious because civilisation is at his command
—this man of blood.' He was losing the sympathy
of the people ; their admiration was converted into
sullen dread of his genius and ambition. For a
considerable time the news of his victories had
ceased to excite them. Even in the theatres of
Paris, their announcement called forth little applause from any but his official supporters. Junot
(Duc d'Abrantès), the most devoted of his generals,
wrote him : 'I, who love you with the adoration
of the savage for the sun, who belong entirely to
you—I wish for peace ; I wish this eternal fighting
to end ; I ask for peace, by the right of twenty-two
years of effective services, and the blood shed from
seventeen wounds, at first for my country and then

for your glory.'[6] Though this remonstrance came
from a man whom he deemed insane, he knew it
expressed the sentiment of France. He was no
longer an idol, but a terror to the world. He recoiled under this defeat of his vanity, and now his
pride alone remained, and was to hurl him on destruction. The battle of Leipsic—'the Battle of
the Nations'—was fought on October 16–18, 1813.
On its eve his oldest generals foresaw its dangers;
they gravely consulted among themselves, and sent
two or three of their number to warn him. His
desperate pride repelled them. 'You, Berthier,'
he said, ' know that your opinion will not have the
weight of a straw in my determination. Save your
words, then. You, Count Daru, are a man of the
pen, not of the sword; your judgment is nothing
here. As for the others, who have sent you, *let
them obey.* This is my answer.'[7] Retributive fate
had another answer for them in the ensuing battle.
Half a million combatants were in the field. Two
hundred thousand cannon shots were fired. The
French were utterly overthrown. One of their own
officers prematurely blew up the bridge over the
Elster, whereby whole battalions were lost, and thou-
sands struggled and died in the river, among them
the heroic Poniatowski. A hundred thousand men
perished; and the great Captain—who might, as
Fichte said, have been the saviour of Europe—

[6] *Mémoires de la Duchesse d'Abrantès*, xvi. 10.
[7] *Ibid.* 12.

met, at last, his irremediable doom.   It was self-incurred.

A favourable authority admits that the defeat at Leipsic was attributable to the fact that Napoleon's ' moral faculties were enfeebled.' [8]   His most flattering historian asserts that his military talents there were as great as ever, but that ' the insatiable demand of his ambition troubled and perverted his immense genius.' [9]   ' He was taken in the snare of his own combinations, and succumbed, after the most terrible battle known—a battle in which were destroyed, a thing horrible to say, more than a hundred thousand men.'   Thiers, in closing the disastrous story, says: ' Alas! men bear, in their own characters, a destiny that they seek around them, above them—everywhere, in a word, except in themselves, where it truly resides, and according to which, as they yield to their passions or reason, they are ruined or saved, whatever else they can do, whatever genius they possess.   And then, when they fail, they attribute their ruin to their soldiers, their generals, their allies ; to men, to gods, declaring themselves betrayed by all, when they have been betrayed only by themselves.'

Madame de Staël was the prey of conflicting emotions, as, day by day, news from the Continent agitated London.   She wished for the overthrow of the Corsican, but not of her countrymen.   When

---

[8] *Biographie Universelle,* sup. vol. lxxv.
[9] *Hist. du Consulat et de l'Empire,* v. 50, by Thiers.

asked by an English Cabinet Minister what she most desired respecting the contest, 'That Napoleon may be victorious but slain,' was her reply.[1] ' It was now,' says her cousin, at the date of the battle of Leipsic, 'that she began to suffer for France.'[2] She had become intimate, in England, with Louis Philippe, Duke of Orleans (afterwards King of the French) and his wife ; and now Louis XVIII. arrived in London, from Hartwell ; their conversations inspired her with the best hopes. ' We shall have,' she wrote, ' a king very favourable to literature.'[3]

Her exiled countrymen were gathering for their return to France ; but she could hardly share in their exultations. The allies pressed forward, fighting their way towards the capital. A battle was fought on March 30, 1814, under the walls of Paris, in which the French were completely routed and the allies entered the city. ' This blow,' she wrote to her son, ' is cruel ; all London is intoxicated with joy, and I alone, in the great city, am a sufferer by this event.'[4]

---

[1] *Considérations,* iv.

[2] *Notice* &c. ii.

[3] *Coppet et Weimar,* vii. Lamartine says that Louis XVIII. had ' as much *esprit* as any statesman, or any man of letters, in his empire. Talleyrand himself did not surpass him in repartee nor the politicians in eloquence, nor the poets in citations, nor the learned in memory. He showed himself equal in conversation to all the distinguished men of his time.' *Histoire de la Restauration,* ii. 15. (8 vols.) Paris, 1854.

[4] *Œuvres Diverses* of Baron Auguste de Staël, i. 51.

She prepared immediately to return to her country. She has recorded the contending feelings with which she witnessed its new condition. 'After ten years of exile,' she writes, 'I landed at Calais thinking of the great pleasure with which I ought to behold again the beautiful France which I had so long regretted ; but my sentiments were quite different from my anticipations. The first men I saw upon the shore wore the Prussian uniform. They were the masters of the city, and had acquired that right by conquest ; but it seemed to me that I was beholding the re-establishment of the old feudal system, such as the historians describe it, when the inhabitants of the land were there only to cultivate the earth, the fruits of which were to be consumed by German warriors. O France ! France ! was it necessary that a foreign-born tyrant should reduce thee to this state ? A French sovereign, whosoever he might be, would have loved thee too much to have exposed thee to such a humiliation. I continued my journey, my heart incessantly suffering from the same thought. I approached Paris : Germans, Russians, Cossacks everywhere presented themselves to my eyes. They were encamped around the church of St. Denis, where the remains of the kings of France reposed. Their discipline prevented any harm, except the oppression of soul which it was impossible not to feel. At last I entered the city where I had passed the most happy and most brilliant days of my life.

I seemed to be in a painful dream. Was I in Germany? In Russia? Had they imitated the streets and public places of the capital of France, in order to recall scenes which no longer existed? In short, all was troubled within me; for, notwithstanding the acuteness of my grief, I esteemed the foreigners for having broken our yoke. I admired them without restriction, at this period; but to see Paris occupied by them, the Tuileries and the Louvre filled by troops from the confines of Asia, to whom our language, our history, our great men, were all less known than the name of the last Khan of Tartary—this was an unendurable mortification. If such was the impression on me, who could not return to France under the reign of Napoleon, what must have been the suffering of our warriors, covered with wounds!' [5]

She wished to see her countrymen, and went to the Opera, but the stairs were guarded by Russian sentinels; in the *salle* she looked on all sides to discover a face known to her, and saw only foreign uniforms; a few citizens were in the pit, 'from old habit,' but, with this exception, all the spectators were changed; 'the spectacle alone remained the same; the decorations, the music, the dance, had lost nothing of their charm. I felt humiliated at French grace being lavished before these sabres and moustaches, as if it were the duty of the conquered to amuse the conquerors. At the Théâtre

[5] *Considérations*, v. 6.

Française, the tragedies of Racine and Voltaire were represented before the foreigners, who were more jealous of our literary glory than eager to recognise it. We were ashamed even of the talents of our poets when they seemed, like ourselves, chained to the car of the invaders. I take pleasure in saying that no officer of the French army appeared at the theatre while the allied troops occupied the capital; they walked about the streets sadly, without uniform, unwilling to wear their military decorations, as they were no longer able to defend the sacred territory, the guardianship of which had been confided to their arms. The irritation which they felt did not permit them to understand that it was their ambitious, egotistical, and reckless chief who had reduced them to this humiliation.'

She records her joy that, by a singular coincidence, Louis XVIII. signed at St. Ouen, the old home of her father in the vicinity of Paris, the declaration which was to guarantee the liberties of the nation, and that it comprised all the articles that Necker had proposed to Louis XVI. in 1789, before the Revolution of July 14 broke out: ' As if,' remarks Lamartine, ' he wished to recall the memory of a popular minister whom he had supported in the Convention of the States.' The King delighted in her company, and esteemed her a powerful support of the government, an ' ally to his crown, because she represented the European spirit.' 'Louis XVIII. by the elevation of his mind, by his literary tastes, by his graceful admiration, consoled her for the disdain and brutalities of Napoleon. Her *salon* in Paris' became one of the forces of the Restoration.'[6] The King soon admitted her claim to the two millions which her father had lent to the national treasury.

Her return to Paris was the greatest of her social triumphs. Its highest society gathered around her, and her *salon* was again the intellectual centre of the capital. Her two dearest friends hastened from their exile to join her : Mathieu de Montmorency returned to occupy an honourable place at Court; Madame Récamier came from Italy, to embellish, with her undiminished beauty, the renewed circle. 'I passed last evening at Madame de Staël's,' wrote Pictet de Rochemont, ' for the Emperor Alexander was to be there, and I wished to speak to him in behalf of Geneva; he has the best inclination towards us. I found there also Talleyrand, Lafayette, Lally-Tollendal, the two Montmorencys, M. de Sabran, the Duchess of Courland, and a crowd of princes and ambassadors. It was a true triumph for the mistress of the house, a triumph of high interest, and one which was prolonged until three o'clock in the morning with continually increasing *éclat*.'[7] 'She is crowned with success,' wrote Bonstetten; 'the

---

[6] Lamartine's *Histoire de la Restauration*, ii. 14. Paris 1851.
[7] Unpublished *Souvenirs* of M. Pictet de Sergy, of Geneva.

Emperor of Russia, kings, generals, all who have a name, frequent her mansion in Paris.'[8]

Villemain, then a young man, rich in the promise of talents which afterward secured him literary distinction, became acquainted with her at this time, and has given us some interesting recollections of her conversations, and of the effect of her 'Allemagne,' now for the first time admitted into France. 'She was one of those privileged beings,' he says, 'one of those superior souls, of whom nothing is forgotten; who take possession alike of the imagination and the heart; whose features remain always vivid before your eyes, and could be painted, after the lapse of thirty years, without mistaking a single trait, if the hand were as able as the memory is moved and faithful. For us young men of letters, under the enchantment of the first love of the arts and of eloquence, she bore, and bears still, rays of light on her brow, the splendour of a new and admirable work, the " Allemagne," that book, proscribed under the Empire, but given back to us by the Restoration as one of the liberties it bore with it. A mixture of the recital of travel, of the painting of manners, of critical analysis, of even free and ideal invention, this book astonished us, enchanted us, on coming forth from that prison in which, notwithstanding our extended frontiers, the Empire had incarcerated our minds. It was a burst of light in a new

[8] *Briefe* &c. ii.

heaven, the sky of the north, pouring an unexpected illumination on our antique studies, ele-
vating the heart to the worship of moral beauty,
that we might bear it into the arts; reminding us
that there is no genius without soul, no soul without religion, without liberty, without love; and,
whilst all these unusual truths displayed themselves to our eyes in pages glowing with intellect
and eloquence, the entirely literary character of
this proscribed book, the speculative height of the
views of art and of taste which it offered, the
absence of all direct polemics, and, meanwhile, the
striking human dignity and civil virtue which
pervaded its sentences, made us better comprehend
the abyss of insipid sterility and moral apathy into
which the absolute power that prohibited such
thoughts, wished apparently to plunge the intelligence of this French nation, which it had so much
abused on battle fields. To this common revelation that our youth received from the publication
of such a writing, was added for me the privilege
of hearing the conversations of the author, her
familiar conversations which were believed to be
superior to her writings, but which, proceeding
from the same source, marked by the same imprint, had only more of the charm of the perfect
unity of thought with the expression of the living
voice. I have often seen Madame de Staël illuminate, with a vivid light, accidental conversations on
politics, letters, art; glance over the past and the

present as two regions entirely open to her view;
divine that which she knew not; evoke into life
and brightness, by the lightning of thought, that
which was only a dead souvenir buried in history;
portray men as she recalled them; judge, for
example, the Cardinal de Richelieu with a profound sagacity, and, I may add, with a noble
womanly wrath; then the Emperor Napoleon, who
combined in her estimation all despotisms, and
whom her eloquent speech disclosed, at all points
of the horizon, as a gigantic shadow obscuring
them all. And how frequently, in the midst of
these animated discussions, this sudden display of
virile reason and eloquence, have I seen her pass
suddenly to private interests, treating them with
the same ardour; giving to some modest or dis-
graced merit a decisive support, by those words of
imperative fascination or touching pathos which
she knew how to address to men of the world, the
most self-defended against emotion. Sometimes by
that conciliatory ardour which was a tie between
the best representatives of all parties, and that
legitimate right of her intellect which gave her
hardly less power over M. de Blacas or M. de Montmorency, than over M. de Lafayette or Baron
Louis, I have seen her, in the same evening, obtain
admission to the household of the King for a man
of merit as independent as unfortunate, re-establish
in their employments functionaries who had been

devoted, but with honour, to the imperial power that she had combated, and serve with her credit men of letters who, during her exile, had denied her talents.'[9]

[9] ' Les Cent Jours :' second volume of *Souvenirs Contemporains.* Paris, 1855.

CHAPTER XL.

AGAIN IN PARIS.

Her Salon reopened in Paris—The Duke of Wellington on his knees—
Alexander of Russia—Letters to the Duchess of Weimar—Her
'Considerations on the French Revolution'—The 'Ten Years of
Exile.'

SOPHIE GAY introduces us to Madame de Staël's
restored *salon*, now more brilliant than ever. 'The
presence of the Cossacks in our streets,' she says,
' was unendurable to me. I shut myself up in my
house, where the letters of my friends kept me
informed of what was passing.' A man of intellect, known since in literature, M. A. de Gustine,
wrote her an account of an evening spent with
Madame de Staël. It is dated at two o'clock on
the morning of March 8, 1814,[1] and says :—'The
salon of Madame de Staël is a mirror which represents the history of the times. What one sees
there is as instructive as many books, and gayer
than many comedies. You ask me why I read so
little? What is the use of my reading when I can

[1] Evidently a mistake (probably typographical) of the month;
for the allies did not take Paris till two weeks later, and Wellington,
mentioned in this letter, was still fighting in the south, on his way to
join them at the capital. The evening party would have been possible
in May.

draw here, from their source, all the ideas of our times? It is life, it is intellect, that shines here, the illuminations of genius. How shall we live if ever we lose her! What most charms, in the society of this woman, is that you feel that she has a regard for you. This gives you immediately the command of all your faculties, and then she lends you some of her own; for her mind is not avaricious, it is only the dispenser of the treasures of her soul: and what I prefer above all things is the soul of people of intellect. How delightful, after her admirable eloquence has been expended on the company, to be able to approach her as a more intimate friend. Then, re-entering into herself, abandoning herself with the confidence which a creative mind always feels the need of, she remains, with one or two persons, to speak about them and herself. It is then that we discover, with admiration, all that God has placed in this heart. What sublime sincerity! What luminous views of the human soul, of the world! What discoveries she causes you to make in nature, in history, in yourself, in all that you had believed yourself to know as well as she. One thanks the Creator that one is, as she, a human creature. Complaining of the indifference of certain persons, she said, How is it that not one of these people can love me as much as I love them all? Her charity is almost divine. I admire her, as all the world does, but few persons love her as I love her; in fact, I find her beautiful.

The Duke of Wellington was to pass the evening with
her. I arrived early, she had not yet appeared; some
habitués were impatient for her; the most marked
were the Abbé de Pradt, Constant, and Lafayette.
They conversed, but I remained in a corner to hear.
At last Madame de Staël came; a great number of
guests entered; they announced Madame Récamier;
she alone could indemnify Madame de Staël for the
delay of Wellington. They remained aside, speaking by themselves in whispers, till the Duke came.
He entered at last; the nobleness of his face, the
simplicity of his manners, produced on us a most
agreeable effect. His pride (for he ought to have
some) has even the grace of timidity. Madame de
Staël, herself impressed by his bearing and language, so little French, remarked, " He bears his
glory as if it were nothing." Then, with a return
of her patriotism, she whispered in my ear, " It is
necessary to admit, however, that never did nature
make a great man at so little expense." It seems
to me that the entire man is described in these few
words. You would suppose that, after this *début*,
we greatly enjoyed the evening; but the Duke had
hardly advanced into the *salon*, when the Abbé de
Pradt seized him, and forced him to listen for
nearly an hour to his ideas of military tactics.
Imagine the wrath of Madame de Staël, and the
ennui of all the company. Schlegel said that it
seemed like hearing that rhetorician who delivered
a discourse on the art of war to Hannibal. Among

the few words that the English general could interpolate, there was one remark which struck me. While the Abbé was taking breath and using his handkerchief a moment, the warrior had time to say that the most frightful day to a man who commands an army, is that on which he gains a battle; because, before he can spend the night on the field, and assure himself the next day of the course of the enemy, the conqueror cannot certainly know that he is not himself conquered. Many guests retired, discouraged by the conduct of the Abbé de Pradt; the hero himself evidently thought of flying, when Madame de Staël came to disengage him from the pertinacious Abbé. She retained him near the door, where a conversation on the English Constitution followed. She could not reconcile political liberty with the servile forms which remained in the individual relations of a society so proud of this liberty. " Words and forms shock nobody in a truly free community," said the Duke; " we keep our old formulas as a homage to the past, just as an old monument is kept up when its original object no longer exists." " Is it true," she asked, " that your Lord Chancellor speaks to the King kneeling, in the session of Parliament? " " It is true." " How is it done? " " Why, Madame, as I say, he kneels when he speaks." " But how? " she continued. " Would you see? " responded the Duke, and he cast himself at the feet of our Corinne. " I wish that all the world saw it," exclaimed Madame de Staël. The whole company applauded; I will not answer for their unanimity at the bottom of the stairs. After all had left, I remained two hours with her and Schlegel, whose wrath against the rhetorical Abbé could not be appeased. During these two hours the conversation of Madame de Staël enchanted me, and proved to me how much reason I had to be attached to a being who saw the world, at the same time, so near and so far. She said to me, in the enthusiasm of her talent, " What happiness if one could be a queen for twenty-four hours! How many beautiful things one could say." These words are like those which made my uncle, the Count de Sabran, say that " she wished the whole world were a *salon*, and she the centre light of it." It is possible that this pointed pleasantry may have been applicable to certain moments of her life. But the same person said of her that, " to comprehend all, was to pardon all." I cannot recount all the details of this evening. There were more than enough materials for a book, in a two hours' conversation with Madame de Staël. I prefer to go to sleep, that I may the better tell you to-morrow, what I have now only enabled you to guess.'

She met in Paris, Alexander of Russia and the Duke of Saxe-Weimar, who had treated her with so much hospitality, the first at St. Petersburg, the second at Weimar. In her conversations with the former she saw increased cause for her admiration.

She had left him great in his misfortunes ; she now found him magnanimous in victory. ' Alexander,' she writes, ' entered Paris quite alone, without guard, without any precaution ; the people were delighted with this generous confidence ; the crowd pressed around his horse, for the French, so long victorious, did not yet feel humiliated in the first moments of their defeat. All parties hoped for a liberator in the Emperor of Russia, and certainly he bore in his heart the desire to be such.'[2] The Duke of Weimar recalled the brilliant days she had spent in his classic capital. She wrote to her correspondent the Duchess : ' I have seen his Highness the Duke, and we have talked much of you. During all my wanderings I have thought of you, and of your kindness to me. For your sake I ought to be willing to endure exile. That exile, which has cost me so much suffering, has been the cause of great good to me. We have witnessed a singular spectacle at Paris ; but it was more frightful at a distance, than near. The strangers have been received here with a perfect cordiality ; nothing now awakens the sad apathy of the nation. Fifteen years of tyranny have extinguished all public spirit. I believe, meanwhile, that the actual government is well established. The King has intellect and address ; and all the means taken by Bonaparte to establish tyranny serve to make the new order of things sure. The history of England

[2] *Considérations* &c. v.

repeats itself here. Would that we could only repeat the Restoration of 1688 ! I shall go to Switzerland in a month, and return to pass the winter in Paris. If your Highness has any orders to give me, I will receive them with gratitude. I have not given up the hope of seeing you again in Germany ; I have lost the habit of being sedentary, and change pleases me. After the marriage of my daughter I shall go to Greece, to compose there a poem on the Crusades. It is necessary to be doing something in this sad life, where one has always the idea of a happiness which flies before us as the clouds. It is true nevertheless that these clouds are the presentiment of another life. Adieu, madame ; adieu, you who have been able to make so noble a use of your years, and have not a single recollection which ought not to honour you in your own eyes. Deign to mention my name to Goethe, and to Madame de Shardt. The Emperor of Russia is adored at Paris.' [3]

This letter shows that she still retained her design of writing the poem on ' Richard Cœur de Lion,' of which we have had several intimations. She was also, at intervals, busy with her ' Considerations on the French Revolution,'—the vindication of her father and one of her greatest productions. We may here, properly enough, take final leave of this and her other posthumous work, the ' Ten Years of Exile.' Of the former, Sainte-Beuve says that ' to

---

[3] *Coppet et Weimar*, viii.

study her in her completeness, at her highest development, we must consider her in 1818,[4] that is to say, at the beginning of the Restoration, which she so well comprehended, and of which she was the historic and political muse, by her able essay. She is perfect only from this day; the full influence of her star is only at her tomb.'[5] Elsewhere this able critic says: 'Its publication, in 1818, was an event. It was the splendid public obsequies of the authoress. Its politics were destined to long and passionate discussions, and a durable influence. Benjamin Constant, in the "Minerve," and M. de Fitz-James, in the "Conservateur," discussed them from opposite standpoints. Bailleul and Bonald wrote essays upon them. The influence that Madame de Staël exercised by this work on the young philosophic, liberal party, represented by the "Globe," was direct; a party that really emanated from her.'[6]

This book is unique. Its motive, which is never for a moment lost sight of, is the defence of Necker. It is not so much a narrative as a philosophic investigation of the principal events of the Revolution, their causes and their significance. It presents more dissertation than narration; it is a thorough

---

[4] The next year after her death, in which the *Considérations* was published by her family. It appeared in three vols. 8vo. A second edition was issued in Paris the same year, and, two years later, a third. Five works were published, for or against it, within four years.

[5] *Chateaubriand et son Groupe,* i. 2.

[6] *Critiques et Portraits Littéraires,* iii. Paris, 1841.

study of the British Constitution, as well as of the political history and needs of France. It abounds in brief personal episodes, which are never, however, irrelevant to its subject. It is often colloquial in its style ; the writer converses freely and brilliantly, and this is one of the chief charms of the work. It is a scathing criticism of Napoleon ; but, apart from this partisan aspect, it is so profoundly thoughtful and suggestive, so vigorous and luminous in style (especially in the first two parts, which alone received her final revision), as to justify Vinet's criticism : ' I think,' he says, ' that no other book written on the subject has given a more complete knowledge—a more simple, and at the same time more luminous idea of the French Revolution ; considered in its causes, its principles, and its course.'[7]

Villemain says that 'splendour of historic colouring, energy of moral sentiment, some partiality which gives force to the expression but does not injure the truth for the future—these are characteristics of this work. Wherefore did life fail in this noble attempt, to aid by the apostleship of talent, the movement of a people towards institutions which elevate and illuminate them ? Never could her pen have been more useful. Her genius was still rising when she was overtaken by death. A great reputation was acquired which ought to bind her to the new destinies of France.'[8] Ville-

---

[7] Vinet's *Etudes sur la Littérature Française au* 19ᵉ *Siècle,* i. 11.
[8] *Littérature* &c. iv. 61.

main's assertion, that never could her influence have been more salutary than in the later liberal struggles of France, is just. It is one of the distinctive powers of science, that, having ascertained principles or laws, it can be predictive; but genius itself is often also prescient. Madame de Staël was the Sibyl, the prophetess of the political future of her country. Modern French Liberals cannot study a better text-book of their cause than the 'Considérations.'

When the book was published, in less than a year after her death, Bonstetten wrote to the German poet Matthisson: 'Are you not all in ecstasy over the Staël? I am. The first edition of eleven thousand is already gone. No work shows more noble feeling for freedom and the rights of man, than this. She invoked liberty for the world even when she was leaving it. The good, the beloved Staël! Dear Matthisson, what awaits us in the future? My heart palpitates whenever I see the tops of the sycamores bending over her tomb, and I too, with nature, bow my head.'[9]

Her cousin, Madame Necker de Saussure, becomes enthusiastic over it, and remarks that 'though she communicated to her friends successively the different parts of her manuscript, yet, when this monumental book was presented to them in its completeness, they were astonished by its imposing grandeur. Whatever idea Madame

---

[9] *Briefe von Bonstetten an Matthisson.* Zürich, 1827.

de Staël had given of her capacity, there is such a
height of thought in this work, that it is necessary
to have before one's eyes all her past, to believe
that she wrote it.   It is the fruit of all her intelligence, all her experience, occupied with the future.
Her political education, in the two administrations
of her father, and the different stages of the Revolution ; her observation of the evils inflicted by
tyranny ; her travels all over Europe—above all,
her residence in England, where her ideas of legis-
lation were matured by discussions with the most
distinguished men—these were her preparations
for the composition of the book.'[1]

Her other posthumous work—the ' Dix Années
d'Exil '—begins in 1800, two years before her first
formal banishment ; its narrative is suspended in
1804, after the death of her father ; it is resumed
in 1810, and abruptly ends at her arrival in
Sweden, in 1812.   Vinet would qualify its severe·
reflections on Napoleon, but admires its talent,
especially its style.   ' It tells its story,' he says,
' with a charming vivacity and naturalness.   The
steeds, which have borne the intellectual traveller,
have never, in any other instance, however fleet,
struck more brilliant scintillations from the stones
in their path.   Luminous traits, piquant epigrams,
dart from her rapid pen.   She seems, like Madame
de Sévigné, to gallop along with the reins on the
courser's neck.   Her style, though so easy, is not·

---

[1] *Notice &c.* i.

careless, not incorrect ; all is light and movement.' Her biography could never have been written without the aid of the ' Dix Années.' It is her grand accusation of Napoleon before posterity. A critic of high authority says, ' All is frank in this work ; it tells its story with simplicity. It refutes the accounts given in the narratives, from St. Helena, of her discords with Napoleon. No one will have any difficulty in recognising the language of truth in Madame de Staël's recital.'[2]

These unfinished works gave way to more urgent interests. She was absorbed in preparations for the marriage of her daughter to the Duc de Broglie, and in anxiety for the declining health of Rocca. Her own health began also to betray ominous symptoms, for her constitution had been shattered by her protracted sufferings.

[2] *Biographie Universelle,* tome xl.

CHAPTER XLI.

THE HUNDRED DAYS.

At Coppet again—Letter to the Duchess of Weimar—Poor Health—
Labours against the African Slave Trade—The ' Reflections on Sui-
cide '—Letters to Madame Récamier—In Paris again—Bonaparte's
Return—The Hundred Days—Madame de Staël in the Salon of
Madame de Rumford—She flees to Coppet—Letters to Madame
Récamier—Bonaparte attempts to conciliate her—Thiers' Mistake
—She remains firm.

AFTER two months spent in the new excitements
of the capital, Madame de Staël's declining health
compelled her to seek relief in her home at Coppet,
from which she had now been a wanderer for
more than two years. The old château, in its
tranquil beauty, amidst some of the most picturesque scenery of Lake Leman, welcomed her to
repose ; but her vigorous constitution had been
broken by her long struggle with misfortune, and
her life was hastening towards its close. She
wrote again (June 8, 1814) to the Duchess of
Weimar : ' The memory of your kindness accompanies me to the tomb which I have chosen for
my asylum.[1]   I will certainly return to you, for I

---

[1] The family cemetery is visible from the windows of the château
at Coppet.

am, alas! free to transport my life wherever I may wish, but I shall never be what I have been, and your affection will henceforth attach itself only to the shadow of my former self. I think I may go this winter to Italy; my nerves are so impaired that I shall be incapable of my remaining duties if my health is not restored.—To sustain me in my prostration I frequently retrace the proofs of your esteem. Adieu, Madame! I transport myself, in thought, to the beautiful garden, the charming château, where I have found so much hospitality. You have seen the last days of my life of hope, of youth, of happiness. At present I exist, as the aged do, with effort, with resignation, but the natural fountain of life is dried up. Adieu yet once more.'[2]

Bonstetten wrote (July 10) to Charlotte Brun: '·Madame de Staël has arrived at Coppet. Rocca comes in four days. She is very much changed, but, as usual, good and *spirituelle*. I hope you have read and re-read her book, the "Allemagne."' To Frederica Brun he writes: 'She is as brilliant as ever. Since the appearance of the "Allemagne" they have been learning German in Geneva and also in France.'[3]

Neither physical nor mental depression could extinguish her love of labour. Work was still,

---

[2] *Coppet et Weimar,* viii.
[3] *Briefe von K. V. von Bonstetten an Friederike Brun,* ii. Frankfurt a. M. 1829.

indeed, as it had always been, her relief and solace. While in England she had become intimate with Wilberforce, Clarkson, and the elder Macaulay; her fervid sympathies allied her with them in their attacks on the Slave Trade, and she now procured the translation of Wilberforce's work on that subject and wrote a preface for it,[4] condensing the history of the movement, and eloquently advocating a general European interest in its behalf. This could not suffice for her generous zeal; she again spent some time in the French capital, and issued there an ' Appeal to the Sovereigns, united in Paris, for the Abolition of the Negro Slave Trade.'[5] She reminded them of the example of England in breaking up the atrocious traffic within her own dominions, and of the sublime opportunity the Allies now had of arraying all Europe against it. ' The sovereigns assembled in France,' she said, ' should give a pledge, for the protection of Africa, to that propitious Heaven from which they have obtained the deliverance of Europe. Many political interests have been discussed by them, but some hours given to so grand, so religious an interest would not be useless even to the affairs of this world. It will be said hereafter that, at this Peace of Paris, the African Slave Trade was abolished by all Europe; this Peace is then holy, for it has been sanctified by such an act of devotion to the God of Armies.'

<hr/>

[4] *Œuvres complètes*, ii.　　　　[5] *Ibid.*

She imbued her children with her sentiments regarding the Slave Trade. A few years later her son, Auguste, advocated its suppression both with his pen and his voice, in public assemblies in France ; her daughter became an active Anti-Slavery philanthropist, in the highest circles of Paris ; and her son-in-law, the Duc de Broglie, eloquently represented the same cause in the French Senate in 1822, and had the honour to sign, after the Revolution of 1830, a conclusive treaty with Great Britain against the traffic. Madame de Staël followed her appeal for the Negro with her 'Response to an Article of a Journal,' which had recently attacked her 'Reflections on Suicide.' Though she never replied to purely literary criticisms, yet, as this essay (now for the first time introduced into France) was accused of teaching anti-Christian opinions, she promptly answered her critics and conclusively refuted the charge.[6]

She returned to Coppet, whence she wrote (July 22) to Madame Récamier : 'I marvel, dear friend, at my courage. I assure you that I am astonished to find myself here again, and I can hardly keep up the fine love of solitude which has brought me back. I have been received with salutes, with flowers and verses, but my soul is not sufficiently rustic not to regret your little apartment, our conversations and disputes, and all

[6] *Œuvres complètes,* ii.

the life that belongs to you. General Filangière has brought me a charming little letter from you. I often see the Davys :[7] the wife is very agreeable ; she admires you much, but fears a little lest her husband may do so. There is also here *she* who was, twenty years ago, *you*, in England, Lady Charlotte Campbell. Her life has been very different from yours ; she married the man whom she loved, and has had eight children ; but he died a drunkard after ill-using her for nearly fourteen years, without her ever speaking of her sorrows to anyone. She is without an intimate friend in this world, and will be till her children can understand her. You have much more intelligence than she, a means of happiness, whatever may be said to the contrary. Albertine requests to be remembered to you. I shall never have rest till I see her in a happy and fixed situation—happy at least so far as God permits in this world.'

She was again in Paris through the winter of 1814–1815. The *salons* of its polished society were now in full vogue, and her own immediately became the chief. Lamartine says, ' Her society was composed of some few republicans, faithful survivors of the Gironde or of Clichy ; some remnants of the constitutional party of the Constituent Assembly ; some new royalists ; of philo-

[7] Sir Humphry and his wife were favourite guests at Coppet and Geneva ; his grave is in the latter place. Lady Davy was particularly admired by Madame de Staël, who said that she was the best realisation of Corinne she had ever met.

sophers, orators, poets, writers and journalists of all dates. She was the centre of all these opinions, of all these talents, naturalised in her *salon* by the goodness of her soul and the tolerance of her genius. She loved everyone, because she comprehended everyone. She was universally loved, because her own opinions had never been tinged with hatred, though with enthusiasm; and this enthusiasm was the natural ardour of her heart and her speech. Her conversation was an endless ode. Her guests pressed around her to witness the continual display of high ideas and magnanimous sentiments, expressed in the inoffensive eloquence of a woman. They went forth passionate against tyranny, and for liberty, for genius, for the unlimited foresights of the imagination. The fire of this *salon* warmed all Europe. Madame de Staël was the Mirabeau of conversation and of letters. A sublime and ravishing delirium took possession of her auditors. The world had not seen, since the Sibyl, the incarnation of virile genius in a woman; she was the Sibyl of two ages, of the eighteenth and nineteenth centuries; of the Revolution in its cradle, of the Revolution in its tomb.'[8] She was not only the irresistible attraction of her own *salon*, but the centre of interest in every similar circle which she entered. Her faculties had never been more vigorous, her conversation never more brilliant, and her personal history gave

[8] *Histoire de la Restauration,* ii. 15.

her an extraordinary prestige ; she was recognised as the foremost woman not only of Paris, of France, but of Europe, that is to say, of the world.

While in the full sway of her restored social empire, the capital was startled by the most unexpected of events. Her exiled persecutor, whose life she had saved, on Elba, from conspirators, had escaped from the island and had landed on the coast of France. Day by day astonishing news arrived of the falling away of cities, provinces, and the army, to his standard. Villemain has left us an account of the effect of this event on her and her associates. He was present, on the evening of ' March 18, 1815,' [9] in the *salon* of the widow of the celebrated Lavoisier, now the wife of the scientific American, Benjamin Thompson (Count Rumford), where a distinguished company had gathered— Lafayette, Benjamin Constant, Sismondi, Lemercier, Cuvier, Jaucourt (whom Madame de Staël had saved from the guillotine, and who had attained high political places), Maine de Biran, the philosopher, and many others, with a crowd of splendid women, and numerous young officers who hastily passed in and out with tidings of the advancing conqueror.

---

[9] Villemain, writing years later, has evidently mistaken the date of the interview at Madame de Rumford's, and also some of the local allusions in Madame de Staël's conversation. His 18th of March may have been the 8th, or more probably the 9th. Madame de Staël dates her visit to the King on the 9th, as will presently be seen ; she wrote a letter to Madame Récamier on her route to Coppet, on the 12th.

'But,' remarks Villemain, ' this evening an eminent woman, the most observed of all, a woman whose rank in the world, the renown of whose works and conversation, the sovereignty of whose intellect, placed her in advance of most statesmen, Madame de Staël, arrived late in the troubled *salon*, drawing to herself all attention and suspending all conjectures. All her vivacity of free thought and original *verve*, all her warmth of sympathy, seemed extinguished by a single and absorbing interest. In the dress that she ordinarily wore, at once brilliant and negligent, under the scarlet turban which half enclosed her abundant black hair and agreed so well with the dazzling expression of her eyes, she seemed no longer the same person. Her visage was changed as if by sickness and sadness ; the fire of her mind, which habitually animated it with a thousand rapid variations, now only marked it with a singular mobile expression of penetrating inquietude, a sort of divination in grief. We had no longer before our eyes the historian, but the victim, of the " Dix Années d'Exil ; " the woman who had sustained, at the cost of so much suffering, a long defiance against absolute power ; had reckoned, almost with despair, every stage of its victorious progress, anticipating still more oppressive ones ; and had been, at last, delivered from peril and fear by a brave flight, uttering from Geneva to London, through Russia and Sweden, her protest against

universal conquest—her oath of resistance through
life. Judging by her great affliction, and her agitated features, it seemed that all this series of trials,.
successively exhausted by her, was about to re-
appear afresh, now that she was advanced in years.
and languishing with ill health. One would, ne--
vertheless, have said, seeing the courage which
dominated her sadness, that she resigned herself
to be struck with death, by the triumph of him
whom she had most detested and most dreaded, but
whom she expected with more indignation than
personal fear—that she dreaded him more for the
calamities of the world, and especially of France,
and the great cause which she loved so much, than
for herself. Some days before, her mind had been
entirely devoted to family cares, the worthy union
arranged for her daughter with a young man of a
noble name and great hopes, whom her daughter
and she had chosen ; and now this soul, which the
ordinary uncertainties of life could so seriously
trouble, was filled with thoughts of a new flight,.
the expectation of a new overthrow of Europe, a
public ruin in which all private happiness might
be submerged. She had come from the interior of
the Tuileries, where all hope was lost ; her resolution was taken, to be executed at once ; she
indulged in no general conversation, only some
expressive words were exchanged with the most
distinguished persons in the *salon*. To some news,
falsely favourable, her answer was only a smile of

inexpressible sadness. She pressed the hand of Lafayette a long time, before two friends who mingled their wishes with hers. " In the chaos which is coming," she said to him, " you must remain ; you must appear, in order to resist, in the name of the law, and to represent 1789. As for me, I have only the power to fly. This is frightful ! " She made a few more marked, or more intimate adieus. To Madame de Rumford, who, in spite of her ordinary calmness and her philosophy, began to be agitated with the universal inquietude, she said, " Remain quiet here, dear madame ; your name will protect you. Your house will be at times, as mine was, the hospital of the politically wounded of all parties. You can yet have, for the advantage of the persecuted, some access to the Court of this man, who departed a conquered despot, and returns a disguised tyrant. He will be obliged, at first, to manage, a little, even those whom he calls the idealogues—your friends, Tracy, Siéyès, Volney, Garat—but me, he hates me ; hates me for my father, my friends, our opinions, and everything ; for the spirit of 1789, the Charter, the liberty of France, and the independence of Europe. He will be here to-morrow. What comedy will be played at his *début?* I know not ; but you know what he has done at Lyons, his general promises of amnesty and his posted bills of individual proscriptions. His talons have already reappeared, even before he has sprung upon us.

There is no army between him and me ; I do not wish to be held as his prisoner, and he shall never have me as his suppliant. Adieu, dear Madame." In a few minutes, Madame de Staël, and some of her confidential friends, went forth from the *salon,* and escaped the same night.' [1]

She has herself given us some allusions to these remarkable days—the memorable *Cent Jours,* the mightiest struggle of the mightiest captain in the history of the world ; the agonizing struggle of the man of destiny against destiny. ' No, never,' she says, ' can I forget the moment when I learned, from one of my friends, on the morning of the 6th of March, 1815, that Bonaparte had landed on the coast of France. I had the misery of fore-seeing, at once, the consequences of this event, such as afterwards came to pass, and it seemed that the earth opened beneath my feet. During many days after the triumph of this man, the succours of prayer failed me entirely, and in my trouble it appeared that God had retired from the earth and would no longer communicate with the beings he had placed upon it. I suffered, in the depth of my soul, from the personal circumstances in which I found myself, but the situation of France absorbed every other thought. I said to M. de Lavalette, whom I met the same hour in which this news burst upon us, " Liberty is lost if Bonaparte triumphs, and the national independence

[1] *Souvenirs Contemporains* &c. ii. 1.

if he is defeated." It seems to me that the event has justified this prediction. A continual fear had possessed my soul many weeks before his landing. In the evening, when the beautiful edifices of the city were illuminated by the rays of the moon, my happiness, and that of France, appeared as a dying friend whose smile is the more precious as it is about to disappear for ever. When they told me that this terrible man was at Cannes, I recoiled before the certainty as before a poignard; I knew he would be in Paris in about fifteen days.—During three days the Royalists indulged in vain hopes.—At last, on the evening of the 9th of March, I went to the Tuileries to see the King; he had courage, but wore an expression of sadness; nothing could be more touching than his noble resignation at such a moment.' [2]

Meanwhile she could not but admire the genius of the desperate soldier. 'I will not,' she adds, ' abandon myself to declamations against Napoleon. He did what was natural for the restoration of his throne; and his march, from Cannes to Paris, was one of the grandest conceptions of audacity that can be cited from history.'

She hastened from Paris, in order to reach Coppet before the roads should be obstructed by the military movements which she knew would immediately ensue. She urged Madame Récamier to escape with her, for the proscription of that

[2] *Considérations* &c. v. 13.

lady, by the Imperial Government, had never been formally revoked ; but she remained and took charge of Madame de Staël's interests in Paris. While on the way to Coppet, Madame de Staël wrote her (March 12), 'How much have I been affected, my dear friend, by again experiencing, under the same misfortune, the same protection, the same interest in my good angel. Render me yet one more service : induce Benjamin Constant to escape; I have the greatest anxiety for him after what he has written.[3]   My route I find perfectly safe; nothing should detain any of you at Paris.   Ah, that I could see you again on the shores of this lake !   You are a divinity, in great events.—I write to my son what you know.—I place all my affections under your protection. Alas, what sufferings ! '

Napoleon, on arriving in the capital, regretted her departure, and 'sent her reassuring words by his brother Joseph, wishing to engage her to return.' [4]   This fact is confirmed by her next letter to Madame Récamier, dated Coppet, March 31, in which she alludes to the 'goodwill which the Emperor has made known to me through his brother.' [5]   These particulars are important, as set-

---

[3] Besides his *L'Esprit d'Usurpation et de Conquête*, published in London the preceding year, he had lately written a violent article, for the *Journal de Paris*, against Napoleon; she had probably seen the manuscript. Compare *Coppet et Weimar*, viii.; and Villemain's *Souvenirs*, ii. 1.

[4] *Coppet et Weimar*, viii.   [5] *Ibid.*

tling a question respecting which the historian, Thiers, has made a grave mistake. He assumes that she remained in the capital during the Hundred Days,[6] and made important concessions to Bonaparte. The author of ' Coppet et Weimar ' refers to her contemporaries, ' still living,' who knew of her departure ; notably Villemain, who, as we have seen, records her leave-taking, at the *salon* of Madame de Rumford, and her immediate return to Coppet. Her first letter to Madame Récamier, of March 12, was written on the route ; her next, dated at Coppet on March 31, not only proves her arrival there, but also that she had not returned to Paris ; she says in it, ' Give me some advice, some news of our friends. Your letter has afforded me the only moment of comfort that I have had for *three weeks.*' The ' three weeks ' correspond with the time between the date of her letter and the date of her departure from Paris ; and in this same letter she says ' I have not the least intention of quitting Coppet this year.'[7] Evidently she had no confidence in Napoleon's overtures, and no disposition to sanction his new liberal

---

[6] *Histoire du Consulat et de l'Empire,* xix.

[7] There is a passing, but decisive, allusion to her, at this time, in one of Bonstetten's letters to Frederica Brun. He says, ' You know all by the newspapers; yesterday I saw the Staël, for the first time at Coppet. After what has passed, Coppet rose before me as a dream ; no one knows France better than the Staël; you would be surprised to hear from her about this revolution; I did not sleep the whole night after hearing her.' This letter is dated March 23, 1815. It is therefore conclusive of the question.

pretensions. Had she entertained, for a time, any such disposition, it could hardly have compromised her seriously, in the estimation of considerate readers. We, who judge the events of that period long after their occurrence, and in the full light of their results, can hardly imagine their impression on contemporary observers. These could judge of them only in the light of the unparalleled military genius and successes of Bonaparte. All France was again rallying to him ; the army, proud of his and their splendid prestige, was again his own. Who could then say that his power was not to be permanent ? He had conquered Europe; he might do so again. And now he came affirming that he had learned the lesson of his misfortunes well ; and promising to France liberty and constitutional government, and to Europe durable peace. Many wise men believed him ; for to them his promised policy seemed the only practicable one, and they esteemed him too shrewd not to perceive that obvious fact. Even Benjamin Constant, who had the courage to publish in a Paris journal an indignant article against him, while he was triumphantly approaching the capital, accepted his liberal pledges, and edited his ‘ Acte Additionnel,’ guaranteeing those pledges ; and Sismondi, whose sober judgment Madame de Staël profoundly respected, had declared his adhesion to him.[8] Had she, in such

[8] ‘ I am of your opinion about Sismondi ; he is a man of the best faith in the world. We have had some terrible quarrels, by letters,

overwhelming circumstances, and without any presage of the fate of the restored Empire, accepted
these pledges, for the sake of her country and the
peace of Europe, she would not thereby have compromised her own liberal principles, for they essentially conceded her principles. But, amidst the
whirlwind of renewed enthusiasm for the conqueror,
and the compromising credulity of some of her
own friends, to whom the astonishing reappearance
of Napoleon at the head of the army seemed the
greatest miracle of history and an irreversible fact,
she remained calmly and resolutely incredulous of
his policy, and hostile to the man. He could not
draw her from her retirement at Coppet. He in-
timated to his brother Joseph something about a
letter, from her, approving the ' Acte Additionnel,'
but no such letter has ever been produced.[9]

concerning Bonaparte; he sees liberty where it is impossible.'
(Madame de Staël to the Comtesse d'Albany, Dec. 8, 1815; Sismondi's *Lettres inédites*). Thiers represents (*Histoire du Consulat
et de l'Empire*, livre lix.) that 'under the influence of Madame de
Staël and Benjamin Constant, the most enlightened of the Genevese
publicists approved Napoleon's *Acte Additionnel*, among them Sismondi.' This letter to the Comtesse d'Albany proves precisely the
contrary, as far as Madame de Staël is concerned; and confirms our
view of Thiers' error.

[9] *Mémoires du Roi Joseph*, vol. x. Paris, 1854. In one place the
letter is said to have been addressed to Napoleon (p. 228), and to have
been conveyed to him by her son Auguste; in another Joseph says it
was addressed to himself (p. 377). At the most it is said to have but
approved the principles of the *Acte Additionnel*. We have seen how little
confidence can be placed in Napoleon's word, in instances from Las
Cases' *Mémorial*; Joseph's *Mémoires* are obnoxious to similar criticism.
In the volume (x.) in which the above alleged intimation is given,

Thiers' impossible assumption, that she remained in the capital, was made in order to give probability to his intimation that she wrote to the statesmen of London in favour of Napoleon. Had she done so, with the qualifications above stated, it would have been, as we have said, no serious compromise of her principles, but it would have been a contradiction of all her antecedent, and subsequent, records regarding her opinions of the man himself.[1] Thiers would have us suppose that she believed in the conversion of Bonaparte. Alluding to the course adopted by Benjamin Constant, he says, 'The highly enlightened school of Geneva publicists approved the Acte Additionnel,' and affirms that 'Madame de Staël, whose rare mind and perfect knowledge of England guaranteed her against the prevailing errors, highly approved it.' Mr. Craw-

Madame de Staël's letters to him, for years, are inserted (Appendix): attempts are made several times in this volume to show that she relented towards Napoleon, but this most important letter is not given : an extraordinary omission, if the letter was addressed to King Joseph. We have the *Correspondance de Napoléon, publiée par ordre de l'Empereur Napoléon III.* in thirty-two huge volumes (Paris, 1858–1869) but look in vain for any trace of the alleged letter in them. It is a curious fact that Savary (Duc de Rovigo—Napoleon's Minister of Police) cites the same letter as addressed to 'the Prince * * *,' a title which could not apply to Napoleon, or King Joseph, at this time. (*Méms.* viii. 3.) No candid reader of the Duke's ridiculous remarks about Madame de Staël (vi. 14) can doubt that he was capable of any duplicity in a case like this. The 'confusion worse confounded' in which this alleged letter is involved, betrays the hand of an official manager like Savary, who could not forgive Madame de Staël's preface to the London edition of the *Allemagne*.

[1] Compare the *Dix Années* and the *Considérations,* passim.

furd, the American Minister at Paris, was about to return home through England, and bore a package of letters in favour of peace, written to leading personages of London. 'Madame de Staël, who,' says Thiers, ' through her long opposition to the Empire, was little suspected of partiality for Napoleon, and who, by her intellect and brilliant renown, could exercise some influence over the British Ministers, addressed them letters, pressing them to withdraw from the coalition. " If accepted and believed, literally, in accordance with his pledges," she said, " Napoleon would give the peace and liberty which he promised ; if repulsed, he would no longer regard the Treaty of Paris, and perhaps not even the Acte Additionnel. The interests of Europe, of humanity, of liberty, were therefore agreed in demanding a pacific policy." The reasons given by Madame de Staël were, we see, as specious as they were rationally and patriotically presented.' We are assured on good authority, that ' there exists in none of the letters of Madame de Staël, addressed to English political personages or others, any such plea for the maintenance of Napoleon's power, or endorsement of his liberalism.' [2] In the posthumous collection of Lord Castlereagh's papers (a miscellaneous mass of private letters and official despatches) may be seen a letter, addressed to him by Crawfurd (April 29), in which he says that he had received many letters from Madame de Staël, the most recent

[2] *Coppet et Weimar*, ix.

of which he ' enclosed.' The editor then inserts a letter *without a signature*, and entitles it ' Madame de Staël to Mr. Crawfurd.' [3] ' This letter,' remarks the author of ' Coppet et Weimar,' ' was evidently written in Paris to Crawfurd while he was still there.' It says, ' I saw yesterday the note you wrote to your neighbour ; if peace continues all heads will be calmed, and we shall have liberty and repose here.' The word *here* is used twice, and could not have been thus used by a writer who was not in Paris nor in France, but among the mountains of Switzerland. But the date of the letter determines this question. It is dated April 23 ; it was received by Mr. Crawfurd before he left Paris ; he left on the 25th. In those days the mail required seventy-two hours, between Geneva and Paris ; this anonymous letter could not then have been written from Coppet, where Madame de Staël certainly was at the time of its date. In the week preceding its date, she wrote to Madame Récamier stating her resolution not to return, but to leave her affairs at Paris in the hands of her son, who still remained there.[4] The letter could not then have been written by Madame de Staël. ' It might well have been one of the enclosures, sent by Crawfurd to Lord Castlereagh, with those which he had received before leaving Paris, on the situation of

[3] *Correspondence, Despatches, and other Papers of Viscount Castlereagh*, edited by his brother, vol. x.

[4] *Coppet et Weimar*, ix.

France, but it was not from Madame de Staël; it
not only has not her signature, but it is not in her
style, and is contrary to her sentiments.'[5]   It dis-
parages the Emperor of Russia, whom she so much
esteemed, and with whom she still maintained a
direct correspondence in 1816.   Thiers, in 'adopt-
ing the English editor's attribution of this anonymous document, was therefore absolutely deceived.
But, in fact, the secretary of the Marquis of London-
derry, discovering a French note, and attributing
it to Madame de Staël, because Crawfurd mentioned
as " enclosed," a letter from this celebrated person,
committed a more excusable error than did the
secretary of M. Thiers, who analysed with so little
exactness, in the interests of his cause, a document
written in his own language, a document in which,
it should be remarked, there is no allusion whatever even to the Acte Additionnel.'[6]   Madame de
Staël, writing the twelfth part of her 'Considerations on the French Revolution,' at the beginning
of the next year,[7] denounces the credulity of those
who sustained Napoleon during the Hundred Days.
After acknowledging, as we have seen, the genius
of the man who could achieve such an unprece-
dented feat of audacity as the return from Elba,
she remarks: 'But what shall we say of the enlightened men who did not see the woe of France,
and of the world, in this return?   Will they dare to

[5] *Coppet et Weimar,* ix.   [6] *Ibid.*

[7] Note of her Editors, v. 1.

pretend that it was for the interests of liberty that they could recall the man who, through fifteen years, had shown himself the most able in the art of being its master ?   They spoke of his conversion, and they found some credulous enough to believe such a miracle; certainly it would require less faith to believe those of Mahommed.'   She alludes to Sismondi, Constant, and her other associates, who succumbed to Napoleon.   She was incapable of the self-stultification which such phrases would imply, had she shared their defection.   Thiers, as we have remarked, attributes the defection of the 'Genevese publicists,' particularly of Sismondi, to her influence. Sismondi, then, should certainly have been aware of so extraordinary a change in her views.   We have positive evidence, however, to the contrary, from his own pen.   His correspondence from Paris, with his mother, at Geneva, was incessant, during the Hundred Days, and has recently been published.[8] Not an intimation is given of any vacillation, on her part, respecting Napoleon.   Eight weeks after the end of the Hundred Days, he rejoined her at Coppet, as we shall soon see; he had misgivings regarding his reception there, and went to seek reconciliation with his old friend.   In a letter from the château, he writes gratefully of her kind treatment of him; he speaks of the 'combat' in her mind between her early republican opinions and her sentiments towards

---

[8] *Revue Historique.*   Paris, 1877–1878.

the restored Bourbons, but affirms that 'her old principles are inherent in her, and always reappear,' and that ' her resentment against Bonaparte has become a violent and blind hatred.' [9]

Schlegel, who knew her opinions better perhaps than any other man, repelled, after her death, in the ' Hamburg Correspondent,' the charge that she had ever compromised with Napoleon. ' I can attest,' he wrote, ' that from the time of the suppression of her " Allemagne," that is to say, when her persecution by Bonaparte was most active, a public functionary made semi-official overtures to me on her behalf, to relieve her exile on condition that she would write something in favour of Napoleon's dynasty. She revolted at this proposition ; she would not devote a single line to the eulogy of tyranny. She resolved rather to seek refuge in England, across Russia and Sweden. If, during the Hundred Days, she had only consented to write in his favour, she would not have been reduced to seek refuge in Switzerland before his arrival in Paris.' [1] Evidently,

---

[9] *Revue Historique*, Paris, 1877–1878 ; thirty-ninth letter, dated August 21, 1815. Sainte-Beuve, while temporarily under the influence of the third Napoleon, favoured Thiers' view of the case. The great critic, usually inflexibly candid, showed, in his latter years, the influence of his changed standpoint ; his theological changes affected his views of Chateaubriand, his political changes his views of Madame de Staël, so long the object of his literary idolatry. His last paper, regarding her, is a pitiable example of his transient Napoleonism, in more than one respect.

[1] *Staëlliana*, by Cousin d'Avalon, p. 106. Paris, 1820.

then, she had taken 'refuge in Switzerland' at the time that Thiers supposed she was in Paris.

The marvellous Hundred Days passed, and Bonaparte, overwhelmed by the catastrophe of Waterloo, fell to rise no more; but Madame de Staël did not return to France; she wished not to witness its second invasion, for it now bristled with six hundred thousand foreign bayonets. Her health continued to decline and, above all, that of Rocca required a better climate.

CHAPTER XLII.

ROCCA—MARRIAGE OF HER DAUGHTER.

Sismondi again at Coppet—Pictet de Sergy—Annette de Gérando—
Mysticism—Madame de Staël's Devotion to Rocca—Again in
Italy—Letters to Madame Récamier—Marriage of her Daughter
—The Duc de Broglie—His Family and Character—Character
of the young Duchess—Her Good Works—Her Salon in Paris—
Lamartine, Ticknor, and Guizot's Opinions of her.

AFTER the downfall of Napoleon, Sismondi hastened
to Coppet, to justify, if possible, his conduct in
Paris. He gives us a momentary glimpse of the
interior of the château. On August 19, 1815, he
writes to his mother : ' I have been received with
strong testimonies of friendship and pleasure by
Madame de Staël and Mademoiselle Randall. They
made known to me the state of opinion regarding
my course—and my restoration to favour. Then
I recounted all I had witnessed. The conversation
was kept up, with vivacity, till after midnight.
Schlegel, who is ardent for the Allies, was not
present. Albertine was also absent, at a ball,
whence she was to return the next day ; but,
according to Mademoiselle Randall, she is more
favourable than ever towards me. Auguste had
set off for Paris at the same time that I left there.

Rocca was in his bed. I passed some time with him; he is very ill, and can never be restored. Madame de Staël appears to me more devoted to him than ever. She has the air of caring for him, both as for a son and a husband. She shows a mixture of conjugal attachment and of protection to which we are not accustomed; and, above all, it is not thus that love usually reveals itself.' The next day he writes: 'Thank God, our intercourse is again absolutely re-established. I have been separated from my Parisian associates, but I am far from having lost my true friends.' On the 21st he continues: 'I have passed my day here very agreeably. I arrived with Dumont and Madame Rilliet, who are very good company, in addition to that of the château. Albertine, who was absent the other day, has received me not only as an old friend, but also as a new ally. I had to relate many anecdotes, many events and conversations which I had witnessed, and, at last, my conversations with the Emperor. All this interested Madame de Staël very much.'[1] After intimating, as we have quoted, her profound hatred of Napoleon, and the struggle of her mind between her early liberalism and her sympathy with the Restoration, prompted, as he supposes, partly by her expectation of the payment of her father's loan, he speaks of the agreeable resumption of his literary labours in the château, and of his

[1] *Revue Historique,* Jan. and Feb. Paris, 1878.

invitation to accompany the family to the south. Madame de Staël never sacrificed a friend for the sake of opinions. Bonstetten writes, in September, to Frederica Brun: 'I went yesterday to Coppet with Saussure, the Princess of Mecklenburg, &c. Sismondi has, for fifteen days, had an obstinate fever. Schlegel has received a decoration from the Czar, who writes excellent letters. The Staël is ill, suffering terribly with her teeth, and in her soul also, because Rocca is very ill, and is not likely to recover. I go thither to console them as much as possible. She is indeed afflicted, but as rich as ever in spirit. The Czar has advised her to go to Milan. Wellington writes to her. He will probably come to Switzerland.'[2]

Meanwhile the kindness of her heart, and the brilliancy of her intellect, could not be repressed by her sufferings. The young Pictet de Sergy visited her with his father (one of her favourite guests) in August. 'Her kindness,' writes the former, 'led her to encourage me by particular attentions. She took a seat near me, and after some words of kindness, which I can never forget, she said : " You are going to Germany; I congratulate you and envy you. I have seen Germany only in its prostration; you will now see it erect. With what interest will you be inspired by the sight of the young heroes, who, after having

---

[2] Bonstetten's *Briefe an Friederike Brun*, by F. von Matthisson, ii.

quitted their studies to deliver their country, have returned to reseat themselves on the benches from which they departed, and to reopen their books at the page where they closed them! Remember me to all my friends there. Study hard, and at your return we will compose together a fourth volume of the Allemagne." I was touched with, and proud of these words. The next morning many persons arrived from Geneva, in time for breakfast. Among them was Dumont, who had successively served, with his modest but invaluable assistance, Mirabeau and Bentham. His fine and discreet mind had a peculiar attraction for Madame de Staël. The breakfast hour was, as is well known, the time at which her intellect, calm and rested, displayed its full riches. The conversation was about the Congress of Vienna, then one of the great European events. They spoke of its characters, its labours, and its fêtes. In reference to the latter, allusion was made to the grand tournaments of the Middle Ages. Opposite Madame de Staël sat the young Count of Woyna, son of one of the Grand Masters of the Court of Vienna. In his character of aide-de-camp of the Prince of Schwarzenberg, he had been appointed to conduct the Duchess of St. Leu (Queen Hortense) out of France, and was then residing with her near Geneva.' Madame de Staël extorted from him, in spite of his diffidence, an account of his share in a tournament at the Court, and of

the name of the lady whose colours he wore on the
occasion.   She then launched into one of her remarkable conversations, one that reminds us of Carl
Ritter's description of her colloquial eloquence. ' It
was,' continues the writer, ' a magnificent poem. All
the Middle Ages, with their chivalry, their devotion, their marvellous characteristics, passed before the enchanted assembly.   Corinne was entirely
herself.   Electrified herself, she electrified the
coldest of the *convives* ; the forks were motionless
in their hands, every ear was intent, all eyes and
mouths eagerly open.   Nobody thought any longer
of the breakfast.' [3]

To Annette de Gérando she wrote, September
27, from Martigny : ' From the midst of the Alps of
the Valais I respond to you, my dear friend.   It
seems to me that this solitude places me in more
intimate sympathy with you.   I am much struck
by what you say of the relations of Madame de
Krüdner with the Emperor Alexander.   I admire
him much, and if, contrary to what is usual with
sovereigns, he is less praised than he merits, it is
because the liberal opinions which he cherishes
in his heart of hearts have few partisans in the
salons.   I need not tell you that liberty and religion absorb my thoughts—enlightened religion,
just liberty.   This is the true path.   I believe in
Mysticism, that is to say, in the religion of Fénelon,
that which has its sanctuary in the heart, which

[3] Manuscript *Souvenirs.*

joins love to works. I believe in a reformation of the *Reformation*, a development of Christianity which shall combine what is good in Catholicism and Protestantism, and which shall separate religion entirely from the political influence of priests. What a splendid thing it would be if Alexander could become the leader of these two noble interests of the human race—personal religion and representative government! Express heartily, I pray you, to Madame de Krüdner my desire to see her; she has truly great grace of soul. Our friend Mathieu has exaggerations, but he possesses great goodness, which makes him recognise the truth, even when he does not avow it. My noble, my pure-minded friend, if my affairs recall me, I shall perhaps in six months return from Rome and see you again. Write to me. Permit me to embrace you tenderly, and to commend me to your thoughts, which ascend towards heaven as prayers.'

She left Coppet, for Italy, in October 1815. Several reasons, besides her reluctance to witness the second invasion of France, induced her to turn southward, rather than towards Paris. The health of Rocca alarmed her; he was slowly dying of pulmonary consumption, the consequence of one of his wounds received in Spain. Her romantic affection for him made his sufferings her own, as we shall presently see from intimations in her letters. During more than three years she had realised, with him, her ideal of woman's happiness—'Love in marriage.' The biographer of her friend Madame Récamier, alluding to her at this time, says that, ' after having known the pleasure, the intoxication of renown, she writes : " Fame is, for woman, only a splendid mourning for happiness." Conjugal affection had ever been, for Madame de Staël, the supreme, the complete blessedness of this world.'[4] The carefully maintained secrecy of their marriage did not allow the world to witness their intimate affection, but allusions in her letters, especially now as the end approaches, confirm her cousin's testimony that ' it is certain this union rendered her happy ; a new day had dawned upon her ; happiness was reborn in her desolate heart, and the dream of all her life had become a reality.'[5] And yet, such was the excessive sensibility of her temperament, that with this satisfaction of her affections was combined continual suffering from anxiety for his health. Her cousin says that though she would disguise to herself his danger, and, ' after cruel alarms,' force herself to believe that ' his life was not in peril and his symptoms were only accidental,' yet she ' devoted incessant attention to him. The whole of her great mind was employed in this service. But who can describe what she suffered at critical moments ! At Pisa, where he was near dying, she compared herself to Marshal Ney, who was then momentarily expecting

[4] *Coppet et Weimar*, ix.   [5] *Notice &c.* ii.

his sentence.   Endowed with talents which preserved her from no pains, but which rather aug-
mented them all, she, nevertheless, said then that
she would write a book with the title: " The
only affliction in life—the loss of an object that we
love." That affliction in her case was the dangerous
state of the young and unfortunate Rocca—that
threatened life, that frail reed which had for a
short time served to support an existence apparently so strong, a reed more frail than herself.
He had not long to live.   After her death, his
grief, his indifference for his own life, were to cut
short his career ; he was to die under the beautiful sky of Provence, where a brother was to receive
his last sighs.'

Her own health, shattered by these and so
many other anxieties, also required this journey ;
but she found relief in her preparations for the
marriage of her daughter, which had been suspended by the reappearance of Napoleon in France.
From Milan she writes to Madame Récamier (Oct.
27) : ' You have the kindness to say that it would
be better for me to be at Paris.   No, in truth, I do
not wish to see the concession of a few popular
liberties—I, who believe that nations are *free born*.
I should pronounce certain words which are not
à la mode, and which would make for me enemies
unnecessarily.   When everything shall have been
arranged for the marriage of Albertine, I will live
in retirement at Paris ; but at present, I have done

well, believe me, in leaving Auguste to represent
me there.   Mathieu, whom I do not wish to wound,
is in an entirely false position.[6] The foreigners, who
are good to me, would do me harm at Paris; the
divisions of parties are such that it would be impossible to reunite them all again in a single *salon*,
unless they could be like you—you an angel of goodness covering all things with your wings.   Believe
me, I am right, and Auguste is of the same opinion.
Please remember me to our Prince of Madrid.[7]
I do not hold the opinion he expressed to you, but
I love him with all my heart.   Circumstances
keep him cautiously near the shore; his spirit
would naturally lead him farther.   I am leaving
Milan to avoid the fêtes, which do not harmonise
with my French heart.   I agree with you in thinking more favourably than ever of Victor de Broglie,
and I will be very happy if nothing hinders the
marriage.   I agree with you also about Madame
de Krüdner; she is the herald of a new and grand
religious epoch which is at hand.   Pray remember
me to her, and tell her that I am devoted to her.
I am going to Genoa, but only for eight days;
continue to write to me at Milan, where they know

---

[6] Mathieu de Montmorency (who had fought for the Republican
Americans, had zealously favoured the French Revolution, and was
the first to propose the motion for the abolition of titles of nobility,
&c.) had now changed his politics.   Their friendship was, however,
soon restored.

[7] The Prince (Adrien de Montmorency, Duc de Laval), who was
an intimate guest of her *salon*, and of that of Madame Récamier, was
now ambassador at Madrid.

my movements. The health of M. de Rocca always disquiets me. I have had no happiness since the landing of Bonaparte.'

About four months later she had the happiness of seeing her daughter married, at Leghorn, by 'civil marriage' on February 15, by the French consul, and at Pisa, on the 20th, by a double religions ceremony, consecrated by a Catholic parish priest of the city, and by a Protestant clergyman of the English Church. She immediately wrote again to Madame Récamier: 'Our marriage, dear Juliette, has passed off exceedingly well; no other emotion of my life compares with this; my attachment to M. de Broglie increases hourly. All his conduct has shown true delicacy and sensibility. His character is virtuous; and I bless God, and my father who has obtained from the all-bountiful God a companion for my daughter so worthy of esteem and of affection.'

Her best beloved child was thus established in one of the most distinguished families of her country, one which, through five hundred years and more, especially since its removal from Italy to France, had given to history numerous statesmen and prelates and captains. Victor, Duc de Broglie, was now about thirty years old, his bride about nineteen. His father, sometime President of the National Assembly, perished on the scaffold in 1794. Eminent by his culture, his devotion to political and economical science, and his 'humanitarian' principles, the young duke was to be distinguished, through the remainder of his long life, by his activity in the political events of his country, especially in the critical times of 1830, 1832, and 1848. His son, the grandson of Madame de Staël, and actual Duc de Broglie, has been conspicuous in the French politics of our own day.

The Duchesse de Broglie honoured her new and exalted position by her virtues and accomplishments. She attained to rare intellectual culture. Her *salon*, in Paris, became almost as attractive as her mother's, and, for many years, was crowded by the best writers, artists, and statesmen of the capital. She presided among them with talent and ease. 'In it,' says Lamartine, ' were assembled the friends of Madame de Staël ; foreigners of high birth and fame ; the orators of the Opposition in both chambers ; the writers and publicists of the rising generation ; republicans in theory, who accommodated themselves to the times and adjourned their hopes. Lafayette, Guizot, Villemain the Fontenelle of the age, Montlosier, were there. Great tolerance prevailed. Men and opinions, youth, prospective ideas, literature, eloquence, poetry, grace of manners, soared above all and tempered all. Many men, pledged to ambition, to glory, or to misfortune, elbowed one another there before separating to pursue their diverse routes. It was a halt before the combat.'[8] A zealous, but catholic

[8] *Histoire de la Restauration,* ii. 15.

Protestant, the Duchess reflected honour on her religion. Like her brother, Auguste, she was an active philanthropist, and the blessings of the poor and those ' who were ready to perish ' came upon her. She was prominent among the best women of France in the promotion of missionary and Bible societies, and all kinds of useful charities. She wrote able essays on the capabilities of her sex, and their religious and philanthropic duties. She edited the works of her brother, and published with them a touching record of his life. After her death, in 1838, some of her own writings were given to the public, bearing the title of ' Fragments sur divers sujets de Religion et de Morale ' (Paris, 1840). They reveal a character beautiful in both its moral and intellectual traits. Her portrait at Coppet, by Ary Scheffer, never fails to arrest attention by its exquisite spiritual loveliness. Ticknor, the American author, who had familiar access to the De Staël and De Broglie *coteries* of Paris, often alludes to her.[9] ' The Duchesse de Broglie,' he writes, ' is quite handsome and has fine talents ; her manners are naïve to a fault, without being affected ; but her beauty and talents make one forget it. The best literary talent of Paris is found at her *salon.* I have seldom seen anyone with deeper and more sincere feelings of tenderness and affection, and never a French woman with stronger religious feelings ; and when, to this, are added

[9] *Life* &c. passim.

great simplicity and frankness, not a little personal beauty, and an independent, original way of thinking, I have described one who would produce considerable effect in any society. In her own she is sincerely loved and admired.' Guizot, who, in spite of his natural coldness and severity, fairly idolised her, and was constantly at her *salon*, says : ' She was one of the most noble, most rare, most charming creatures I have seen in the world, and of her I will say, as St. Simon said of the Duc de Bourgogne when deploring his death, " may it please God, in His mercy, that I may see her for ever where His goodness has without doubt placed her."'[1] Lamartine equally admired her. ' She was trained,' he says, ' by her mother, in the enthusiasm of genius. But her enthusiasm, more pious than that of her mother, was, above all, the ardour of virtue. Piety sanctified, to the eye, the pensive loveliness of her features. It was the interior hymn of a beautiful soul revealed in an angelic, thoughtful face. She seemed the most beautiful, the purest thought of her mother incarnated in an angelic form, to raise one's thoughts to heaven, and represent saintliness by beauty.'[2]

In the joy of the bridal scenes at Pisa, Madame de Staël wrote her last letter to her faithful correspondent, the Grande Duchesse Louise of Weimar, with whom she wished to share her happiness.

[1] *Mémoires de mon Temps,* iv. 259.
[2] *Histoire de la Restauration,* ii. 15.

She asks, through her, the ' poetic benediction ' of
Goethe on the young couple ; and adds, ' During
my ten years of exile I owed to you the sweetest
moments of my existence.'[3] Sismondi and Schlegel
had accompanied the bridal party to Italy ; and
the former wrote to the Comtesse d'Albany of
their expected visit to Florence. ' She always,' he
says, ' has need of intellectual society nourished
by thought and sentiment. You will make the
acquaintance of her son-in-law, a man of great
intelligence and of noble character.'

Her life was failing ; thenceforth she scarcely
wrote to anyone, except Madame Récamier ; but,
with her usual persistence in labour, she was still
writing her ' Considerations.' She accompanies
the bridal party to Florence, whence she writes to
Madame Récamier (May 23) : ' I am suffering much
in Italy, but I am glad I came, for the health of
M. de Rocca improves. Without the sun I can do
nothing at Florence ; Rome is much better for me.
However, life declines so much, at my age, that one
feels nothing more vividly than sadness ; one remains young only in that respect. The marriage
is a happy one, thank God ! They truly love one
another very much, and the qualities of M. de Broglie
will permit no change in him.—I love Mathieu
too much to risk displeasing him by blaming what
he approves, and my opinion is that I shall not stay
in Paris. I have taken a fancy to go to Grenada,

[3] *Coppet et Weimar*, ix.

or Valencia, if Adrien '—the Duc de Laval—' can obtain permission for me. I have been cruelly alarmed during the last month by a cold which M. de Rocca has been suffering from. Thank God, he is better. But, some day, I will tell you all that passed in my heart during this time. You would be astonished to see how much he has gained in all respects. So much patience, so much study, so much gratitude for my care, make him the most perfect friend that my imagination can paint.'

CHAPTER XLIII.

LAST SCENES—DEATH.

Again at Coppet—Byron there—Brougham there—Bonstetten there—
Rocca's Health—Bonstetten's last Adieu—Again in Paris—Madame
de Krüdner—Alexander of Russia and Benjamin Constant with
her—Madame de Staël's Salon—Her last Illness—Chateaubriand's
Visit—Ticknor's Visit—Madame Récamier—Madame de Staël's
Opinion of America—Her Affection for Rocca—Her Death—Sismondi and Bonstetten at her Burial—Bonstetten's Conversation
with Rocca—Ticknor at Coppet—Chateaubriand and Madame
Récamier at her Grave.

THE bridal party returned to the home, at Coppet,
about June 21, 1816. Byron was now frequently
a guest there; he had fled to Switzerland for refuge from the 'persecutions' which his own conduct
had provoked in London, and was living in the
Diodati Villa, at Cologny, near Geneva, where
his desperate cynicism found some relief in the
conversation of Shelley and his accomplished wife,
in the composition of some of the finest pages
of 'Childe Harold,' and in excursions, on the lake,
to Coppet. Madame de Staël alone, of all the
neighbouring society, received him. Her good
influence softened, somewhat, his misanthropic
spirit; for, though he had tried hard, in London,

to treat her with his usual irony towards women, he could not, as we have seen, resist the charm of her brilliant and genial nature. He now sought her company. 'Madame de Staël,' he wrote, 'wishes to see the " Antiquary," and I am going to take it to her to-morrow. She has made Coppet as agreeable to me as society and talent can make any place on earth. Bonstetten is there a good deal. He is a fine, lively old man, and much esteemed by his compatriots. All there are well, excepting Rocca, who, I am sorry to say, looks in a very bad state of health. Schlegel is in high force, and Madame de Staël is as brilliant as ever.' The sight of the young married couple had charms even for him ; he admired the Duchesse de Broglie, and writes that 'nothing is more pleasing than to see the development of domestic affections in a very young woman.' Madame de Staël faithfully reproved his conduct towards his own young wife, and so far subdued him as to induce him to write to a friend in London, proposing to be reconciled to her.[1] Bonstetten wrote to his friend, the poet Matthisson : 'Lord Byron inquires eagerly about you. I had to tell him, and Hobhouse, his fellow traveller, where and how you live ; your poetry dazzles him ; he compares it with that of Bürger and Salis. We rode in the moonlight from Coppet to Genthod, whence the two friends took boat for their villa. Hobhouse is exceedingly amiable, and

---

[1] Moore's *Byron*, ii.

full of spirit and fire. I spent a whole evening with these imaginative beings, and the Staël and her beautiful daughter, the Duchesse de Broglie, at Coppet. Gaiety and wit flew all around. The Staël surpassed us all. I cannot compare Byron with any other creature. His voice is music; his features those of an angel; but an only half-honest little demon lightens through his sarcasm.'[2]

Sismondi writes to the Countess of Albany: 'M. Rocca is in a better state of health than he has enjoyed for some time. She even thinks of a journey to Paris by September 1, and she is so delusively sanguine about him as to hope to avoid a return to the south next winter. Madame Brun speaks of you with constant gratitude. She is very happy; her beloved daughter Ida is married; all the dreams of the mother's imagination are centred in this child. Bonstetten is at Geneva, as gay and as young as ever. Byron is still at Geneva; he came there with two girls of suspicious morals, and an Italian physician; they all have too little respect for public decency, in their way of travelling; and this offence, joined to the resentment of the English against him, for his treatment of his wife, has led all society to refuse to see him. Brougham has dined at Coppet. In company he has been demure and very taciturn, showing neither the logical force with which he conducts so admirably the questions of which he is master,

[2] *Briefe von Bonstetten an Matthisson.* Zürich, 1827.

nor the impetuosity which has frequently troubled
the measures of the Opposition by rendering him
insubordinate to the tactics of others.'[3]   Bonstetten
is now more frequently than ever at the château,
and constantly writes about it to his old friend
Madame Brun.   In August he says : ' I have just returned from Coppet.   No court is so animated.   All
the remarkable people in Europe come together
there.   The Emperor of Russia continues to write to
Madame de Staël ; she is a power in all the nations.'
The next week he writes : ' I have conducted Bell,
the coadjutor of Lancaster in the new mode of
instruction, to our dear Coppet.   I found there
the charming Lady Anna Maria Elliot, the eldest
daughter of Lord Minto, of whom Madame de Staël
said that she is the most intelligent Englishwoman
she had ever seen.   The *salon* was full of eminent
personages.   Madame de Staël and Bell did the
talking, all the rest of the company listened.   At
five o'clock there arrived Lord Byron, Madame de
Mongelas, who, they say, reigns over Bavaria, Lady
Hamilton, one of the Pictets, an illustrious Italian,
the Duc and Duchesse de Broglie, and so on.   I was
never at so intellectual a dinner party or a more
agreeable one.   At eight o'clock the *salon* was
again filled.   Lord Breadalbane, the De Saussures,
and others arrived.   I returned with Dumont.'
Never indeed had Coppet been a centre of more
social and intellectual power than during this

---

[3] Taillandier's *Lettres inédites de Sismondi*.

summer. ' It was,' says Pictet de Sergy, ' the period of the supreme reign ' of Madame de Staël. Stendal (Bayle), writing the next year, says, ' There was here, on the coast of Lake Leman, last autumn, the most astonishing reunion : it was the States General of European opinion. To my eyes the phenomenon rises even to political importance. Had it continued, all the Academies of Europe would have paled before it. I know not what could be set off against a *salon* where Dumont, Bonstetten, Prevost, the Pictets, Romilly, Brougham, Schlegel, De Broglie, De Brême, Byron, discussed the grandest questions of ethics and the arts before Mesdames Necker de Saussure, de Broglie, and de Staël. There were here six hundred persons, the most distinguished of Europe. Men of intellect, of wealth, of the greatest titles, all came here to seek pleasure in the *salon* of the illustrious woman for whom France weeps.' ' Coppet,' says a living French writer, ' was an intellectual Coblenz on the frontier of France.' It made ' energetic war and reprisals,' at times, on her literary domain ; ' a Coblenz liberal and parliamentary, whence came forth political doctrines, a programme of ideas, a race of statesmen, a school of thinkers, which have filled, with their combats, their triumphs, or their defeats, more than half a century of our history.' [4]

About five months after the marriage of her

[4] M. Caro, *Revue Politique et Littéraire*, Sept. 1880.

daughter, Madame de Staël writes again from Coppet to Madame Récamier : ' I have had no new anxiety for Rocca, but his health is always wavering, and this poignard is ever suspended over my life. Ah ! I was not born to be happy. The marriage of my daughter, nevertheless, is a success. She is to be a mother, as I believe ; this will modify my plans, for I cannot leave her in this condition. On the other hand, I am really frightened at the society of Paris, and the expected violent Assembly. I am resolved to be silent ; but I see, by even the style of Mathieu, what an alarming party spirit reigns in France. I have always foreseen it. Ah, happiness ! But at my age it is in the goodness of God alone that one can trust.' In the following October she writes : ' My plans for the end of this year are still uncertain, for at the commencement of autumn M. de Rocca was again afflicted by his old sufferings. I hope yet that this is only a passing attack. With the condition of my daughter and his illness, what can I do ? My heart is in a state of cruel anguish. Must it be thus even till one dies ? As you tell me, with your sweet words, that Mathieu still loves me, I wrote him yesterday ; but did he perceive that I had ceased to write ?' [5]

She was now herself slowly sinking under a mortal disease. This fact should be a sufficient apology for the extreme anguish which she felt

[5] *Coppet et Weimar,* ix.

for others and which pervades her letters. She made one more strenuous effort to rally her energies and reach Paris again. Bonstetten records his last interview with her. 'I see yet,' he writes to Frederica Brun, 'the place in the *salon* where she took leave of me before her departure. I was gay and content and gave her my hand, saying *au revoir*. But she cast upon me a look so profoundly sad that, after leaving, I asked myself if I ought not to return to her. I thought, nevertheless, that this look was addressed to my old age, and that she thought she should never see me again. I continued my route; it was an eternal adieu.'[6] To his friend Matthisson he wrote, 'The Staël is very ill; I shall lose in her a well-tried friend. Her death will be a loss for the whole cultivated world.'

In Paris, during the winter of 1816–1817, her *salon* was again thronged by representative men of all parties. Madame de Krüdner had returned, and her mansion was frequented by the most eminent men and women of the capital, who heard, with respectful wonder, her spiritualistic discussions. We have witnessed her conversations with Madame de Staël; it is not improbable that her influence tended to deepen the religious interest with which the latter now contemplated the daily increasing uncertainty of her own life. The verification of one of Madame de Krüdner's most extraordinary

[6] Steinel's *Bonstetten*, ch. ix.

vaticinations gave *éclat* to her mission in Paris. She had predicted the return of Bonaparte from Elba, stating the very year of that event. That his irrepressible ambition was still dangerous, no one could doubt; but that he should so soon attempt to regain his throne, and attempt it in so startling a manner, while all Europe was still armed and jubilant over his downfall, few could have apprehended. To the Allies, whose armies and kings were again thronging Paris, and exulting in the glories of Waterloo, she was now, as Sainte-Beuve says, 'the Evangelic Valleda, the Prophetess of the North.' She became 'the habitual counsellor of Alexander.' He avoided the gay resorts and festivities of the city; and ascribed the recent great events entirely to the hand of God. 'He went forth,' continues Sainte-Beuve, 'from the Elysée-Bourbon, through a garden gate, to go to her house, close at hand, many times a day; and there they prayed together, invoking the light of the Spirit.' Benjamin Constant, whose opinions on religion, as on all other subjects, were of great weight with Madame de Staël, felt, for a time at least, the magical power of the Sibyl. His restless soul was now contending between a profound but unsuccessful passion for Madame Récamier, and the influence of Madame de Krüdner. He passed from the *salon* of the one to that of he other, in almost delirious agitation, finding in the characters of both a purity which tacitly rebuked his own moral feebleness. ' He received,' continues Sainte-Beuve, ' from Madame de Krüdner consolation in his difficulties, and sustenance for his soul. He spent hours with her, seeking repose, and sharing in her prayers ; it was Adolphe, still the same, by the side of a regenerated Valérie.' ' She has produced on me an effect,' wrote Constant to Madame Récamier, ' which I have never before experienced.' The intellectually strong man ' dissolved in tears,' under the sense of his own moral weakness. ' Excellent woman !' he exclaims, ' she sees that a frightful suffering is consuming me. She retained me three hours comforting me.' Sainte-Beuve errs in saying that ' Madame de Staël prized Madame de Krüdner as author of 'Valérie,' but had too political and historic a mind to enter into her prophetic exaltation ; she smiled at it, but Benjamin Constant could not smile.' On the contrary, Madame de Staël had said to Madame Récamier, as we have seen, ' I think as you do about Madame de Krüdner ; she is the herald of a grand religious epoch.' The strongest minds could hardly fail to feel her influence in these marvellous times. Constant defended her, later, in the ' Journal de Paris,' against an attack by the philosopher De Bonald in the ' Journal des Débats.' [7]

Notwithstanding her declining health, Madame de Staël attained, in the winter of 1816–1817,

[7] Eynard's *Vie de Madame de Krüdner,* ii. 25.

her highest power in the society of Paris. Every evening, says one of her guests, ' her *salon* was crowded with all that was distinguished and powerful, not in France only, but in all Europe, which was then represented in Paris by a remarkable number of its most extraordinary men. She had, to a degree perhaps never possessed by any other person, the rare talent of uniting around her the most distinguished individuals of all the opposite parties, literary and political, and making them establish relations among themselves which they could not afterwards entirely shake off. There might be found Wellington and Lafayette, Chateaubriand, Talleyrand, and Prince Laval; Humboldt and Blucher from Berlin; Constant and Sismondi from Switzerland; the two Schlegels from Hanover; Canova from Italy; the beautiful Madame Récamier, and the admirable Duchesse de Duras; and from England such a multitude that it seemed like a general emigration of British talent and rank.' [8]

Bonstetten kept up a constant correspondence with Paris, and as constantly sent his news to Frederica Brun. In March (1817) he writes: ' Alas, the Staël is dying! I have no hope for her. The agitations of 1813 have been fatal to her. I love her and know how to appreciate her; I shall

---

[8] Child's *Memoirs of Madame de Staël and Madame Roland.* I attribute the citation to Ticknor's manuscript Lectures on French Literature, which were in the hands of Mrs. Child.

lose very much in her, and you will also. She
appreciates and loves you. The work she is still
writing (on the French Revolution) will excite
great attention. Each of her works has made
sonorous chords vibrate through all Europe.
What she has written on social life is admirable.
No one is better acquainted with the " grand
monde " than she. In conversation she has
never had a rival.' In May he writes : ' Ah!
the poor Staël, I shall never see her again ! She
is so feeble that they have to feed her like a little
child. You may be sure, and steadfastly maintain,
that it is certainly and solely to her that France
owes the diminution of 30,000 troops which has
been made in the army of occupation. The
sovereigns had abandoned the decision of this
point to Wellington, and he wished not to spare a
single man. Madame de Staël alone changed his
opinion in this respect. It is to her that France
may owe its salvation.'

Day by day her malady advanced ; her daughter entertained her company ; she was confined to
her sick chamber, where she still received her most
intimate friends. Those among them whose politics had lately, more or less, separated them
from her, were now reconciled to her, and were
again daily with her—Benjamin Constant, Mathieu
de Montmorency, Sismondi, Chateaubriand. Chateaubriand records one of his sad visits at this time.
' It was a mournful time for France,' he says,

'when I again met Madame Récamier, the epoch of the death of Madame de Staël. Re-entering Paris, after the Hundred Days, the author of "Delphine" had returned only to suffer. I saw her at her own house and at that of the Duchesse de Duras. Little by little her health became worse, and she was at last obliged to keep her bed. One morning I called at her house, in the Rue Royale ; the window shutters were two-thirds closed. She reclined, supported by pillows. I approached her, and at first could hardly see the invalid. An ardent fever animated her cheeks. Her quick glance recognised me in the darkness, and she said, "Good day, my dear Francis. I am suffering, but not too much to love you still." She extended her hand, which I pressed and kissed. On lifting my head I perceived at the other side of the bed a pale and wasted figure—it was M. de Rocca. He also was dying. I had never seen him before, and was never to see him again. He did not speak, but bowed as he passed me—his steps could not be heard ; he departed like a shadow. Pausing a moment at the door, he turned towards the bed and, with a motion of the hand, took leave of Madame de Staël. A few days later she changed her lodgings. She invited me to dine with her in the Rue Neuve des Mathurins. I went, but she was not in the *salon* and could not even be present at the dinner ; yet she knew not that the fatal hour was so near. The last letter that she wrote to Madame de Duras was traced in great characters, irregular as those of a child ; it had an affectionate word for *Francis*. The expiration of a great talent affects more than the dying individual : society is struck by a general disaster ; each member of it suffers a loss. With Madame de Staël closed a momentous portion of my times. Her death made one of those breaches which the fall of a superior intellect produces once in an age, and which can never be closed.' [9]

George Ticknor was now in Paris, with access to its polished society such as probably no American had enjoyed since the days of Franklin. He was often at the mansion of the Duchesse de Broglie, where her mother was staying, but could not, for some time, see the invalid. On May 11, 1817, he writes : 'At last I have seen Madame de Staël. Ever since I presented my letters she has been so ill that her physician refused her permission to see above three or four persons a day, and those such of her most familiar friends as would amuse without exciting her. She was in bed, pale, feeble, and evidently depressed in spirits, and the mere stretching out of her hand to me, or rather making a slight movement, as if she desired to do it, cost an effort it was painful to witness. Observing, with that intuition for which she has always been so famous, the effect her situation produced on me, she said, "It is necessary that you should not judge of me

[9] *Mémoires d'Outre-Tombe,* viii.

from what you see here. This is not me—it is only
the shadow of what I was four months since—and
a shadow which will probably soon disappear." I
told her that M. Portal and her other physicians
did not think so. " Yes," said she, " yes, I know it,
but their opinions have always so much of the
vanity of authors that I place no reliance on them.
I shall never rise from this sickness, I am sure of
it." She saw at this moment that the Duchesse de
Broglie had entered the apartment, and was so
much affected by the last remark that she had
gone to the window to hide her feelings. She
therefore began to talk about America. Everything she said was marked by that imagination
which gives such a peculiar energy to her works,
and which has made her so long the idol of French
society; but, whenever she seemed to be aware
that she was about to utter any phrase of force or
aptness, her languid features were kindled with an
animation which made a strong contrast with her
feeble condition. Especially when she said of
America, " You are the advanced guard of the
human race; you have the future of the world!"
—there came a slight tinge of colour in her face
which spoke plainly enough of the pride of genius.
As I feared to weary her with conversation, I asked
her daughter if I should not go ; but she said she
was glad to see her mother interested, and wished
rather that I should stay. I remained therefore for half an hour longer—until dinner was

announced—during which we talked chiefly of the prospects of Europe, of which she despairs. When I rose to go, she gave me her hand and said, under the impression that I was soon going to America : " You will soon be at your home, and I, I am going to mine also." I pretended not to understand her, and told her I was sure I should see her in Switzerland much better. She looked on her daughter, while her eyes filled with tears, and said in English, " God grant me that favour," and I left her. The impression of this scene remained on us all during the dinner, but in the evening old M. St. Léon, Lacretelle, and Villemain (the latter one of the most eloquent professors in Paris) came in, and gave a gayer air to the conversation.'

There were dinner parties in the house daily, and the usual evening company was received by her daughter, who would often go to the sick chamber to report any remarkable saying or news of the guests that might entertain and relieve the sufferer ; for her love of society, her ruling passion, was strong even in death. Ticknor dined there repeatedly without seeing her, but always with distinguished company—Lafayette, Sir Humphry and Lady Davy, Humboldt, Schlegel, the Duc de Laval, the De Broglies, Villemain, Lacretelle, Pallissot, Benjamin Constant, Barante, Chateaubriand, Madame Récamier, &c. 'Madame de Staël,' he says, ' likes to have somebody every day, for society

is necessary to her.   There is a *coterie* every evening, the best in Paris.' [1]

In an account of one of these dinner parties
Ticknor gives us a passing view of the dearest
feminine friend of the dying authoress, who was
daily with her.   He sat at the table between
Chateaubriand and Madame Récamier, and writes :
' She must now be forty or more, though she has
not the appearance of so much ; and the lustre of
that beauty which filled Europe with its fame is
certainly faded.   I do not mean .to say she is not
still beautiful, for she certainly is, and very beautiful.   Her figure is fine, her mild eyes full of expression, and her arm and hand most beautiful.   I
was surprised to find her with fair complexion, and
no less surprised to find the general expression of
her countenance anything but melancholy, and her
conversation gay and full of vivacity, though, at the
same time, it should be added, always without
extravagance.' [2]

[1] Ticknor's *Life* &c. i. 6.

[2] Senior gives us a later glimpse of her.   In a conversation with
Madame Mohl, in 1860, she said to him : 'F or about eighteen years
I saw Madame Récamier every day.   For four years I lived under the
same roof.   She used to relate to us her early life.   No one told a
story better.   I first knew her in 1831, when she was fifty-three.
Her complexion was fair, but her colour, which had been brilliant, was
gone.   Her eyes were black and both bright and soft.   Her figure,
fine in youth, but never slim, was dignified though not tall.   She was
still pretty, rather than handsome.   With great softness and attrac-
tiveness of manner, she had something about her which repelled
familiarity.   No one ever took a liberty with her.   She read much, and
contrived to do so by having regular hours on which no one intruded.

Rocca, though wasting away with disease, was incessant in his attentions to Madame de Staël, and her ardent affection for him was intensified by the prospect of their separation. The Duchesse d'Abrantès says that, 'Loved with passion, at more than fifty years of age, by a man who was more than twenty years her junior, she still responded to this passion with all the ardour of her soul—a soul which was young and primitive even at this period of her life. He loved her profoundly, because .he had a heart ; for only those who love with the heart can animate the love of others. Rocca loved Madame de Staël as any woman of mediocrity, but good, tender, and devoted, could wish to be loved, and as she had always desired to be loved, though without finding before a heart eager for all the pleasures of such a sentiment. She had been struck with anguish at arriving at that period of woman's life when the world says, " Thou shouldst love no more— thou shouldst no more be loved," for she then felt that she could still love as vividly as she could at twenty. It was then that she found Rocca.

Hers was one of the few houses in which you could hear a subject sifted. She liked discussion. She had early imbibed religious sentiments, which she always retained, but was certainly not at all a professed *dévote.*' Madame Mohl believed in the report that she was the daughter of Récamier, who married her only in form, in order to secure his property to her. 'Their relations were parental, not conjugal.' Senior's *Conversations with Thiers, Guizot,* &c., ii. London, 1878.

During her illness her *femme de chambre* brought
her, as soon as she awoke, her writing materials,
and she wrote in bed till noon; then some of her
friends arrived.—Rocca knelt by the side of her
bed, regarding her with affection; she was revived
by his presence, which revealed a soul all her
own and still young and ardent. She forgot death
and her sufferings for the moment; she re-entered
into life, and a life beautiful with youth and love.
Alas! it was hard to die thus. I believe that her
sensations were then more vivid and more profound than at twenty. The power to love is more
energetic in such circumstances than in youth.
She was good, she was a perfect friend, as indulgent as talented, and she never knew envy.
She was loving, her warm heart animated all the
affections of others; she loved to be loved, and
returned affection a hundred-fold, and her last
days were illuminated by the sweet light of love.
" When I see Rocca enter in the morning," she
said a few days before her death, " it seems to me
that I become better, and that I shall again get up.
I look into his eyes, and there I see love and the
need he has of my heart. Then I wish to live,
since my life is necessary to another." Benjamin
Constant passed the last night at her bedside.
What memories must have been revived in his
soul! What thoughts in a mind like that of Constant's, during such a sad watching at the deathbed

of a woman whom he had so much loved! For he had loved her too, and had attempted to poison himself because she did not love him.'[3]

None of Madame de Staël's friends apprehended her danger; she had no organic disease, but was suffering from a general declension of her constitution. Baron Portal, first physician to the King, attended her frequently, and encouraged them to hope, and to enliven her by their discussions in the adjacent dining-room. But her powerful nature constantly gave way. Members of the Royal family daily inquired at her door, and every day the Duke of Wellington called in person. She frequently said, 'My father awaits me on the other shore.' Her cousin says that she was, 'even to her last sigh, tender and confiding as a child,' and 'profoundly grateful to all around her, especially to the incomparable friend' who, after years of faithful attendance, now chiefly ministered to her in her last hours.[4] The dying authoress was still characteristically sympathetic with other sufferers; she used her influence for a condemned man (Barry), who was pardoned by the King on the day after her death. 'I have always been the same,' she said to Chateaubriand, 'vivid and sad; I have loved God, my father, and my country.'

---

[3] *Mémoires de la Duchesse d'Abrantès*, xvii. 5. Compare her *Mémoires sur la Restauration*, iv. 2.

[4] Miss Randall, her devoted English companion through all her years of exile.

She dictated a letter to Madame Necker de Sanssure, in which, alluding to her daughter, she said, 'With such a treasure of the heart, it is sad to quit life. I should be wretched were all now to end between Albertine and me—were we not to meet in another world.' On coming out of a reverie she said, 'I believe that I know what this passage from life to death is; and I am sure that the goodness of God will make it easy. Our imaginations trouble us about it, but its pains are not severe.'[5] She had said, in the words of her dying Corinne, 'When the designs of Providence are accomplished in us, an internal harmony, a music of the soul, prepares us for the arrival of the angel of death. He has nothing alarming, nothing terrible about him; he has white wings, though he advances through the night.'[6]

She found consolation in the treatise 'De Imitatione Christi.' In her essay ' on the moral design ' of her 'Delphine' she had said, 'How can we reflect in solitude, without discovering that all profound sentiments have a tinge of sadness; and that man cannot elevate himself above the physical life without perceiving the present incompleteness of the moral world? The more he develops his mind and heart, the more he feels the limitations of existence. Religious passions, ambitious passions, all spring from a conscious necessity of filling the void of life. I do not believe that, since the beginning of the

[5] *Notice &c.* xi. [6] *Corinne,* last chapter.

world, a single distinguished mind can be cited, which has not found life to be inferior to its desires and sentiments.' Corinne, in her ' Last Chant,' had sung ' There is nothing restrictive, nothing servile, nothing limited, in religion. It is immensity, it is infinity, it is eternity. Genius cannot turn away from it; the aspirations of the imagination surpass the bounds of life; and the sublime, in anything, is a reflection of God.' For years she had habitually felt that Christianity affords the only, and the sufficient, solution of the problem of life, and that the true end of life is, as she had said, ' the religious education of the heart.' Mortal life developing into immortal life—the moral world environed by the spiritual world—' the incompleteness ' of the one complemented by the transcendent destinies of the other—this was her final philosophy of the subject. And she saw, in the Christian doctrines of the immortality of the soul, of the ' forgiveness of sins,' of a paternal, though disciplinary government of the world—disciplinary mostly by chastening trials—the only rational, as well as the only consolatory, explanation of the order of the universe. Such was her faith, and the integrity of our narrative requires that it be thus distinctly stated. Whatever may be thought of it, we are consoled to know that, now, after the long struggle between her higher and lower sentiments, after some grievous errors of life and much suffering from them, as well as from the usual morbidness of genius, and often from exaggerated evils, this faith enabled her to die at peace with God and all the world.

She expired, without pain, at five o'clock on the morning of July 14, 1817. Portal published a *brochure* on her 'Malady and Death,' in which he says that her body was opened to be embalmed, in order that it might be conveyed to Coppet, and that there was hardly a trace of disease in any of the internal organs; 'her death could be attributed only to cachexia, or an evil condition of the system arising from several antecedent causes. She preserved the energy of her intellectual faculties to the last moment. She passed the whole of her last day seated in her armchair, conversing with her friends.'[7] She slept her usual time that night; 'a few minutes afterwards her attendants perceived that she was dead.'

Baron von Vohgt wrote immediately to De Gérando: 'I cannot tell you how much I have been struck by this death. She was so *full of life*. We shall never again see such a woman. Her enthusiasm for all that is beautiful and good; the soul with which she expressed herself on both these subjects; the vivacity of her brilliant intellect; the grace of her speech; all is before me. I shall never forget her. She was good. Her errors

---

[7] *Notice sur la Maladie et la Mort de Madame la Baronne de Staël.* Paris, 1817. Lacretelle wrote: 'The brain of Madame de Staël has received great honour from the anatomists; its dissection has excited enthusiasm, on account of its greater size than the average among women.' *Testament Philosophique* &c. ii. 22.

were those of her judgment, and could never impair her heart.'

Rocca survived her less than seven months; his bereavement aggravated his malady; he hastened, after her burial, to the south for relief, and found it in death, at Hyères, on January 29, 1818, in the thirty-first year of his age.

Her remains were taken to Coppet and laid to rest in the family cemetery. Schlegel, Sismondi, Bonstetten, the Duc de Noailles, and many other distinguished personages, joined with the family in the funeral solemnities. The common people formed saddened lines from the château to the cemetery. The *cortége* included the municipal functionaries, and most of the 'Councillors of State,' of Geneva.

Bonstetten wrote to Madame Brun: 'I have been to Coppet to assist at the reception of the convoy bringing the body of Madame de Staël; and, from her own chamber, have seen the coffin borne between close hedges of people from all parts of the vicinity. The funeral *cortége* moved slowly towards the little grove, surrounded with walls, where her father and mother repose. The birds, thronging the trees, alone interrupted, by their songs, the solemn silence of the sad ceremony. Men in black moved as funereal shades in the gloom of the deep woods; and, as the coffin was borne through it, the leaves seemed to tremble. Ah! I cannot believe that she no longer lives! It seems to me that I must always see her before me. She was a good, a beautiful soul.'

Sismondi, whose genius she had so early prompted, and whose literary labours she had so long inspired, has left us a few affecting lines respecting the last scene. After the interment he wrote to his mother : ' So, it is ended—this abode where I have so long lived—where I have been so happy with her ! It is ended, that vivifying society, that magic lantern of the world, which I first saw illuminated here, and by which I have learned so much ! My life is painfully changed. I owe more to her than perhaps to any other person. How I suffered at the interment ! A discourse delivered by the minister of Coppet, over the bier, while Albertine (Madame de Broglie) and Mademoiselle Randall were kneeling at the coffin, so touched my heart, and made me so measure the extent of my loss, that I could not restrain my tears.' [8]

A few days later Bonstetten wrote to Madame Brun : ' Rocca was not in the funeral *cortége* ; he was ill, he will soon die of his old wounds. I have again been to Coppet with a friend of the Staël, from Milan. I was so affected that I could not speak ; I hastened to my old chamber in the château. Albertine and Auguste came to me, he with their five-years-old brother in his arms. " I introduce to you my little brother," he said ; " we do," said both, " what we believe would be agree-

[8] *Fragments de son Journal et Correspondance.* Geneva, 1857.

able to our mother, if she saw us. Our first care
has been to establish the legitimacy of our brother."
Little Alfonse inherits his mother's eyes. I could
not look at them. Ah! death is such a serious
thing! Our ordinary life cannot be harmonised
with it. My Italian companion (De Brême) told
me that the Staël took him, but a year ago, to the
sombre woods of the cemetery and, standing before
the walled-up door, said, " When I shall be there,.
promise me that you will visit me." I looked
again on the very place in the *salon* where I took
my final leave of her before her last departure for
Paris. I cannot bring myself to realise that I shall
see her no more. I told her once that I wished to
see her asleep, in order to be sure that she ever
closed her eyes, and was not always thinking.
Now, now!—I am constantly looking to see her
near me. She was a good, a pure, a noble soul!'
Still later he writes: 'One of her best traits was
her cordial, conciliatory disposition; no wish to
injure an enemy could remain two minutes in her
heart. Her whole being was kindness and love,
and what gave greater value to her kindness was
that no one knew men better than she, and none
could more effectively avenge himself against them.
Miss Randall came to me; we wept together..
Hardly had she gone when Rocca came, bringing
his son. How much I have to tell you! Where
shall I begin! How unjust I have been towards
Rocca! He told me all the particulars about the

marriage; it was solemnised both in Coppet and
Sweden, so solicitous was she that it should be un-
questionable in respect to every formality. Rocca
and his son inherit a million livres. She left three
millions and between eight and nine hundred
thousand livres. Rocca told me of her love with
much feeling and many tears. " I know," said he,
" that I am a dying man, and I hoped to die in
her arms; that would have been sweet to me.
Now, what am I? Who can fill for me the place
of this great being? I wish to fly to a desert.
People speak to me of my fortune. Sordid souls!
Had I not all her fortune when she was alive?
What is money to me? No society will henceforth
exist for me. What crowned power can give me
back her who was my life?" He spoke of her last
illness; she came home from an evening gathering where she had been more brilliant than ever.
She went to Rocca's room, and wished to ring the
bell, but had not strength. She attempted to press
his hand, but could not close her own. Thus her
remaining life ebbed away, but without affecting her
intellect; on the contrary, she was never more luminous than during her sickness. But hear further:
she could not, and would not go to sleep, that night,
for fear that she should never see Rocca again. She
dreaded the possibility that her, or his, eyes might
be closed for ever while she slept. He entreated
her to sleep for brief intervals, pledging himself
to wake her at certain periods, as indicated by his

watch; she did so, and in this way she regained confidence and ability to sleep as usual. The thought of Rocca was her life, and in this, and this alone, she found rest. On the evening before her death she took care to instruct those around her to give him his medicine. She said to him, " I have ordered a fire to be lit in your chamber, for it is so cold to-night." Alas! it was the chill of the grave, for the day was very warm. She added, "We will try to spend this winter in Naples;" and then "Good-night," and it was for ever! Her patience was extraordinary. During her entire illness she was all love, sweetness, and devotion. Rocca's presence alone was the support of her life. She required them to bear her often to his sick chamber to assure herself that he was alive. Death was little to her, by his side. What would have become of her if she had outlived him? He is, indeed, a good, noble, and true soul. O my God! when I stand before this tomb, where these three rest in eternal stillness, beneath the overhanging trees, I cannot control my throbbing heart.'[9]

Thenceforward Coppet was to be a shrine for literary pilgrims. Nearly twenty years after her death George Ticknor returned, from his distant country, to renew his youthful recollections of the brilliant scenes of the *salons* of Paris, Geneva, and Coppet. Time had sobered his me-

[9] Bonstetten's *Briefe* &c. ii.

mories, but his brief record of them is not without a touch of feeling. 'We drove to-day,' he says, 'on the beautiful banks of this lake, through the rich fields and vineyards of the Pays de Vaud, and in sight always of the mountains of Savoy, from Lausanne to Geneva. We stopped to see the château at Coppet, which we found a comfortable and even luxurious establishment on the inside, though of slight pretensions outside. The room—a long hall—that Madame de Staël used for private theatricals, was fitted up by Auguste for a library, in which he placed the books of both his mother and his grandfather, and at one end of it a fine statue of Necker by Tieck. The family portraits, Necker and Madame Necker, the Baron and Madame de Staël, Auguste, a bust of Madame de Broglie, are in another room, and Auguste's cabinet is just as he left it. The whole was very sad to me, the more so perhaps because the *concierge* recollected me, and showed the desolation of the place, and its melancholy memorials, with a good deal of feeling. The door of the monument, in which rest the remains of Necker and his wife, with Madame de Staël at his feet, has been walled up. Auguste is buried on the outside, and round the whole is a high wall, the gate to which is not opened at all, as both Necker and Madame de Staël desired their cemetery should never be made a show. Whenever she herself arrived at Coppet, she took the key and visited it quite alone, but otherwise the enclosure was never opened.' 'Geneva is extremely changed: Bonstetten, the head of all that was literary and agreeable, died two years ago, about ninety years old; Simond the traveller, Dumont, &c. &c. are all gone. I have renewed my acquaintance with Madame Rilliet-Huber and M. Hess, the first of whom is the most intimate friend of the De Staëls remaining in Geneva, and the last a man of letters attached to her household. *They are all that survive* of the delightful circle, in which I passed some time most happily nineteen years ago.'

These were not 'all that survived,' however; Ticknor seems not to have been aware that one of the most interesting of them all, Madame Necker de Saussure, still lived, though absent and in declining health. 'Her family,' says one of her literary friends, ' hoping for the good effects of a kindlier air, had established themselves at Morney, in one of the little valleys of the neighbouring Mont Salève, which opens towards the chain of the Alps. It was there that, on the 13th of April, 1841, surrounded by the most tender and vigilant care, she expired, after having silently contemplated, for the last time in this world, the grand spectacle of the day dying slowly on the mountains.' [1] 'She,' says the almost sole survivor of the Coppet *salon*, the venerable Pictet de Sergy,

---

[1] An anonymous *brochure*, without date, with which I have been favoured by her nephew, Professor A. Rilliet, of Geneva.

' she possessed great and varied knowledge, and a rare faculty for meditation, which gave authority to her conversation.   Her first work was a translation of Schlegel's " Dramatic Literature ; " in an original " Introduction " she criticises, with impartiality and talent, his opinions on Sophocles, Shakespeare, and Calderon.   Her " Notice " on Madame de Staël, is a *chef-d'œuvre* of sentiment and delicacy, and will always remain the most interesting document on the very exceptional. personality of its subject.   An increasing infirmity, deafness, isolated her somewhat from society at last, but led her to fortify her faculties, by solitary meditation, to an extraordinary degree and intensity.   Her continued studies resulted in that remarkable work, twice " crowned " in France, the treatise on " Progressive Education."   It sufficed to place her in the first rank of ethical writers.' [2]

Two of Madame de Staël's oldest and dearest friends, who were destined to survive her longer than almost any of her other associates, went together on a pilgrimage to her grave, years after she had been laid to rest there ; two whose impressions, amid the tranquil and picturesque scene, we would be most interested to know.   Her memory still consecrated the mutual sentiments of Chateaubriand and of Madame Récamier.   He was now sixty-four years of age, she fifty-five, but their souls were yet vivid with the poetry, the romance,

[2] Manuscript *Souvenirs.*

of their remarkable lives, so long identified with
hers. Excluding all other companionship, they
spent the day in the solitude of Coppet. Chateaubriand has recorded the visit in his best style and
with genuine pathos. 'The château was closed,'
he says; ' they opened its doors for me; I wandered
in the deserted apartments. The companion of
my pilgrimage recognised all the old places, where
she still seemed to see her friend, seated at her
piano, or entering, or going forth, or conversing
on the terrace which borders the gallery. She
revisited the chamber which she herself used to
occupy; days long passed returned to her; it was
as a repetition of the scene that I have painted in
" René: " " I wandered through the echoing apartments, where I heard only the sound of my own
steps. Everywhere the halls were vacant. How
sweet and rapid are the moments that brothers
and sisters pass in their young years, united under
the wings of their aged parents! The family of
man is of only a day, the breath of God disperses
it as a vapour; scarcely does the son know the
father, the father the son, the brother the sister,
the sister the brother. The oak sees its acorns
germinate around it; it is thus with the children
of men." I recalled also what I have said in
my " Mémoires " of my last visit to Cambourg, in
parting for America. Two worlds, different, but
united by a secret sympathy, occupied the attention
of Madame Récamier and me. Alas! these isolated

worlds, each of us bore them in our souls; for where can two persons be found who have lived sufficiently long together not to have separate memories? From the château we entered the park; the early autumn had commenced to tinge and to detach the leaves, the breeze abated and allowed us to hear a stream which turned a mill. After threading the wooded aisles, through which she had often walked with Madame de Staël, she wished to pay her respects to her ashes. At some distance from the park is a coppice, mingled with larger trees and environed by hoary walls. This coppice resembles those thickets of wood, in the open country, which sportsmen call spinneys; it is there that death has thrust its prey and enclosed its victims. A sepulchre had been built, beforehand, for Necker, his wife and his daughter; when the latter was placed in it the door of the crypt was walled up. The child of Auguste was buried outside of it. Auguste himself, who died before his child, rests under a stone at the feet of his kindred; on the stone are engraved the words of Scripture, " Why seek ye the living among the dead?" I did not enter the cemetery; Madame Récamier alone obtained permission to go into it. I remained seated on a bench outside and, turning away from France, fixed my gaze now on the summit of Mont Blanc, now on the lake of Geneva. Golden clouds covered the horizon behind the sombre line of the Jura; they seemed like a glory extended over a

long coffin. I perceived, on the other side of the
lake, the villa of Byron, the top of which was
touched by the rays of the setting sun. Rousseau
was no longer there to admire the scene; and
Voltaire, long departed, had never cared for it.
In the presence of the tomb of Madame de Staël
how many illustrious persons, once happy amidst
these same scenes, but now for ever absent,
returned to my memory! They seemed to come
back to seek the shade of their old friend, themselves but shades, and fly with her to heaven, her
convoy through the night. At this moment
Madame Récamier, pale and in tears, came forth
from the coppice, as if she herself were but a
shade. If I ever felt, at once, both the vanity
and the reality of glory and of life, and also what
it is to be truly loved, it was at the entrance of
this silent and obscure forest, where she sleeps who
had so much *éclat* and fame.' [3]

I have thus endeavoured to recall this remarkable life, amidst scenes familiar to its heroine, in
frequent view of her home and her tomb; to have
attempted to delineate such a life and such a
character without somewhat of the sensibility
which so much characterised her, would have been
impossible, and incompatible with the truthfulness
of the narrative. With whatever severity we may
reflect on her faults, we must, after this thorough
review of her history, give to her our last adieu as

[3] *Mémoires d'Outre-Tombe,* x.

to one of the noblest intellects, one of the sweetest, most tender, most lovable souls, in literary history. If many distinguished women have had fewer errors, few have had more virtues. No true man will here take a final leave of her without admiration; no true woman without wishing to give her the kiss of charity and peace.

The old château, the forest cemetery, the whole of Coppet, remain as her monument; her native country has, as yet, given her none; but she needs no local memorial. Pericles said, over the heroic dead of Athens, that the whole earth is the monument of great characters. Such a life is still effectively extant in the intellectual world. Her ashes are on the shores of the Leman: her spirit is everywhere.

THE END.

LONDON : PRINTED BY
SPOTTISWOODE AND CO., NEW-STREET SQUARE
AND PARLIAMENT STREET

MR. MURRAY'S LIST.

LIFE OF LORD CAMPBELL, LORD CHIEF JUSTICE, afterwards LORD CHANCELLOR of ENGLAND. Edited by his Daughter, the Hon. Mrs. HARDCASTLE. With Portrait. 2 vols. 8vo. 30s.

INDIA IN 1880. By SIR RICHARD TEMPLE, BART., late Governor of Bombay. Lieutenant-Governor of Bengal, &c., &c. 8vo.

MEMOIR OF THE PUBLIC LIFE OF THE RIGHT HON. J. C. HERRIES, during the REIGNS of GEORGE III. and IV., WILLIAM IV., and QUEEN VICTORIA. Founded on Unpublished Documents. By his Son, EDWARD HERRIES, C.B. 2 vols. 8vo. 24s.

CHRISTIAN INSTITUTIONS; ESSAYS ON ECCLESIASTICAL SUBJECTS. By A. P. STANLEY, D.D., DEAN OF WESTMINSTER. 8vo. 12s.

JAPAN; ITS HISTORY, TRADITIONS, AND RELIGIONS. With the NARRATIVE of a Visit to JAPAN in 1879. By Sir EDWARD J. REED, K.C.B. With Map and Illustrations. 2 vols. 8vo. 28s.

ILIOS; A COMPLETE HISTORY OF THE CITY AND COUNTRY OF THE TROJANS. With an AUTOBIOGRAPHY of the AUTHOR. By Dr. SCHLIEMANN. With nearly 2,000 Illustrations. Imperial 8vo. 50s.

UNBEATEN TRACKS IN JAPAN. TRAVELS OF A LADY in the INTERIOR. By ISABELLA BIRD, Author of 'A Lady's Life in the Rocky Mountains,' &c. With Map and Illustrations. 2 vols. Crown 8vo. 24s.

THE PERSONAL LIFE OF DAVID LIVINGSTONE, LL.D., from his UNPUBLISHED JOURNALS and CORRESPONDENCE. By W. G. BLAIKIE, D.D. With Portrait and Map. 8vo. 15s.

THE MANIFOLD WITNESS FOR CHRIST. An attempt to EXHIBIT the COMBINED FORCE of VARIOUS EVIDENCES of CHRISTIANITY, DIRECT AND INDIRECT. By Canon BARRY, D.D., Principal of King's College, London. 8vo. 12s.

A HANDBOOK TO POLITICAL QUESTIONS OF THE DAY. Being the ARGUMENTS on EITHER SIDE. By SYDNEY C. BUXTON. Second Edition, revised, with additional arguments. 8vo. 5s.

SKETCHES OF EMINENT STATESMEN AND WRITERS WITH OTHER ESSAYS. Reprinted from the 'Quarterly Review,' with Additions and Corrections. By A. HAYWARD, Q.C. 2 vols. 8vo. 28s.

MRS. GROTE. A SKETCH. By Lady EASTLAKE. Post 8vo. 6s.

JOHN MURRAY, Albemarle Street.

RAMBLES AMONG THE HILLS IN THE PEAK OF DERBYSHIRE, AND ON THE SOUTH DOWNS, with Sketches of People by the Way. By LOUIS J. JENNINGS, Author of 'Field Paths and Green Lanes in Sussex.' With Illustrations. Post 8vo. 12s.

DUTY. With Illustrations of COURAGE, PATIENCE, and ENDURANCE. By SAMUEL SMILES, LL.D. Post 8vo. 6s.

A POPULAR ACCOUNT OF PERUVIAN BARK, AND ITS INTRODUCTION INTO BRITISH INDIA, CEYLON, &c., AND THE PROGRESS AND EXTENT OF ITS CULTIVATION. By CLEMENTS R. MARKHAM, C.B. With Maps and Woodcuts. Post 8vo. 14s.

A HISTORY OF GREEK SCULPTURE. From the EARLIEST TIMES down to the Age of PHEIDIAS. By A. S. MURRAY, of the British Museum. With Illustrations. Royal 8vo. 21s.

MEOMIRS OF THE LIFE AND EVENTFUL CAREER OF THE DUKE DE SALDANHA, SOLDIER and STATESMAN. By the CONDE DA CARNOTA. With Portrait and Maps. 2 vols. 8vo. 32s.

THE POWER OF MOVEMENT IN PLANTS. By CHARLES DARWIN, assisted by FRANCIS DARWIN. With Woodcuts. Crown 8vo. 15s.

SIBERIA IN EUROPE. A NATURALIST'S VISIT TO THE VALLEY OF THE PETCHORA IN NORTH-EAST RUSSIA. With Notices of Birds and their Migrations. By HENRY SEEBOHM, F.R.G.S. With Map and Illustrations. Crown 8vo. 14s.

THE PSALMS OF DAVID. With NOTES EXPLANATORY and CRITICAL. By the DEAN OF WELLS, Canon ELLIOTT, and Canon COOK. Medium 8vo. 10s. 6d.

THE GARDENS OF THE SUN; or a NATURALIST'S JOURNAL ON THE MOUNTAINS AND IN THE FORESTS AND SWAMPS OF BORNEO AND THE SULU ARCHIPELAGO. By F. W. BURRIDGE. With Illustrations. Crown 8vo. 14s.

HISTORY OF EGYPT UNDER THE PHARAOHS. DERIVED ENTIRELY FROM THE MONUMENTS. With a MEMOIR on the EXODUS OF THE ISRAELITES and the EGYPTIAN MONUMENTS. By Dr. HENRY BRUGSCH. *Second Edition, revised.* With New Preface and Notes by the Author. Maps. 2 vols. 8vo. 32s.

ENGLISH STUDIES. By Professor J. S. BREWER, M.A., late of the Record Office. 8vo. 14s.

JOHN MURRAY, Albemarle Street.

50 ALBEMARLE STREET, LONDON,
December 1880.

MR. MURRAY'S

LIST OF WORKS

IN

GENERAL LITERATURE,

CONTAINING

THE SPEAKER'S COMMENTARY ON THE BIBLE.

HISTORY, ANCIENT & MODERN.

BIOGRAPHY, MEMOIRS, &C.

GEOGRAPHY, VOYAGES, AND TRAVELS.

HANDBOOKS FOR TRAVELLERS.

THEOLOGY, RELIGION, &C.

SCIENCE, NATURAL HISTORY, GEOLOGY, &C.

ART, ARCHITECTURE, AND ANTIQUITIES.

EDUCATIONAL WORKS.

POETRY, THE DRAMA, &C.

NAVAL AND MILITARY WORKS.

PHILOSOPHY, LAW, AND POLITICS.

RURAL & DOMESTIC ECONOMY

FIELD SPORTS, &C.

MISCELLANEOUS LITERATURE AND PHILOLOGY.

HOME AND COLONIAL LIBRARY.

DR. WM. SMITH'S ATLAS OF ANCIENT GEOGRAPHY.

THE SPEAKER'S COMMENTARY.

Medium 8vo.

THE HOLY BIBLE, according to the Authorised Version, A.D. 1611, with an EXPLANATORY and CRITICAL COMMENTARY, and a REVISION of the TRANSLATION. By BISHOPS and CLERGY of the ANGLICAN CHURCH. Edited by F. C. COOK, M.A., Canon of Exeter, Preacher at Lincoln's Inn, and Chaplain in Ordinary to the Queen.

THE OLD TESTAMENT. 6 VOLS. 8vo, 135s.
Vol. I.—30s.

GENESIS—Bishop of Winchester.
EXODUS—Canon Cook and Rev. Samuel Clark.

LEVITICUS—Rev. Samuel Clark.
NUMBERS—Canon Espin and Rev. J. F. Thrupp.

DEUTERONOMY—Canon Espin.

Vols. II. and III.—36s.

JOSHUA—Canon Espin.
JUDGES, RUTH, SAMUEL—Bishop of Bath and Wells.

KINGS, CHRONICLES, EZRA, NEHEMIAH, ESTHER—Canon Rawlinson.

Vol. IV.—24s.

JOB—Canon Cook.
PSALMS—Dean of Wells, Canon Cook, and Canon Elliott.

PROVERBS—Rev. E. H. Plumptre.
ECCLESIASTES—Rev. W. T. Bullock.
SONG OF SOLOMON—Rev. T. Kingsbury.

Vol. V.—20s.

ISAIAH—Rev. Dr. Kay.

JEREMIAH AND LAMENTATIONS—Dean of Canterbury.

Vol. VI.—25s.

EZEKIEL—Rev. Dr. Currey.
DANIEL—Archdeacon Rose and Rev. J. Fuller.
HOSEA and JONAH—Rev. E. Huxtable.
AMOS, NAHUM, and ZEPHANIAH—Rev. R. Gandell.

JOEL and OBADIAH—Rev. F. Meyrick.
MICAH and HABAKKUK—Rev. Samuel Clark and Canon Cook.
HAGGAI, ZECHARIAH, and MALACHI—Canon Drake.

THE NEW TESTAMENT. 4 VOLS. 8vo.
Vol. I.—18s.

GENERAL INTRODUCTION—The Archbishop of York.
ST. MATTHEW & ST. MARK—Dean Mansel and Canon Cook.

ST. LUKE—Bishop of St. David's.

Vol. II.—20s.

ST. JOHN—Canon Westcott.

THE ACTS—Bishop of Chester.

Vol. III. (*Nearly Ready.*)

ROMANS—Rev. Canon Gifford.
CORINTHIANS—Canon Evans & Rev. J. Waite.
GALATIANS—Dean of Chester.
PHILIPPIANS, EPHESIANS, COLOSSIANS,

THESSALONIANS, and PHILEMON—Dean Jeremie, Rev. F. Meyrick, Dean of Raphoe, and Bishop of Derry.
PASTORAL EPISTLES—Bishop of London.
HEBREWS—Rev. Dr. Kay.

Vol. IV. (*In the Press.*)

ST. JAMES—Dean of Rochester.
ST. JOHN—Bishop of Derry.

ST. PETER and ST. JUDE—Canon Cook, and Rev. Dr. Lumby, D.D.
REVELATION—Archdeacon Lee.

THE STUDENT'S EDITION OF THE SPEAKER'S COMMENTARY on the Old Testament, abridged and edited. By J. M. FULLER, M.A., Vicar of Bexley, late Fellow of St. John's College, Cambridge. 4 vols. Crown 8vo, 7s. 6d. each.

Vol. I. GENESIS to DEUTERONOMY.
Vol. II. JOSHUA to ESTHER.

Vol. III. JOB to SONG OF SOLOMON.
Vol. IV. ISAIAH to MALACHI [*Nearly ready*

HISTORY ANCIENT AND MODERN.

Ancient History.

History of the Ancient World; from the earliest Records to the fall of the Western Empire, A.D. 476. By PHILIP SMITH. Plans. 3 vols. 8vo, 31s. 6d.

Student's Ancient History of the East. From the Earliest Times to the Conquest of Alexander the Great ; including Egypt, Assyria, Babylonia, Media, Persia, Asia Minor, and Phœnicia. By PHILIP SMITH. Woodcuts. Post 8vo, 7s. 6d.

History of Egypt under the Pharaohs. Derived from the Monuments. With Memoir on the Exodus of the Israelites. By Dr. BRUGSCH. Maps. 2 vols. 8vo, 32s.

Nile Gleanings: the Ethnology, History, and Art of Ancient Egypt, as Revealed by Paintings and Bas-Reliefs. With Descriptions of Nubia and its Great Rock Temples to the Second Cataract. By VILLIERS STUART. With 58 Coloured and Outline Plates. Royal 8vo, 31s. 6d.

Manners and Customs of the Ancient Egyptians: their Religion, Arts, Laws, Manufactures, etc. By Sir J. GARDNER WILKINSON. Revised by SAMUEL BIRCH, LL.D. Illustrations. 3 vols. 8vo, £4 : 4s.

Popular Account of the AN-CIENT EGYPTIANS. By Sir J. G. WILKINSON. Illustrations. 2 vols. post 8vo, 12s.

The Five Great Monarchies of the ANCIENT EASTERN WORLD ; or the History, Geography, and Antiquities of Chaldea, Assyria, Babylonia, Media, and Persia. By Canon RAWLINSON. Illustrations. 3 vols. 8vo, 42s.

Herodotus : A new English version. With notes' and essays, historical and ethnographical. By Canon RAWLINSON, Sir HENRY RAWLINSON, and Sir J. G. WILKINSON. Illustrations. 4 vols. 8vo, 48s.

History of Greece, from the Earliest Period to the close of the Generation contemporary with Alexander the Great. By GEORGE GROTE. Library Edition. Portrait and Maps. 10 vols. 8vo, 120s. ; or, Cabinet ed., Portrait and Plans, 12 vols. post 8vo, 6s. each.

Student's History of Greece, from the Earliest Times to the Roman Conquest, with the History of Literature and Art. By Dr. WM. SMITH. Woodcuts. Post 8vo, 7s. 6d.

Student's History of Rome, from the Earliest Times to the Establishment of the Empire. With the History of Literature and Art. By Dean LIDDELL. Woodcuts. Post 8vo, 7s. 6d.

History of the Decline and Fall of the ROMAN EMPIRE, By EDWARD GIBBON, with Notes by MILMAN and GUIZOT. Edited by Dr. WM. SMITH. Maps. 8 vols. 8vo, £3.

Student's Gibbon ; an Epi-tome of the History of the Decline and Fall of the Roman Empire. By EDWARD GIBBON. Woodcuts. Post 8vo, 7s. 6d.

Dictionary of Greek and Roman ANTIQUITIES. Edited by Dr. WM. SMITH. Illustrations. Royal 8vo, 28s.

Dictionary of Greek and Roman BIOGRAPHY and MYTHOLOGY. Edited by Dr. WM. SMITH. Illustrations. 3 vols. royal 8vo, 84s.

Classical Dictionary of Bio-GRAPHY, MYTHOLOGY, and GEOGRAPHY, for the Higher Forms. By Dr. WM. SMITH. Illustrations. 8vo, 18s.

Smaller Classical Dictionary of Mythology, Biography, and Geography. Woodcuts. Crown 8vo, 7s. 6d.

Smaller Dictionary of Greek and Roman Antiquities. Abridged from the large work. By Dr. WM. SMITH. Woodcuts. Crown 8vo, 7s. 6d.

Scripture and Church History.

Student's Old Testament His-tory ; from the Creation to the Return of the Jews from Captivity. By PHILIP SMITH. Woodcuts. Post 8vo, 7s. 6d.

Student's New Testament His-tory. With an Introduction connecting the History of the Old and New Testaments. By PHILIP SMITH. Woodcuts. Post 8vo, 7s. 6d.

History of the Jews, from the Earliest Period to Modern Times. By Dean MILMAN. 3 vols. Post 8vo, 18s.

History of the Jewish Church. By Dean STANLEY. 1st and 2d SERIES, Abraham to the Captivity. Maps. 2 vols. 8vo, 24s. 3d SERIES, Captivity to the Christian Era. Maps. 8vo, 14s.

History of Christianity, from the Birth of Christ to the Extinction of Paganism in the Roman Empire. By Dean MILMAN. 3 vols. post 8vo, 18s.

History of the Christian Church from the Apostolic Age to the Reformation, A.D. 64-1517. By Canon ROBERTSON. 8 vols. post 8vo, 6s. each.

History of Latin Christianity and of the Popes to Nicholas V. By Dean MILMAN. 9 vols. post 8vo, 54s.

Student's Manual of Ecclesiastical History, from the Time of the Apostles to the Full Establishment of the Holy Roman Empire and the Papal Power. By PHILIP SMITH. Woodcuts. Post 8vo, 7s. 6d.

History of the Eastern Church. By Dean STANLEY. Plans. 8vo, 12s.

History of the Gallican Church, from the Concordat at Bologna, 1516, to the Revolution. By Rev. W. H. JERVIS. Portraits. 2 vols. 8vo, 28s.

Student's Manual of English Church History, from the time of Henry VIII. to the Silencing of Convocation in the 18th Century. By Canon PERRY. Post 8vo, 7s. 6d.

History of the Church of SCOTLAND. By Dean STANLEY. 8vo, 7s. 6d.

Dictionary of Christian Antiquities, comprising the History, Institutions, and Antiquities of the Christian Church. Edited by WM. SMITH and Archdeacon CHEETHAM. Illustrations. 2 vols. med. 8vo, £3 : 13 : 6.

Dictionary of Christian Biography, Literature, Sects, and Doctrines, from the Time of the Apostles to the Age of Charlemagne. Edited by Dr. WM. SMITH and Rev. H. WACE. Vols. I. & II. Medium 8vo, 31s. 6d. each.

The Jesuits, their Constitution and Teaching. An Historical Sketch. By W. C. CARTWRIGHT. 8vo, 9s.

Notes on some Passages in the Liturgical History of the Reformed English Church. By Lord SELBORNE. 8vo, 6s.

Mediæval and Modern History.

An Account of the Modern Egyptians. By E. W. LANE. Illustrations. 2 vols. crown 8vo, 12s.

History of Europe during the MIDDLE AGES. By HENRY HALLAM. Library Edition. 3 vols. 8vo, 30s. ; or Cabinet Edition. 3 vols. post 8vo, 12s. Student's Edition. Post 8vo, 7s. 6d.

Student's History of France. From the Earliest Times to the Establishment of the Second Empire, 1852. With Notes on the Institutions of the Country. By W. H. JERVIS. Woodcuts. Post 8vo, 7s. 6d.

History of Charles the Bold, Duke of Burgundy. By J. FOSTER KIRK. Portraits. 3 vols. 8vo, 45s.

Student's Hume ; a History of ENGLAND, from the Earliest Times to the Revolution of 1688. Revised and continued to the Treaty of Berlin, 1878, by J. S. BREWER. With 7 Coloured Maps and 70 Woodcuts. Post 8vo, 7s. 6d.

History of England, from the Accession of Henry VII. to the Death of George II. By HENRY HALLAM. 3 vols. 8vo, 30s.; or Cabinet Edition

vols. post 8vo, 12s. Student's Edition. Post 8vo, 7s. 6d.

Literary History of Europe during the 15th, 16th, and 17th Centuries. Library Edition. 3 vols. 8vo, 36s. Cabinet Edition, 4 vols. post 8vo, 16s.

Historical Memorials of Canterbury. 1. Landing of Augustine—2. Murder of Becket—3. Edward the Black Prince—4. Becket's Shrine. By Dean STANLEY. Woodcuts. Post 8vo, 7s. 6d.

History of the United Netherlands, from the Death of William the Silent to the Twelve Years' Truce, 1609. By J. L. MOTLEY. Portraits. 4 vols. post 8vo, 6s. each.

Life and Death of John of BARNEVELD, Advocate of Holland. With a view of the primary causes and movements of the Thirty Years War. By J. L. MOTLEY. Illustrations. 2 vols. post 8vo, 12s.

Students' History of Modern Europe, from the End of the Middle Ages to the Treaty of Berlin, 1878.

Sir John Northcotes's Note-book during the Long Parliament. From the Original MS. Edited by A. H. A. HAMILTON. Crown 8vo, 9s.

History of India—The Hindoo and Mohammedan Periods. By the Hon. MOUNTSTUART ELPHINSTONE. Edited by Professor COWELL. Map. 8vo, 18s.

Historic Peerage of England, Exhibiting the Origin, Descent, and Present State of every Title of Peerage which has existed since the Conquest. By Sir HARRIS NICOLAS. 8vo, 30s.

Two Sieges of Vienna by the TURKS. From the German. By LORD ELLESMERE. Post 8vo, 2s.

British India from its origin to 1783. By EARL STANHOPE. Post 8vo, 3s. 6d.

History of England, from the Reign of Queen Anne (1701) to the Peace of Versailles (1783). By Earl STANHOPE. 9 vols. post 8vo, 5s. each.

"The Forty-Five;" or, the Rebellion in Scotland in 1745. By Earl STANHOPE. Post 8vo, 3s. 6d.

Historical Essays. By EARL STANHOPE. Post 8vo, 3s. 6d.

French Retreat from Moscow, and other Essays. By EARL STANHOPE. Post 8vo. 7s. 6d.

Scenes from the War of Liberation in Germany. From the German. By Sir A. GORDON. Post 8vo, 3s. 6d.

The Siege of Gibraltar, 1772-1780, with a Description of that Garrison from the earliest periods. By JOHN DRINKWATER. Post 8vo, 2s.

Annals of the Wars of the 18th and 19th Century, 1700-1815. By Sir EDWARD CUST. Maps. 9 vols. 16mo, 5s. each.

State of Society in France BEFORE THE REVOLUTION, 1789. By ALEXIS DE TOCQUEVILLE. Translated by HENRY REEVE. 8vo, 14s.

History of Europe during the FRENCH REVOLUTION, 1789-95. From the Secret Archives of Germany. By Professor VON SYBEL. 4 vols. 8vo, 48s.

English Battles and Sieges of the Peninsular War. By Sir W. NAPIER. Portrait. Post 8vo, 9s.

The Story of the Battle of WATERLOO. By Rev. G. R. GLEIG. Post 8vo, 3s. 6d.

Wellington's Civil and Political Despatches, 1819-1831. Edited by his

Wellington's Supplementary Despatches and Correspondence. Edited by his SON. 15 vols. 8vo, 20s. each. An index. 8vo, 20s.

Campaigns at Washington and NEW ORLEANS. By Rev. G. R. GLEIG. Post 8vo, 2s.

Sir Robert Sale's Brigade in AFFGHANISTAN. By Rev. G. R. GLEIG, Post 8vo, 2s.

French in Algiers; the Soldier of the Foreign Legion—and Prisoners of Abd-el-Kadir. Translated by Lady DUFF GORDON. Post 8vo, 2s.

History of the Fall of the Jesuits in the Nineteenth Century. From the French. Post 8vo, 2s.

English in Spain; or, the Story of the Civil War between Christinos and Carlists in 1834, 1840. By Major F. DUNCAN, R.A. With plates. 8vo, 16s.

Personal Narrative of Events in China during Lord Elgin's Second Embassy. By H. B. LOCH. Illustrations. Post 8vo, 9s.

Origin and History of the GRENADIER GUARDS, from original documents, &c. By Gen. Sir F. W. HAMILTON. Illustrations. 3 vols. 8vo, 63s.

History of the Royal Artillery. Compiled from the original Records. By Major F. DUNCAN, R.A. Portraits. 2 vols. 8vo, 18s.

The Huguenots in England & Ireland, their Settlements, Churches, and Industries. By SAMUEL SMILES. Crown 8vo, 7s. 6d.

Historical Memorials of Westminster Abbey, from its Foundation to the Present Time. By Dean STANLEY. Illustrations. 8vo, 15s.

Notices of the Historic Persons buried in the Chapel of St. Peter, in the Tower of London, with an Account of the Discovery of the Remains of Queen Anne Boleyn. By DOYNE C. BELL. Illustrations. Crown 8vo, 14s.

Handbook to St. Paul's Cathedral. By Dean MILMAN Illustrations. Cr. 8vo, 10s. 6d.

Annals of Winchcombe and Sudeley. By EMMA DENT. With Plates. 4to, 42s.

English Studies of the late Rev. J. S. BREWER. CONTENTS: New Sources of English History. Green's Short History of the English People. The Royal Supremacy. Hatfield House. The Stuarts. Shakspeare. How to Study English History. Ancient Lon-

BIOGRAPHY AND MEMOIRS.

Ecclesiastical and Missionary.

Dictionary of Christian Biography, Literature, Sects, and Doctrines, from the time of the Apostles to the Age of Charlemagne. Edited by Dr. WM. SMITH and Professor WACE. Vols. I. & II. Medium 8vo, 31s. 6d. each.

Life of St. Hugh of Avalon, Bishop of Lincoln. By Canon PERRY. Portrait. Post 8vo, 10s. 6d.

The Life and Times of St. John Chrysostom. A Sketch of the Church and the Empire in the Fourth Century. By Rev. W. R. W. STEPHENS, M.A. With Portrait. 8vo, 12s.

Personal Life of David Livingstone, LL.D., D.C.L. From his unpublished Journals and Correspondence. By WILLIAM G. BLAIKIE, D.D. With Portrait and Map. 8vo, 15s.

Memoir of William Ellis, the Missionary. By his SON. Portrait. 8vo, 10s. 6d.

Memoir of Bishop Milman, Metropolitan of India. With a Selection from his Letters. By his SISTER. Map. 8vo, 12s.

Life of Bishop SUMNER, during an Episcopate of Forty Years. By Rev. G. H. SUMNER. Portrait. 8vo, 14s.

Life of Samuel Wilberforce, Bishop of Oxford and Winchester. By Canon ASHWELL. Portraits. Vol. I. 8vo, 15s.

Life of John Wilson, D.D. (of Bombay); Fifty Years a Philanthropist and Scholar in the East. By GEORGE SMITH. Illustrations. Post 8vo, 9s.

Political and Social.

Memoir of the Public Life of Right Hon. John Charles Herries during the reigns of George III., George IV., William IV., and Victoria. By his Son, ED. HERRIES, C.B. 2 vols. 8vo, 24s.

Monographs : Personal and So-cial. By Lord HOUGHTON. Portraits. Crown 8vo, 10s. 6d.

Self-Help. With Illustrations of Conduct and Perseverance. By Dr. SMILES. Post 8vo, 6s. ; or in French, 5s.

Life and Death of John of BARNEVELD, Advocate of Holland. With a View of the Primary Causes and Movements of "The Thirty Years' War." By J. L. MOTLEY. Illustrations. 2 vols. post 8vo, 12s.

Rheinsberg ; Memorials of Frederick the Great and Prince Henry of Prussia. By ANDREW HAMILTON. 2 vols. crown 8vo, 21s.

Life and Correspondence of Dr. Arnold of Rugby. By Dean STANLEY. Portrait. 2 vols. cr. 8vo. 12s.

Memoir of Edward, Catherine, and Mary Stanley. By Dean STANLEY. Post 8vo, 9s.

Memoirs of Sir Fowell Buxton, with Extracts from his Correspondence. By CHARLES BUXTON. Portrait. 8vo, 16s. ; or post 8vo, 5s.

King William IV.'s Corre-spondence with the late EARL GREY, 1830-1832. Edited by his Son. 2 vols. 8vo, 30s.

Life of Theodore Hook. By J. G. LOCKHART. Fcap. 8vo, 1s,

Memoir of Hon. Julian Fane. By Lord LYTTON. Portrait. Post 8vo, 5s.

Selection from the Familiar Correspondence of Sir CHARLES BELL. Portrait. Post 8vo, 5s.

Madame de Staël, a Study of her Life and Times : the First Revolution and the First Empire. By Dr. A. STEVENS. With portraits. 2 vols. Crown 8vo, 24s.

Adventures on the Road to Paris, 1813-14. From the Autobiography of HENRY STEFFENS. Post 8vo, 2s.

Sketches of Eminent Statesmen and Writers, with other Essays. Reprinted from the *Quarterly Review*, with Additions and Corrections. By A. HAYWARD, Q.C. 2 vols. 8vo, 28s. CONTENTS :—Thiers, Bismarck, Cavour, Metternich, Montalembert, Melbourne, Wellesley, Byron and Tennyson, Venice, St. Simon, Sevigné, Du Deffand, Holland House, Strawberry Hill.

Life of William Pitt. By EARL STANHOPE. Portraits. 3 vols. 8vo, 36s.

Brief Memoir of the Princess CHARLOTTE OF WALES. By Lady ROSE WEIGALL. Portrait. Crown 8vo, 8s. 6d.

Life of William Wilberforce. By his SON. Portrait. Post 8vo, 6s.

Memoirs ; By Sir Robert Peel. Edited by Earl STANHOPE and Lord CARDWELL. 2 vols. post 8vo, 15s.

Mrs. Grote ; a Sketch. By LADY EASTLAKE. Crown 8vo, 6s.

Literary and Artistic.

Dictionary of Greek & Roman BIOGRAPHY and MYTHOLOGY. Edited by Dr. WM. SMITH. 3 vols. 8vo, 84s.

Personal Life of George Grote, the Historian of Greece. Compiled from Family Documents. By Mrs. GROTE. Portrait. 8vo, 12s.

Life of Albert Durer. With a History of his Art. By MORITZ, THAUSING. Illustrations. 2 vols. 8vo.

Michel Angelo, Sculptor, Paint- er, and Architect ; including Documents from the Buonarroti Archives, now for the first time published. By C. HEATH WILSON. Plates. Royal 8vo, 26s.

Titian : his Life and Times, with some Account of his Family from Unpublished Documents. By J. A. CROWE and G. B. CAVALCASELLE. Illustrations. 2 vols. 8vo, 42s.

The Early Life of Jonathan SWIFT. By JOHN FORSTER. 1667-1711. Portrait. 8vo, 15s.

Life of Dr. Samuel Johnson. By JAMES BOSWELL. Edited by J. W. CROKER. With Notes by Lord Stowell, Sir Walter Scott, Sir James Mackintosh, Disraeli, Markland, Lockhart, &c. Medium 8vo, 12s.

Johnson's Lives of the ENGLISH POETS. Edited by CUNNINGHAM. 3 vols. 8vo. 22s. 6d.

Life of Jonathan Swift. By HENRY CRAIK, B.A. 8vo.

Life and Letters of Lord Byron With Notices of his Life. By THOMAS MOORE. Portraits. Royal 8vo, 7s. 6d,: or 6 vols. fcap. 8vo, 18s.

Life of Lord Byron, with an Essay on his Place in Literature. By CARL ELZE. Portrait. 8vo, 16s.

Lives of the British Poets. By THOMAS CAMPBELL. Post 8vo, 3s. 6d.

Memoir of Sir Charles East- LAKE. By Lady EASTLAKE. Prefixed to his Contributions to the Literature of the Fine Arts. 2 vols. 8vo, 24s.

Popular Biographies—BUNYAN, CROMWELL, CLIVE, CONDE, DRAKE, MUNRO. See *Home and Colonial Library,* p. 30.

Life and Times of Sir Joshua Reynolds. With Notes of his Contemporaries. By C. R. LESLIE and TOM TAYLOR. Portraits. 2 vols. 8vo. 42s.

Lives of the Early Italian Painters ; illustrating the Progress of Painting in Italy from Cimabue to Bassano. By Mrs. JAMESON. Illustrations. Post 8vo, 12s.

Lives of the Early Flemish Painters, and Notices of their Works. By CROWE and CAVALCASELLE. Illustrations. Post 8vo, 7s. 6d. ; or large paper, 15s.

Life of Horace. By Dean MILMAN. 8vo, 9s.

Life and Works of Sir CHARLES BARRY, R.A. By Canon BARRY, D.D. Illustrations. 8vo, 15s.

Naval and Military.

Lives of the Warriors of the 17th Century. By Sir EDWARD CUST, D.C.L. 6 vols. crown 8vo, 50s.

Character, Actions, and Writ- ings of Wellington. By JULES MAUREL. Fcap. 8vo, 1s. 6d.

Napoleon at Fontainbleau and Elba. Being a Journal of Occurrences and Notes of Conversations, &c. By Sir NEIL CAMPBELL. Portrait. 8vo, 15s.

Letters and Journals of the EARL of ELGIN, Governor-General of India. Edited by THEODORE WALROND. 8vo, 14s.

Memoirs of the Duke of Sal- danha : Soldier and Statesman. With Selections from his Correspondence. By CONDE DA CARNOTA. With Portrait and Maps. 2 vols. 8vo, 32s.

Memoir of Sir John Burgoyne. By Sir FRANCIS HEAD. Post 8vo, 1s.

Autobiography of Sir John Barrow, Bart. Portrait. 8vo, 16s.

The Life, Letters, and Journals of F.-M. Sir Wm. Maynard Gomm, G.C.B., Commander-in-Chief in India, Constable of the Tower, and Colonel of the Coldstream Guards, 1784-1879. By F. C. CARR GOMM. With Portrait. 8vo.

Private Diary of General Sir ROBERT WILSON : during Missions and Employments with the European Armies in 1812-1814. Map. 2 vols. 8vo, 26s.

Reminiscences of Forty Years' SERVICE IN INDIA. By Lieut.-Gen. Sir GEORGE LAWRENCE. Including the Cabul Disasters, and Captivities in Affghanistan. Crown 8vo, 10s. 6d.

Life of Belisarius. By Lord MAHON. Post 8vo, 10s. 6d.

Legal and Scientific.

Lives of the Lord Chancellors and KEEPERS of the GREAT SEAL of ENGLAND, from the Earliest Times to the death of Lord Eldon, 1838. By Lord CAMPBELL. 10 vols. post 8vo, 6s. each.

Lives of the Chief Justices of ENGLAND, from the Norman Conquest till the death of Lord Tenterden. By Lord CAMPBELL. 4 vols. cr. 8vo, 6s. each.

Life and Letters of Lord Campbell, Lord Chief-Justice, and afterwards Lord Chancellor of England. Based on his Autobiography, Journals, and Correspondence. Edited by his Daughter, the Hon. Mrs. HARDCASTLE. With Portrait. 2 vols. 8vo, 30s.

Life of Lord Chancellor Eldon. By HORACE TWISS. Portrait. 2 vols. post 8vo, 21s.

Biographia Juridica. A Biographical Dictionary of the Judges of England, from the Conquest to 1870. By EDWARD FOSS. Medium 8vo, 21s.

Lives of the Engineers. From the Earliest Times to the Death of the Stephensons. With an Account of the Steam Engine and Railway Locomotive. By SAMUEL SMILES, LL.D. 9 Portraits and 340 Woodcuts, 5 vols. crown 8vo, 7s. 6d. each.

Industrial Biography : or Iron-Workers and Tool-Makers. By SAMUEL SMILES. Post 8vo, 6s.

Life of Thomas Edward (Shoemaker, of Banff), Scotch Naturalist.' By SAMUEL SMILES. Illustrated. Crown 8vo, 10s. 6d.

Life of Robert Dick (Baker, of Thurso), Geologist and Botanist. By S. SMILES. Illustrations. Crown 8vo, 12s.

Memoir of Sir Roderick Murchison. With Notices of his Contemporaries, and a Sketch of Palæozoic Geology in Britain. By Professor GEIKIE. Portraits. 2 vols. 8vo, 30s.

Memoir and Correspondence of Caroline Herschel, Sister of Sir William and Aunt of Sir John Herschel. Portraits. Crown 8vo, 7s. 6d.

Personal Recollections, from Early Life to old Age. By MARY SOMERVILLE. Portrait. Crown 8vo, 12s.

Life of Erasmus Darwin. By CHARLES DARWIN. With a Study of his Scientific Works by Dr. KRAUSE. Portrait, 8vo, 7s. 6d.

GEOGRAPHY, VOYAGES, AND TRAVELS.

The East Indies, China, &c.

India in 1880. By Sir RICHARD TEMPLE, Bart. 8vo.

Students' Manual of the Geography of India. By GEORGE SMITH, LL.D. Post 8vo.

Travels of Marco Polo. A new English version. Illustrated with copious Notes. By Col. YULE, C.B. Illustrations. 2 vols. 8vo, 63s.

A Visit to High Tartary, Yarkand, and KASHGAR, and over the Karakorum Pass. By ROBERT SHAW. Illustrations. 8vo, 16s.

New Japan ; The Land of the Rising Sun. Its Annals during the past twenty years ; recording the remarkable progress of the Japanese in western civilisation. By SAMUEL MOSSMAN. Map. 8vo, 15s.

A Cruise in the Eastern Seas, from the Corea to the River Amur. With an Account of Russian Siberia, Japan, and Formosa. By Capt. B. W. BAX. Illustrations. Crown 8vo, 12s.

British Burma and its People : Sketches of Native Manners, Customs, and Religion. By Capt. FORBES. Crown 8vo, 10s. 6d.

The River of Golden Sand. Narrative of a Journey through China to Burmah. By Capt. WM. GILL, R.E. With a Preface by Col. YULE. With Map. 2 vols. 8vo, 30s.

The Satsuma Rebellion. An Episode of Modern Japanese History. By AUGUSTUS H. MOUNSEY. Map. Crown 8vo, 10s. 6d.

Letters from Madras. By a LADY. Post 8vo, 2s.

Journey to the Source of the River Oxus, by the Indus, Kabul, and Badakhshan. By Capt. WOOD. With the Geography of the Valley of the Oxus, by Col. YULE. Map. 8vo, 12s.

Thirteen Years' Residence at the Court of China, in the Service of the Emperor. By Father RIPA. Post 8vo, 2s.

Popular Account of the Manners and Customs of India. By Rev. CHAS. ACLAND. Post 8vo, 2s.

Nineveh and its Remains. With an Account of a Visit to the Chaldean Christians of Kurdistan, and the Yezedis or Devil Worshippers, &c. By Sir H. LAYARD. Illustrations. 2 vols. 8vo, 36s.; or post 8vo, 7s. 6d.

Nineveh and Babylon; a Narrative of a Second Expedition to the Ruins of Assyria, with Travels in Armenia. By Sir H. LAYARD. Illustrations. 8vo, 21s.; or post 8vo, 7s. 6d.

Unbeaten Tracks in Japan. Travels of a Lady in the Interior, including Visits to the Aborigines of Yezo and the Shrines of Nikko and Isé. By ISABELLA L. BIRD. Map and Illustrations. 2 vols. crown 8vo, 24s.

Japan; Its History, Traditions, and Religions, with the Narrative of a Visit in 1879. By Sir E. J. REED, K.C.B. With Map and Illustrations. 2 vols. 8vo, 28s.

Africa—Egypt.

A Popular Account of Dr. Livingstone's Travels and Adventures in South Africa, 1840-56. Illustrations. Post 8vo, 7s. 6d.

A Popular Account of Dr. Livingstone's Expedition to the Zambesi, Lakes Shirwa and Nyassa, 1858-64. Illustrations. Post 8vo, 7s. 6d.

Dr. Livingstone's Last Journals in CENTRAL AFRICA, 1865-73. With a Narrative of his last moments and sufferings. By Rev. HORACE WALLER. Illustrations. 2 vols. 8vo, 15s.

Livingstonia; Journal of Adventures in Exploring Lake Nyassa, and Establishing a Settlement there. By E. D. YOUNG, R.N. Map. Post 8vo, 7s. 6d.

Explorations in Equatorial Africa, with Accounts of the Savage Tribes, the Gorilla, &c. By P. DU CHAILLU. Illustrations. 8vo, 21s.

Journey to Ashango Land, and Further Penetration into Equatorial Africa. By P. B. DU CHAILLU. Illustrations. 8vo, 21s.

Adventures and Discoveries among the Lakes and Mountains of Eastern Africa. By Captain ELTON and H. B. COTTERILL. With Map and Illustrations. 8vo, 21s.

Wanderings South of the Atlas Mountains, in the Great Sahara. By Canon TRISTRAM. Illustrations. Post 8vo, 15s.

Six Months in Ascension. An Unscientific Account of a Scientific Expedition. By Mrs. GILL. Map. Crown 8vo, 9s.

Five Years' Adventures in the far Interior of S. Africa with the Wild Beasts of the Forests. By R. GORDON CUMMING. Woodcuts. Post 8vo, 6s.

Recollections of Fighting and Hunting in South Africa, 1834-67. By Gen. Sir JOHN BISSET, C.B. Illustrations. Crown 8vo, 14s.

Nile Gleanings: The Ethnology, History, and Art of Ancient Egypt, as revealed by Paintings and Bas-Reliefs. By H. VILLIERS STUART. With 50 coloured Illustrations. Royal 8vo, 31s.6d.

The Country of the Moors. A Journey from Tripoli in Barbary to the Holy City of Kairwan. By EDWARD RAE. Illustrations. Crown 8vo, 24s.

A Residence in Sierra Leone, described from a Journal kept on the Spot. By a LADY. Post 8vo, 3s. 6d.

British Mission to Abyssinia. With Notices of the Countries traversed from Massowah, through the Soodan, and back to Magdala. By HORMUZD RASSAM. Illustrations. 2 vols. 30s.

Sport in Abyssinia. By Earl of MAYO. Illustrations. Crown 8vo, 12s.

Abyssinia during a Three Years' Residence. By MANSFIELD PARKYNS. Woodcuts. Post 8vo, 7s. 6d.

Adventures in the Libyan Desert. By B. ST. JOHN. Post 8vo, 2s.

Travels in Egypt, Nubia, Syria, and the Holy Land. By Captains IRBY and MANGLES. Post 8vo, 2s.

The Cradle of the Blue Nile. A Visit to the Court of King John of Ethiopia. By E. A. DE COSSON. Illustrations. 2 vols. post 8vo, 21s.

An Account of the Manners and Customs of the Modern Egyptians. By EDWARD WM. LANE. Woodcuts. 2 vols. post 8vo, 12s.

Madagascar Revisited; Describing the Persecutions endured by the Christian Converts. By Rev. W. ELLIS. Illustrations, 8vo, 16s.

Mediterranean—Greece,
Turkey in Europe.

Travels in Asia Minor: With Antiquarian Researches and Discoveries, and Illustrations of Biblical Literature and Archæology. By H. VAN LENNEP. Illustrations. 2 vols. post 8vo, 24s.

Ilios; a History of the City and Country of the Trojans, including all Recent Discoveries on the Site of Troy and the Troad in 1871-3 and 1878-9. With an Autobiography. By Dr. SCHLIEMANN. Illustrations. Imperial 8vo, 50s.

Discoveries on the Sites of Ancient Mycenæ and Tiryns. By Dr. SCHLIEMANN. With a Preface by the Right Hon. W. E. GLADSTONE, M.P. Illustrations. Medium 8vo, 50s.

Cyprus; its Ancient Cities, Tombs, and Temples. A Narrative of Researches and Excavations during Ten Years' Residence in that Island. By LOUIS P. DI CESNOLA. Illustrations. Medium 8vo, 50s.

Bulgaria before the War: a Seven Years' Experience of European Turkey and its Inhabitants. By H. C. BARKLEY. Post 8vo, 10s. 6d.

Between the Danube and the Black Sea, or, Five Years in Bulgaria. By H. C. BARKLEY. Post 8vo, 10s. 6d.

Researches in the Highlands of Turkey. With Notes on the Classical Superstitions of the Modern Greek. By Rev. H. F. TOZER. Illustrations. 2 vols. crown 8vo, 24s.

Lectures on the Geography of Greece. By Rev. H. F. TOZER. Map. Post 8vo, 9s.

Twenty Years' Residence among the Bulgarians, Greeks, Albanians, Turks, and Armenians. By a Consul's Wife. 2 vols. crown 8vo, 21s.

Reminiscences of Athens and the Morea, during Travels in Greece. By Lord CARNARVON. Crown 8vo, 7s. 6d.

Asia, Syria, Holy Land.

England and Russia in the East. A Series of Papers on the Political and Geographical Condition of Central Asia. By Sir H. RAWLINSON. Map. 8vo, 12s.

The Caucasus, Persia and Tur- key in Asia. A journey to Tabreez, Kurdistan, down the Tigris and Euphrates to Nineveh and Babylon. and across the Desert to Palmyra. By Baron THIELMANN. Illustrations. 2 vols. post 8vo, 18s.

Sketches of the Manners and Customs of Persia. By Sir JOHN MALCOLM. Post 8vo, 3s. 6d.

Journal of Researches in the Holy Land in 1838 and 1852. With Historical Illustrations. By EDWARD ROBINSON, D.D. Maps. 3 vols. 8vo, 42s.

Sinai and Palestine; in Con- nection with their History. By Dean STANLEY. Plans. 8vo, 14s.

The Bible in the Holy Land. Extracts from the above Work. Woodcuts. Fcap. 8vo, 2s. 6d.

Damascus, Palmyra, Lebanon; with Travels among the Giant Cities of Bashan and the Hauran. By Rev. J. L. PORTER. Woodcuts. Post 8vo, 7s. 6d.

The Jordan, the Nile, Red Sea, Lake of Gennesareth, etc. The Cruise of the Rob Roy in Palestine, Egypt, and the Waters of Damascus. By JOHN MACGREGOR. Illustrations. Post 8vo, 7s. 6d.

The Land of Moab. Travels and Discoveries on the East Side of the Dead Sea and the Jordan. By Canon TRISTRAM. Illustrations. Cr. 8vo, 15s.

The Bedouins of the Euphrates Valley. By Lady ANNE BLUNT. With some account of the Arab Horses. Illustrations. 2 vols. crown 8vo, 24s.

A Pilgrimage to Nejd, the Cradle of the Arab Race, and a Visit to the Court of the Arab Emir. By Lady ANNE BLUNT. With Illustrations from the Author's Drawings. 2 vols. post 8vo.

Australia, Polynesia, &c.

Discoveries in New Guinea. A Cruise in Polynesia, and Visits to Torres Straits, etc. By Capt. MORESBY, Illustrations. 8vo, 15s.

The Gardens of the Sun; or a Naturalist's Journal on the Mountains and in the Forests and Swamps of Borneo and the Sulu Archipelago. By F. W. BURBIDGE. With Illustrations. Crown 8vo, 14s.

A Boy's Voyage Round the World. Edited by SAMUEL SMILES. Woodcuts. Small 8vo, 6s.

Hawaiian Archipelago; Six Months among the Palm Groves, Coral Reefs, and Volcanoes of the SANDWICH ISLANDS. By ISABELLA BIRD. Illustrations. Crown 8vo, 7s. 6d.

Ride Through the Disturbed Districts of NEW ZEALAND to Lake Taupo at the time of the Rebellion; with notes of the South Sea Islands. By Hon. H. MEADE. Illustrations. 8vo, 12s.

Typee and Omoo; or the Marquesas and South Sea Islanders. By H. MELVILLE. 2 vols. post 8vo, 7s.

Notes and Sketches of New South Wales. By Mrs. MEREDITH. Post 8vo, 2s.

Mutineers of the "Bounty," and their Descendants; with their Settlements in Pitcairn and Norfolk Islands. By Lady BELCHER. Illustrations. Post 8vo, 12s.

America, West Indies, Arctic Regions.

A Lady's Life in the Rocky Mountains. By ISABELLA BIRD. Illustrations. Post 8vo, 10s. 6d.

Mexico and the Rocky Mountains. By GEORGE F. RUXTON. Post 8vo, 3s. 6d.

Pioneering in South Brazil. Three Years of Forest and Prairie Life in the Province of Paraña. By T. P. BIGG WITHER. Illustrations. 2 vols. crown 8vo, 24s.

The Naturalist on the River AMAZONS, with Adventures during Eleven Years of Travel. By H. W. BATES. Illustrations. Post 8vo, 7s. 6d.

Voyage up the River Amazons, and a visit to Para. By WILLIAM H. EDWARDS. Post 8vo, 2s.

Voyage of a Naturalist round the World. By CHARLES DARWIN. Post 8vo, 9s.

The Patagonians; a Year's Wandering over Untrodden Ground from the Straits of Magellan to the Rio Negro. By Capt. MUSTERS. Illustrations. Post 8vo, 7s. 6d.

Voyage of the "Fox" in the ARCTIC SEAS, and the Discovery of the Fate of Sir John Franklin and his Companions. By Sir LEOPOLD M'CLINTOCK. Illustrations. Post 8vo, 7s. 6d.

Perils of the Polar Seas. True Stories of Arctic Discovery and Adventure. By Mrs. CHISHOLM. Illustrations. Small 8vo, 6s.

Communistic Societies of the UNITED STATES; their Religious Creeds, Social Practices, and Present Condition. By CHARLES NORDHOFF. Illustrations. 8vo, 15s.

Europe.

Etchings on the Mosel: a Series of Twenty Plates, with Descriptive Letterpress. By ERNEST GEORGE. Folio, 42s.

Etchings from the Loire and South of France. In a Series of Twenty Plates, with Descriptive Text. By ERNEST GEORGE. Folio, 42s.

Field Paths and Green Lanes. Being Country Walks, chiefly in Surrey and Sussex. By LOUIS J. JENNINGS. Illustrations. Post 8vo, 10s. 6d.

Rambles among the Hills; or Walks on the Peak of Derbyshire and in the South Downs. By L. J. JENNINGS. With Illustrations. Post 8vo, 12s.

Twenty Years in the Wild

The Ascent of the Matterhorn. By EDWARD WHYMPER. 100 Illustrations. Medium 8vo, 10s. 6d.

Siberia in Europe; a Naturalist's Voyage to the Valley of the Petchora in N.E. Russia. By HENRY SEEBOHM. With Map and Illustrations. Crown 8vo, 14s.

A Month in Norway. By J. G. HOLLWAY. Fcap. 8vo, 2s.

Letters from the Shores of the Baltic. By a LADY. Post 8vo, 2s.

Letters from High Latitudes: An Account of a Yacht Voyage to Iceland, Jan Mayen, and Spitzbergen. By Lord DUFFERIN. Illustrations. Crown 8vo, 7s. 6d.

The Bible in Spain; or the Journeys, Adventures, and Imprisonments of an Englishman in the Peninsula. By GEORGE BORROW. Post 8vo, 5s.

The Gypsies of Spain; their Manners, Customs, Religion, and Language. By GEO. BORROW. Post 8vo, 5s.

Gatherings from Spain. By RICHARD FORD. Post 8vo, 3s. 6d.

Bubbles from the Brunnen of NASSAU. By Sir FRANCIS HEAD. Woodcuts. Post 8vo, 7s. 6d.

General Geography.

A History of Ancient Geography among the Greeks and Romans, from the Earliest Ages till the Fall of the Roman Empire. By E. H. BUNBURY. 2 vols. 8vo, 42s.

Art of Travel; or Hints on the Shifts and Contrivances available in Wild Countries. By FRANCIS GALTON. Woodcuts. Post 8vo, 7s. 6d.

Dictionary of Greek and Roman Geography. Edited by Dr. WM. SMITH. 2 vols. royal 8vo, 56s.

Atlas of Ancient Geography Biblical and Classical, compiled under the superintendence of Dr. WM. SMITH and Mr. GEORGE GROVE. Folio, £6 : 6s.

Student's Manual of Ancient Geography. By Canon BEVAN, M.A. Woodcuts. Post 8vo, 7s. 6d.

Student's Manual of Modern Geography, Mathematical, Physical, and Descriptive. By Canon BEVAN, M.A. Woodcuts. Post 8vo, 7s. 6d.

A School Manual of Modern Geography, Physical and Political. By JOHN RICHARDSON, M.A. Post 8vo, 5s.

A Smaller Manual of Modern Geography. Physical and Political. Post 8vo, 2s. 6d.

Journal of the Royal Geogra-

HANDBOOKS FOR TRAVELLERS.

Foreign.

Handbook — Travel Talk ;—
English, French, German, and Italian.
16mo, 3s. 6d.

Handbook—Holland and Belgium. Maps and Plans. Post 8vo, 6s.

Handbook — North Germany ;
the Rhine, the Black Forest, the Hartz, Thüringerwald, Saxon Switzerland, Rügen the Giant Mountains, Taunus, Odenwald, Elass, and Lothringen. Map and Plans. Post 8vo, 10s.

Handbook—Switzerland ; The
Alps of Savoy, and Piedmont. Maps and Plans. In Two Parts. Post 8vo, 10s.

Handbook — South Germany ;
Tyrol, Bavaria, Austria, Salzburg, Styria, Hungary, and the Danube from Ulm to the Black Sea. Maps and Plans. Post 8vo, 10s.

Handbook—France. Part I.
Normandy, Brittany, The French Alps, the Loire, Seine, Garonne, and Pyrenees. Maps and Plans. Post 8vo, 7s. 6d.

Handbook—France. Part II.
Auvergne, the Cevennes, Burgundy, the Rhone and Saone, Provence, Nimes, Arles, Marseilles, the French Alps, Alsace, Lorraine, Champagne, etc. Maps and Plans. Post 8vo, 7s. 6d.

Handbook—Paris and its Environs. Maps and Plans. 16mo, 3s. 6d.

Handbook — Mediterranean :
Its principal Cities, Seaports, Harbours, and Borderlands. With nearly 50 Maps and Plans. Post 8vo.

Handbook—Algeria and Tunis ;
Algiers, Constantin, Oran, the Atlas Range, etc. Maps and Plans. Post 8vo, 10s.

Handbook — Spain ; Madrid,
The Castiles, Basque, Asturias, Galicia, Estremadura, Andalusia, Ronda, Granada, Murcia, Valencia, Catalonia, Aragon, Navarre, Balearic Islands. Maps and Plans. Post 8vo, 20s.

Handbook—Portugal ; Lisbon,
Oporto, Cintra, etc. Map. Post 8vo, 12s.

Handbook—North Italy ; Piedmont, Nice, Lombardy, Venice, Parma, Modena, and Romagna. Maps and Plans. Post 8vo, 10s.

Handbook—Central Italy ; Tuscany, Florence, Lucca, Umbria, The Marches, and the Patrimony of St. Peter Maps and Plans. Post 8vo, 10s.

The Cicerone ; or, Art Guide
to Painting in Italy. By Dr. JACOB BURCKHARDT. Post 8vo, 6s.

Handbook—Rome and its Environs. Map and Plans. Post 8vo.

Handbook—South Italy ; Two
Sicilies, Naples, Pompeii, Herculaneum, Vesuvius, Abruzzi. Maps and Plans. Post 8vo, 10s.

Handbook—Egypt ; the Nile,
Egypt, Nubia, Alexandria, Cairo, The Pyramids, Thebes, Suez Canal, Peninsula of Sinai, The Oases, the Fyoom. Map and Plans. In Two Parts. Post 8vo, 15s.

Handbook — Greece ; Ionian
Islands, Athens, Peloponnesus, Ægæan Sea, Albania, Thessaly, and Macedonia. Maps and Plans. Post 8vo.

Handbook — Turkey in Asia ;
Constantinople, The Bosphorus, Dardanelles, Brousa, Plain of Troy, Crete, Cyprus, Smyrna, Ephesus, the Seven Churches, Coasts of the Black Sea, Armenia, Mesopotamia. Maps and Plans. Post 8vo, 15s.

Handbook—Denmark ; Sleswig-Holstein, Copenhagen, Jutland, Iceland. Maps and Plans. Post 8vo, 6s.

Handbook—Sweden ; Stockholm, Upsala, Gothenburg, the Shores of the Baltic, etc. Maps and Plans. Post 8vo.

Handbook—Norway ; Christiania, Bergen, Trondhjem, the Fjelds, Iceland. Maps and Plans. Post 8vo, 9s.

Handbook—Russia ; St. Petersburg, Moscow, Poland, Finland, The Crimea, Caucasus, Siberia, and Central Asia. Maps and Plans. Post 8vo, 18s.

Handbook — Bombay. Map.
Post 8vo, 12s.

Handbook — Madras. Maps
and Plans. Post 8vo, 15s.

Handbook—Holy Land ; Syria,
Palestine, Sinai, Edom and the Syrian Deserts, Jerusalem, Petra, Damascus, and Palmyra. Maps and Plans. Post 8vo, 20s.

Travelling Map of Palestine,
Mounted and in a Case. 12s.

English.

Handbook—London as it is.
Map and Plans. 16mo, 3s. 6d.

Handbook—Environs of London, within 20 miles round of the Metropolis. 2 vols. Post 8vo, 21s.

Handbook—England & Wales.
Condensed in one Volume. Forming a Companion to Bradshaw's Railway Tables. Map. Post 8vo, 10s.

Handbook—Eastern Counties;
Chelmsford, Harwich, Colchester, Maldon, Cambridge, Ely, Newmarket, Bury, Ipswich, Woodbridge, Felixstowe, Lowestoft, Norwich, Yarmouth, Cromer. Map and Plans. Post 8vo, 12s.

Handbook — Kent ; Canterbury, Dover, Ramsgate, Rochester, Chatham. Map and Plans. Post 8vo, 7s. 6d.

Handbook—Sussex ; Brighton, Eastbourne, Chichester, Hastings, Lewes, Arundel, etc. Map. Post 8vo, 6s.

Handbook—Surrey and Hants;
Kingston, Croydon, Reigate, Guildford, Dorking, Boxhill, Winchester, Southampton, New Forest, Portsmouth, Isle of Wight. Maps and Plans. Post 8vo, 10s. •

Handbook—Berks, Bucks, and Oxon ; Windsor, Eton, Reading, Aylesbury, Henley, Oxford, Blenheim, and the Thames. Map and Plans. Post 8vo.

Handbook—Wilts, Dorset, and Somerset ; Salisbury, Stonehenge, Chippenham, Weymouth, Sherborne, Wells, Bath, Bristol, etc. Map. Post 8vo, 10s.

Handbook—Devon ; Exeter, Ilfracombe, Linton, Sidmouth, Dawlish, Teignmouth, Plymouth, Devonport, Torquay. Maps and Plans. Post 8vo, 7s. 6d.

Handbook—Cornwall ; Launceston, Penzance, Falmouth, The Lizard, Land's End. Maps. Post 8vo, 6s.

Handbook—Gloucester, Hereford, and Worcester ; Cirencester, Cheltenham, Stroud, Tewkesbury, Leominster, Ross, Malvern, Kidderminster, Dudley, Evesham. Map. Post 8vo.

Handbook — North Wales ;
Bangor, Carnarvon, Beaumaris, Snowdon, Llanberis, Dolgelly, Cader Idris, Conway. Map. Post 8vo, 7s.

Handbook — South Wales ;
Monmouth, Llandaff, Merthyr, Vale of Neath, Pembroke, Carmarthen, Tenby, Swansea, the Wye. Map. Post 8vo, 7s.

Handbook—Derby, Notts, Leicester, and Stafford ; Matlock, Bakewell, Chatsworth, The Peak, Buxton, Hardwick, Dovedale, Ashborne, Southwell, Mansfield, Retford, Burton, Belvoir, Melton Mowbray, Wolverhampton, Lichfield, Tamworth. Map. Post 8vo, 9s.

Handbook—Shropshire & Cheshire, Shrewsbury, Ludlow, Bridgnorth, Oswestry, Chester, Crewe, Alderley, Stockport, Birkenhead. Maps and Plans. Post 8vo, 6s.

Handbook—Lancashire; Warrington, Bury, Manchester, Liverpool, Burnley, Clitheroe, Bolton, Blackburn, Wigan, Preston, Rochdale, Lancaster, Southport, Blackpool. Map. Post 8vo, 7s. 6d.

Handbook—Northamptonshire and Rutland ; Northampton, Peterborough, Towcester, Daventry, Market Harborough, Kettering, Wallingborough, Thrapston, Stamford, Uppingham, Oakham. Maps. Post 8vo, 7s. 6d.

Handbook—Yorkshire ; Doncaster, Hull, Selby, Beverley, Scarborough, Whitby, Horrogate, Ripon, Leeds, Wakefield, Bradford, Halifax, Huddersfield, Sheffield. Map and Plans. Post 8vo, 12s.

Handbook — Durham and Northumberland ; Newcastle, Darlington, Bishop Auckland, Stockton, Hartlepool, Sunderland, Shields, Berwick, Tynemouth, Alnwick. Map. Post 8vo, 9s.

Handbook—Westmorland and Cumberland ; Lancaster, Furness Abbey, Ambleside, Kendal, Windermere, Coniston, Keswick, Grasmere, Ulswater, Carlisle, Cockermouth, Penrith, Appleby. Map. Post 8vo.

Travelling Map of the Lake District, 3s. 6d.

Handbook—Scotland ; Edinburgh, Melrose, Abbotsford, Glasgow, Dumfries, Galloway, Ayr, Stirling, Arran, The Clyde, Oban, Inverary, Loch Lomond, Loch Katrine and Trossachs, Caledonian Canal, Inverness, Perth, Dundee, Aberdeen, Braemar, Skye, Caithness, Ross, and Sutherland. Maps and Plans. Post 8vo, 9s.

Handbook—Ireland ; Dublin, Belfast, The Giant's Causeway, Bantry, Glengariff, etc., Donegal, Galway, Wexford, Cork, Limerick, Waterford, Killarney. Maps and Plans. Post 8vo, 10s.

Handbook—Herts, Beds, Warwick. Map. Post 8vo. [*In preparation.*

Handbook — Huntingdon and Lincoln. Map. Post 8vo.
[*In preparation.*

ENGLISH CATHEDRALS.

Handbook — Southern Cathedrals. Winchester, Salisbury, Exeter, Wells, Rochester, Canterbury, Chichester, and St. Albans. Illustrations. 2 vols. Crown 8vo, 36s.

Handbook — Eastern Cathedrals. Oxford, Peterborough, Ely, Norwich, and Lincoln. Illustrations. Crown 8vo, 18s.

Handbook — Western Cathedrals. Bristol, Gloucester, Hereford, Worcester, and Lichfield. With 60 Illustrations. Crown 8vo, 16s.

Handbook — Northern Cathedrals. York, Ripon, Durham, Carlisle, Chester, and Manchester. Illustrations. 2 vols. Crown 8vo, 21s.

Handbook—Welsh Cathedrals. Llandaff, St. David's, Bangor, and St. Asaph's. Illustrations. Crown 8vo, 15s.

Handbook—St. Alban's Cathedral. Illustrations. Crown 8vo, 6s.

Handbook—St. Paul's. Illustrations. Crown 8vo, 10s. 6d.

RELIGION AND THEOLOGY.

The Speaker's Commentary on THE BIBLE. Explanatory and Critical, With a Revision of the Translation. By Bishops and Clergy of the Anglican Church. Edited by Canon COOK. Medium 8vo. Old Testament, 6 vols., 135s. New Testament, 4 vols. See p. 2, *ante.*

The New Testament : Edited, with a short Practical Commentary, by Archdeacon CHURTON and Bishop BASIL JONES. With 100 Illustrations. 2 vols. Crown 8vo, 21s.

The Student's Edition of the Speaker's Commentary on the Bible. Abridged and Edited by JOHN M. FULLER, M.A. Crown 8vo, See p. 2.

Dictionary of the Bible ; its Antiquities, Biography, Geography, and Natural History. By various Writers. Edited by Dr. WM. SMITH. Illustrations. 3 vols. 8vo, 105s.

Concise Bible Dictionary. For the use of Students and Families. Condensed from the above. Maps and 300 Illustrations. 8vo, 21s.

Smaller Bible Dictionary ; for Schools and Young Persons. Abridged from the above. Maps and Woodcuts. Crown 8vo, 7s. 6d.

Dictionary of Christian Antiquities ; comprising the History, Institutions, and Antiquities of the Christian Church. Edited by Dr. WM. SMITH, and Archdeacon CHEETHAM. Illustrations. 2 vols. 8vo, £3 : 13 : 6.

Church Dictionary. By Dean HOOK. 8vo, 16s.

Dictionary of Christian Biography, Literature, Sects, and Doctrines ; from the Times of the Apostles to the Age of Charlemagne. Edited by Dr. WM. SMITH and Professor WACE. Vols. I. & II. 8vo, 31s. 6d. each.

A Dictionary of Hymnology ; A Companion to existing Hymn Books. Setting forth the Origin and History of the Hymns in the most popular Hymnals, together with Biographical Notices of their Authors and Translators, and their Sources and Origins. By Rev. JOHN JULIAN. 8vo.

The Student's Manual of English Church History. From the reign of Henry VIIIth to the Silencing of Convocation in the Eighteenth Century. By Canon PERRY. Post 8vo, 7s. 6d.

Student's Manual of Ecclesiastical History. From the Times of the Apostles to the Establishment of the Holy Roman Empire and the Papal Power. By PHILIP SMITH, B.A. Woodcuts. Post 8vo, 7s. 6d.

Student's Old Testament History. From the Creation to the return of the Jews from Captivity. By P. SMITH. Woodcuts. Post 8vo, 7s. 6d.

Student's New Testament History. With an Introduction connecting the History of the Old and New Testaments. By PHILIP SMITH. Woodcuts. Post 8vo, 7s. 6d.

History of Latin Christianity, including that of the Popes to the Pontificate of NICHOLAS V. By Dean MILMAN. 9 vols. crown 8vo, 54s.

Book of Common Prayer ; with Historical Notes. By Rev. THOMAS JAMES. With Initial Letters, Vignettes, etc. 8vo, 18s.

The Convocation Prayer Book, Showing what would be the Condition of the Book if Amended in conformity with the Recommendations of the Convocations of Canterbury and York, 1879. Post 8vo, 5s.

Signs and Wonders in the Land of HAM. With Ancient and Modern Parallels and Illustrations. By Rev. T. S. MILLINGTON. Woodcuts. 8vo, 7s. 6d.

The Talmud : Selected Extracts, chiefly Illustrating the Teaching of the Bible. With an Introduction. By Bishop BARCLAY. Illustrations. 8vo, 14s.

Notes on some Passages in the Liturgical History of the Reformed English Church. By Lord SELBORNE, 8vo, 6s.

History of the Christian Church from the Apostolic Age to the Reformation, A.D. 64-1517. By Canon ROBERTSON. 8 vols. post 8vo, 6s. each.

Undesigned Scriptural Coincidences in the Old and New Testaments ; a Test of their Veracity. By Rev. J. J. BLUNT. Post 8vo, 6s.

History of the Christian Church in the First Three Centuries. By Rev. J. J. BLUNT. Post 8vo, 6s.

The Parish Priest; His Duties, Acquirements, and Obligations. By Rev. J. J. BLUNT. Post 8vo, 6s.

Biblical Researches in Palestine and the Adjacent Regions. A Journal of Travels and Researches. With Historical Illustrations. By EDWARD ROBINSON, D.D. Maps. 3 vols. 8vo, 42s.

Psalms of David ; with Notes, Explanatory and Critical. By Dean WELLS, Canon ELLIOTT, and Canon COOK. Medium 8vo, 10s. 6d.

The Witness of the Psalms to Christ and Christianity. The Bampton Lectures for 1876. By the Bishop of Derry. 8vo, 14s.

The Manifold Witness for Christ : being an Attempt to Exhibit the Combined Force of Various Evidences, Direct and Indirect, of Christianity. By Canon BARRY. 8vo. 12s.

University Sermons. By Rev. J. J. BLUNT. Post 8vo, 6s.

Church and the Age : a Series of Essays on the Principles and Present Position of the Anglican Church. By various writers. 2 vols. 8vo, 26s.

The Synoptic Gospels,—The Death of Christ,—The Worth of Life,—Design in Nature, and other Essays. By Archbishop THOMSON. Cr. 8vo, 9s.

Companions for the Devout Life. Lectures delivered at St. James' Church. 1875-76. By Archb. of Dublin —Bps. of Ely and Derry—Deans of St. Paul's, Norwich, Chester, and Chichester — Canons Ashwell, Barry, and Farrar—Revs. Humphry, Carter, and

Classic Preachers of the English Church.
FIRST SERIES. 1877. Donne, Barrow, South, Beveridge, Wilson, Butler. With Introduction. Post 8vo, 7s. 6d.
SECOND SERIES. 1878. Bull, Horsley, Taylor, Sanderson, Tillotson, Andrewes. Post 8vo, 7s. 6d.

Masters in English Theology. Lectures delivered at King's College, London. By Canon BARRY, Dean of St. Paul's, Prof. PLUMPTRE, Canons WESTCOTT and FARRAR, and Archdeacon CHEETHAM. Post 8vo, 7s. 6d.

Essays on Cathedrals. By various Authors. Edited, with an Introduction, by Dean HOWSON. 8vo, 12s.

The Cathedral : its Necessary Place in the Life and Work of the Church. By the BISHOP of TRURO. Crown 8vo, 6s.

The Gallican Church. From the Concordat of Bologna, 1516, to the Revolution. With an introduction. By W. H. JERVIS. Portraits. 2 vols. 8vo, 28s.

Continuity of Scripture, as declared by the Testimony of Our Lord and of the Evangelists and Apostles. By Lord HATHERLEY. 8vo, 6s. ; or cheap edition, 2s. 6d.

Bible Lands. Their Modern Customs and Manners, illustrative of Scripture. By HENRY VAN LENNEP, D.D. Illustrations. 8vo, 21s.

The Shadows of a Sick Room. With Preface by Canon LIDDON. 16mo, 2s. 6d.

Manual of Family Prayer ; arranged on a card. 8vo, 2s.

Treatise on the Augustinian Doctrine of Predestination. By Canon MOZLEY. Crown 8vo, 9s.

Foundations of Religion in the Mind and Heart of Man. By Sir JOHN BYLES. Post 8vo, 6s.

Hymns adapted to the Church Service. By Bishop HEBER. 16mo, 1s. 6d.

The Nicene and Apostles' CREEDS. Their Literary History, with some account of "The Creed of St. Athanasius." By Canon SWAINSON. 8vo, 16s.

The Limits of Religious Thought examined. Bampton Lectures. By Dean MANSEL. Post 8vo, 8s. 6d

Christian Institutions ; Essays on Ecclesiastical Subjects. By Dean

Epistles of St. Paul to the
Corinthians. The Greek Text; with Critical Notes and Dissertations. By Dean STANLEY. 8vo, 18s.

Lectures on the History of the
EASTERN CHURCH. By Dean STANLEY. 8vo, 12s.

Lectures on the History of the
JEWISH CHURCH. By Dean STANLEY. 1st and 2d SERIES, Abraham to the Captivity. Maps. 2 vols. 8vo, 24s. 3d SERIES, Captivity to the Christian Era. Maps. 8vo, 14s.

Sermons preached during the
Tour of the Prince of Wales in the East. By Dean STANLEY. With Notices of the Localities visited. 8vo, 9s.

Sermons preached in Lincoln's-
Inn. By Canon COOK. 8vo, 9s.

Benedicite : or, Song of the
Three Children. Being Illustrations of the Power, Beneficence, and Design, manifested by the Creator in His Works. By G. C. CHILD CHAPLIN, M.D. Post 8vo, 6s.

Sermons preached at Lincoln's-
Inn. By Archbishop THOMSON, 8vo, 10s. 6d.

Life in the Light of God's
Word. By Archbishop THOMSON. Post 8vo, 5s.

Life in Faith. Sermons
preached at Cheltenham and Rugby. By T. W. JEX-BLAKE, D.D. Small 8vo, 3s. 6d.

A History of Christianity, from
the Birth of Christ to the Abolition of Paganism in the Roman Empire. By Dean MILMAN. 3 vols. post 8vo, 18s.

History of the Jews, from the
earliest period, continued to Modern Times. By Dean MILMAN. 3 vols. post 8vo, 18s.

A Smaller Scripture History of
the Old and New Testaments. Edited by Dr. W. SMITH. Woodcuts. 16mo 3s. 6d.

The Jesuits : their Constitu-
tion and Teaching ; an Historical Sketch. By W. C. CARTWRIGHT. 8vo, 9s.

Rome and the Newest Fashions
in Religion. By the Right Hon. W. E. GLADSTONE. Containing The Vatican Decrees—Vaticanism—Speeches of Pius IX. 8vo, 7s. 6d.

Eight Months at Rome, during
the Vatican Council, with a Daily Account of the Proceedings. By POMPONIO LETO. 8vo, 12s.

Worship in the Church of
ENGLAND. By A. J. B. BERESFORD-HOPE. 8vo, 9s.; or, *Popular Edition.* 8vo, 2s. 6d.

SCIENCE NATURAL HISTORY, GEOLOGY, ETC.

Science.

Connexion of the Physical
Sciences. By MARY SOMERVILLE. New Edition. Revised by A. B. BUCKLEY. Plates. Post 8vo, 9s.

Molecular and Microscopic
Science. By MARY SOMERVILLE. Illustrations. 2 vols. post 8vo, 21s.

Six Months in Ascension ;
an Unscientific Account of a Scientific Expedition. By Mrs. GILL. Map. Crown 8vo, 9s.

The Admiralty Manual of
Scientific Inquiry, prepared for the use of Officers, and Travellers in General. Map. Post 8vo, 3s. 6d.

Reports of the British Associa-
TION for the Advancement of Science, from 1831 to the present time. 8vo.

Philosophy in Sport made
Science in Earnest; or, the First Principles of Natural Philosophy explained by aid of the Toys and Sports of Youth. By Dr. PARIS. Woodcuts. Post 8vo, 7s. 6d.

Metallurgy ; The Art of Ex-
tracting Metals from their Ores. By JOHN PERCY, F.R.S. With Illustrations. 8vo.
FUEL, WOOD, PEAT, COAL, &c. 30s.
LEAD, and Part of SILVER. 30s.
SILVER and GOLD, 30s.

The Manufacture of Russian
Sheet-iron. By JOHN PERCY, 8vo, 2s. 6d.

A Manual of Naval Architec-
ture for the Use of Officers of the Royal Navy, Mercantile Marine, Yachtsmen, Shipbuilders, and others. By W. H. WHITE. Illustrations. 8vo, 24s.

Ironclad Ships; their Qualities,
Performances, and Cost, with Chapters on Turret Ships, Rams, &c. By Sir E. J. REED, C.B. Illustrations. 8vo, 12s.

Natural Philosophy ; an Intro-
duction to the study of Statics, Dynamics, Hydrostatics, Light, Heat, and Sound ; with numerous Examples. By SAMUEL NEWTH. Small 8vo, 3s. 6d.

Letters from Russia in 1875.
By Sir E. J. REED. 8vo, 5s.

Mathematical Examples. A
Graduated Series of Elementary Examples in Arithmetic, Algebra, Logarithms, Trigonometry, and Mechanics. By SAMUEL NEWTH. Small 8vo, 8s. 6d.

Elements of Mechanics, including Hydrostatics, with numerous Examples. By SAMUEL NEWTH. Small 8vo, 8s. 6d.

Patterns for Turning; to be cut on the Lathe *without* the use of *any* Ornamental Chuck. By W. H. ELPHINSTONE. Illustrations. Small 4to, 15s.

Natural History and Medicine.

Siberia in Europe. A Naturalist's Visit to the Valley of the Petchora in North-East Russia. With Notices of Birds and their Migrations. By HENRY SEEBOHM, F.R.G.S. With Map and Illustrations. Crown 8vo, 14s.

Life of a Scotch Naturalist (THOMAS EDWARD). By S. SMILES. Illustrations. Crown 8vo, 10s. 6d.

The Cat; an Introduction to the Study of Backboned Animals, especially Mammals. By ST. GEORGE MIVART. With numerous Illustrations. 8vo.

The Origin of Species, by MEANS OF NATURAL SELECTION; or the Preservation of Favoured Races in the Struggle for Life. By CHARLES DARWIN. Post 8vo, 7s. 6d.

Voyage of a Naturalist; being a Journal of Researches into the Natural History and Geology of the Countries visited during a Voyage round the World. By CHARLES DARWIN. Illustrations. Post 8vo, 9s.

Variation of Animals and Plants UNDER DOMESTICATION. By C. DARWIN. Illustrations. 2 vols. cr. 8vo, 18s.

The Various Contrivances by which ORCHIDS are FERTILISED by INSECTS. By CHARLES DARWIN. Woodcuts. Post 8vo, 9s.

The Effects of Cross and Self Fertilization in the Vegetable Kingdom. By CHARLES DARWIN. Crown 8vo, 12s.

Expression of the Emotions in Man and Animals. By CHARLES DARWIN. Illustrations. Crown 8vo, 12s.

Descent of Man and Selection in Relation to Sex. By CHARLES DARWIN. Illustrations. Crown 8vo, 9s.

Insectivorous Plants. By CHARLES DARWIN. Post 8vo, 14s.

The Movements and Habits of Climbing Plants. By CHAS. DARWIN. Post 8vo, 6s.

The Different Forms of Flowers on Plants of the same Species. By CHARLES DARWIN. Woodcuts. Crown 8vo, 10s. 6d.

The Power of Movement in Plants. By CHARLES DARWIN, assisted by FRANCIS DARWIN. Woodcuts. Crown 8vo, 15s.

Facts and Arguments for Darwin. By FRITZ MULLER. Illustrations. Post 8vo, 5s.

Geographical Hand-book of all the known Ferns, with Tables to show their Distribution. By K. M. LYELL. Post 8vo, 7s. 6d.

The Gardens of the Sun; or a Naturalist's Journal on the Mountains and in the Forests and Swamps of Borneo and the Sulu Archipelago. By F. W. BURBIDGE. With Illustrations. Crown 8vo, 14s.

Harvest of the Sea. An Account of the British Food Fishes. With Sketches of Fisheries and Fisher-Folk, By JAMES G. BERTRAM. Illustrations. Post 8vo, 9s.

Kirkes' Handbook of Physiology. By W. MORRANT BAKER. 420 Woodcuts. Post 8vo, 14s.

Gleanings in Natural History. By EDWARD JESSE. Woodcuts. Fcap. 3s. 6d.

Geography and Geology.

Student's Elements of Geology. By Sir CHARLES LYELL. Woodcuts. Post 8vo, 9s.

Principles of Geology; or, the Modern Changes of the Earth and its Inhabitants, as Illustrative of Geology. By Sir CHARLES LYELL. Woodcuts. 2 vols. 8vo, 32s.

Antiquity of Man, from Geo-logical Evidences; with Remarks on Theories of the Origin of Species. With special reference to man's first appearance on the earth. By Sir CHARLES LYELL. Illustrations. 8vo, 14s.

Physical Geography. By MARY SOMERVILLE. New Edition, Revised by Rev. J. RICHARDSON. Portrait. Post 8vo, 9s.

Physical Geography of the Holy Land. By EDWARD ROBINSON, Post 8vo, 10s. 6d.

Siluria; a History of the Oldest FOSSILIFEROUS ROCKS and their Foundations; with a Brief Sketch of the Distribution of Gold over the Earth. By Sir RODERICK MURCHISON. Illustrations. 2 vols. 8vo, 18s.

Records of the Rocks; or, Notes on the Geology, Natural History, and Antiquities of North and South Wales, Devon, &c. By Rev. W. S. SYMONDS. Illustrations. Crown 8vo, 12s.

Life of a Scotch Geologist and Botanist (ROBERT DICK). By S. SMILES. Illustrations. Crown 8vo, 12s.

Scepticism in Geology, and the Reasons for it. An assemblage of Facts from Nature opposed to the Theory of "Causes now in Action," and refuting it. By VERIFIER. Post 8vo, 6s.

The Freedom of Science in the Modern State. By RUDOLF VIRCHOW Fcp. 8vo, 2s.

FINE ARTS, ARCHITECTURE, & ANTIQUITIES.

The National Memorial to the PRINCE CONSORT at KENSINGTON. A Descriptive and Illustrated Account, consisting of Coloured Views and Engravings of the Monument and its Decorations, its Groups, Statues, Mosaics, Architecture, and Metalwork. With descriptive text by DOYNE C. BELL. Folio, £12 : 12s.

A Handbook to the Albert Memorial. Fcap. 8vo, 1s. ; or with Illustrations, 2s. 6d.

Ancient Pottery and Porcelain: Egyptian. Assyrian, Greek, Etruscan, and Roman. By SAMUEL BIRCH. Illustrations. Medium 8vo, 42s.

Mediæval and Modern Pottery and PORCELAIN. By JOSEPH MARRYAT. Illustrations. Medium 8vo, 42s.

Old English Plate : Ecclesias-tical, Decorative, and Domestic; its Makers and Marks. With Illustrations and Improved Tables of the Date Letters used in England, Scotland, and Ireland. By WILFRED J. CRIPPS. Illustrations. Medium 8vo.

Old French Plate : Furnishing Tables of the Paris Date Letters, and Facsimiles of other marks. By W. J. CRIPPS. With Illustrations. 8vo, 8s. 6d.

Cyprus; its Ancient Cities, Tombs, and Temples. A Narrative of Researches and Excavations during Ten Years' Residence in that Island. By LOUIS P. DI CESNOLA. 400 Illustrations. Medium 8vo, 50s.

A History of Greek Sculpture, from the Earliest Times down to the age of Pheidias. By A. S. MURRAY. With Illustrations. Royal 8vo, 21s.

Ancient Mycenæ; Discoveries and Researches on the Sites of Mycenæ and Tiryns. By Dr. SCHLIEMANN. With Preface by the Right Hon. W. E. GLADSTONE. 500 Illustrations. Medium 8vo, 50s.

Ilios; a Complete History of the City and Country of the Trojans, including all Recent Discoveries and Researches made on the Site of Troy and the Troad in 1871-3 and 1878-9. With an Autobiography of the Author. By Dr. SCHLIEMANN. With nearly 2000 Illustrations. Imperial 8vo, 50s.

Nile Gleanings : the Ethno-logy, History, and Art of Ancient Egypt, as Revealed by Paintings and Bas-Reliefs. With Descriptions of Nubia and its Great Rock Temples to the Second Cataract. By VILLIERS STUART. With 50 Coloured Plates. Royal 8vo, 31s. 6d.

The Cities and Cemeteries of Etruria. By GEORGE DENNIS. 200 Illustrations. 2 vols. medium 8vo, 42s.

History of Painting in North Italy, 14th to 16th Century. Venice, Padua, Vicenza, Verona, Ferrara, Milan, Friuli, Breschia. By CROWE and CAVALCASELLE. Illustrations. 2 vols. 8vo, 42s.

Titian : his Life and Times. By CROWE and CAVALCASELLE. Illustrations. 2 vols. 8vo, 42s.

Handbook to the Italian Schools of Painting: Based on the work of Kugler. Revised by Lady EASTLAKE. 140 Illustrations. 2 vols. crown 8vo, 30s.

Handbook to the German, Dutch, and Flemish Schools of Painting. Based on the work of Kugler. Revised by J. A. CROWE. 60 Illustrations. 2 vols. post 8vo, 24s.

Lives of the Italian Painters ; and the Progress of Painting in Italy. Cimabue to Bassano. By Mrs. JAMESON. Illustrations. Post 8vo, 12s. .

Lives of the Early Flemish Painters, with Notices of their Works. By CROWE and CAVALCASELLE. Illustrations. Post 8vo, 7s. 6d. ; or large paper, 8vo, 15s.

The Cicerone ; or, Art Guide to Painting in Italy. By Dr. BURCKHARDT. Post 8vo, 6s.

History of Architecture in all COUNTRIES, from the Earliest Times to the Present Day. By JAMES FERGUSSON. With 1600 Illustrations. 4 vols. Medium 8vo.

I. & II. Ancient and Mediæval, 63s.
III. Indian and Eastern, 42s.
IV. Modern, 31s. 6d.

Rude Stone Monuments in all COUNTRIES : their Age and Uses. By JAMES FERGUSSON. Illustrations. Medium 8vo, 24s.

The Temples of the Jews and other Buildings in the Haram Area at Jerusalem. By JAMES FERGUSSON. Illustrations. 4to, 42s.

The Holy Sepulchre and the Temple at Jerusalem. By JAS. FERGUSSON. Woodcuts. 8vo, 7s. 6d.

Leaves from My Sketch-Book, By E. W. COOKE, R.A. 50 Plates. With Descriptive Text. 2 vols. Small folio, 31s. 6d. each. 1st SERIES, Paris, Arles, Monaco, Nuremberg, Switzerland, Rome, Egypt, etc. 2d SERIES, Venice, Naples, Pompeii, Poestum, the Nile, etc.

Albert Durer's Life and Works. By Dr. THAUSING. From the German. With Portrait and Illustrations. 2 vols. Medium 8vo. [*In the Press.*

Life of Michel Angelo, Sculptor, Painter, and Architect, including unedited Documents in the Buonarroti Archives, by CHARLES HEATH WILSON. Royal 8vo, 26s.

A Descriptive Catalogue of the Etched Work of Rembrandt ; with Life and Introductions. By CHAS. H. MIDDLETON. Plates. Medium 8vo, 31s. 6d.

The Rise and Development of Mediæval Architecture. By Sir G. GILBERT SCOTT. 450 Illustrations. 2 vols. Medium 8vo, 42s.

Secular and Domestic Architecture. By Sir G. SCOTT, R.A. 8vo, 9s.

The Gothic Architecture of ITALY. By G. E. STREET, R.A. Illustrations. Royal 8vo, 26s.

The Gothic Architecture of SPAIN. By G. E. STREET, R.A. Illustrations. Royal 8vo, 30s.

Notes on the Churches of Kent. By Sir STEPHEN GLYNNE. With a Preface by W. H. GLADSTONE. Illustrations. 8vo, 12s.

Handbooks to English Cathedrals. See p. 15.

Purity in Musical Art. By A. F. J. THIBAUT. With Memoir by W. H. GLADSTONE. Post 8vo, 7s. 6d.

Handbook for Young Painters. By C. R. LESLIE. Illustrations. Post 8vo, 7s. 6d.

Life and Times of Sir Joshua Reynolds, with notices of his Contemporaries. By C. R. LESLIE and TOM TAYLOR. Portraits. 2 vols. 8vo, 42s.

Lectures on Architecture. Delivered before the Royal Academy. By EDWARD BARRY, R.A. 8vo.

Contributions to the Literature OF THE FINE ARTS. By Sir C. LOCK EASTLAKE, R.A. With a Memoir by Lady EASTLAKE. 2 vols. 8vo, 24s.

School Architecture. Practical Information on the Planning, Designing, Building, and Furnishing of Schoolhouses, etc. By E. R. ROBSON. Illustrations. Medium 8vo, 18s.

Small Country House. A brief
Discourse on the Planning of a Residence to cost from £2000 to £5000. With Supplementary Estimates to £7000. By ROBERT KERR. Post 8vo, 3s.

The Choice of a Dwelling; a
Practical Handbook of useful information on all points connected with a House. Plans. Post 8vo, 7s. 6d.

Life of Sir Charles Barry, R.A.,
Architect. By Canon BARRY. Illustrations. Medium 8vo, 15s.

London — Past and Present:
alphabetically arranged. By PETER CUNNINGHAM. A new and revised edition. 3 vols. 8vo. [In the Press.

PHILOSOPHY, LAW, AND POLITICS.

The Eastern Question. By the
late Viscount STRATFORD DE REDCLIFFE, K.G., G.C.B. Being a Selection from his Writings during the last Five Years of his Life. With a Preface by Dean STANLEY. Post 8vo.

Letters on the Politics of
Switzerland, pending the outbreak of the Civil War in. 1847. By GEORGE GROTE. 8vo, 6s.

Constitutional Progress. A
Series of Lectures. By MONTAGUE BURROWS. Post 8vo, 5s.

Constitution and Practice of
Courts-Martial. By Capt. SIMMONS. 8vo, 15s.

Administration of Justice under
Military and Martial Law, as applicable to the Army, Navy, Marine, and Auxiliary Forces. By C. M. CLODE. 8vo, 12s.

Student's Blackstone. A Sys-
tematic Abridgment of the entire Commentarles. By R. MALCOLM KERR. Post 8vo, 7s. 6d.

Communistic Societies of the
United States. With Accounts of the Shakers and other Societies; their Creeds, Social Practices, Industries, etc. By C. NORDHOFF. Illustrations. 8vo, 15s.

The English Constitution; its
Rise, Growth, and Present State. By DAVID ROWLAND. Post 8vo, 10s. 6d.

A Handbook to the Political
Questions of the day, with the Arguments on Either Side. By SYDNEY C. BUXTON. 8vo, 5s.

Laws of Nature the Foundation
of Morals. By DAVID ROWLAND. Post 8vo, 6s.

A Manual of Moral Philo-
sophy. With Quotations and References. By WILLIAM FLEMING. Post 8vo, 7s. 6d.

Lessons from Nature; as mani-
fested in Mind and Matter. By ST. GEORGE MIVART, F.R.S. 8vo, 16s.

Gleanings of Past Years, 1843-
78. By the Right Hon. W. E. GLADSTONE, M.P. Small 8vo, 2s. 6d. each. I. The Throne, Prince Consort, Cabinet, and Constitution. II. Personal and Literary. III. Historical and Speculative. IV. Foreign. V. and VI. Ecclesiastical. VII. Miscellaneous.

Speeches and Addresses, Poli-
tical and Literary. Delivered in the House of Lords, in Canada, and elsewhere. By the Right Hon. the EARL OF DUFFERIN. 8vo.

Philosophy of the Moral Feel-
INGS. By JOHN ABERCROMBIE. Fcap 8vo, 2s. 6d.

The Intellectual Powers, and
the Investigation of Truth. By JOHN ABERCROMBIE. Fcap. 8vo, 3s. 6d.

Hortensius; an Historical
Essay on the Office and Duties of an Advocate. By WILLIAM FORSYTH. Illustrations. 8vo, 7s. 6d.

Lectures on General Jurispru-
dence; or, the Philosophy of Positive Law. By JOHN AUSTIN. Edited by ROBERT CAMPBELL. 2 vols. 8vo, 32s.

Student's Edition of Austin's
Lectures on Jurisprudence. Compiled from the larger work. By ROBERT CAMPBELL. Post 8vo, 12s.

An Analysis of Austin's Juris-
prudence for the Use of Students. By GORDON CAMPBELL, M.A. Post 8vo. 6s.

England and Russia in the East.
A Series of Papers on the Political and Geographical Condition of Central Asia. By Sir H. RAWLINSON. Map. 8vo, 12s.

Ancient Law : its Connection with the Early History of Society, and its Relation to Modern Ideas. By Sir HENRY S. MAINE. 8vo, 12s.

Village Communities in the East and West. By Sir HENRY S. MAINE. 8vo, 12s.

The Early History of Institu-tions. By Sir HENRY MAINE. 8vo, 12s.

Local Taxation of Great Britain and Ireland. By R. H. I. PALGRAVE 8vo, 5s.

Plato and other Companions of Socrates. By GEORGE GROTE. 3 vols. 8vo, 45s.

Artistotle. By GEORGE GROTE. Second Edition. With Additions. 8vo, 18s.

Minor Works of George Grote. With Critical Remarks on his Intellectual Character, Writings, and Speeches. By ALEX. BAIN. Portrait. 8vo, 14s.

The Bengal Famine. How it will be Met, and how to Prevent Future Famines. By Sir BARTLE FRERE. Maps. Crown 8vo, 5s.

India in 1880. By Sir R. TEMPLE. 8vo.

Results of Indian Missions. By Sir BARTLE FRERE. Small 8vo, 2s. 6d.

Eastern Africa viewed as a Field for Mission Labour. By Sir BARTLE FRERE. Crown 8vo, 5s.

Researches into the Early History of Mankind, and the Development of Civilisation. By E. B. TYLOR. 8vo, 12s.

The Lex Salica; The Ten Texts, With the Glosses and the Lex Emendata. Synoptically Edited by J. H. HESSELS. With Notes on the Frankish Words in the Lex Salica by Professor KERN. 4to, 42s.

Primitive Culture : Researches into the Development of Mythology, Philosophy, Religion, Art, and Custom. By E. B. TYLOR. 2 vols. 8vo, 24s.

Ricardo's Political Works. With a Biographical Sketch. By J. R. M'CULLOCH. 8vo, 16s.

The Moral Philosophy of Aris-totle. Consisting of a Translation of the Nicomachean Ethics, and of the Paraphrase attributed to Andronicus of Rhodes; with Introductory Analysis of each Book. By the late WALTER M. HATCH, M.A. 8vo, 18s.

History of British Commerce, and of the Economic Progress of the Nation, 1763–1878. By LEONE LEVI. 8vo, 18s.

Ideas of the Day on Policy. By CHARLES BUXTON. 8vo, 6s.

Judgments of the Privy Council, with an Historical Account of the Appellate Jurisdiction in the Church of England. By G. C. BRODRICK and W. H. FREMANTLE. 8vo, 10s. 6d.

A Little Light on the Cretan Question. By A. F. YULE. Post 8vo. 2s. 6d.

History of the English Poor Laws. By Sir G. NICHOLLS. 2 vols. 8vo.

Consolation in Travel; or, The Last Days of a Philosopher. By Sir HUMPHRY DAVY. Woodcuts. Fcap. 8vo, 3s. 6d.

GENERAL LITERATURE AND PHILOLOGY.

The Quarterly Review. 8vo, 6s.

Prince Albert's Speeches and Addresses on Public Occasions; with an outline of his Character. Portrait. Fcap. 8vo, 1s.

The Talmud and other Literary Remains of EMANUEL DEUTSCH. With a Memoir. 8vo, 12s.

Letters, Lectures, and Reviews, including the Phrontisterion, or Oxford in the 19th Century. By Dean MANSEL. 8vo, 12s.

The Novels and Novelists of the 18th Century; in Illustration of the Manners and Morals of the Age. By WM. FORSYTH. Post 8vo, 10s.6d.

Principles of Greek Etymology. By PROFESSOR CURTIUS. Translated by A. S. WILKINS, M.A., and E. B. ENGLAND, M.A. 2 vols. 8vo, 15s. each.

The Greek Verb. Its Struct-ure and Development. By Professor CURTIUS. Translated by A. S. WILKINS and E. B. ENGLAND. 8vo, 18s.

Miscellanies. By Earl STAN-
HOPE. 2 vols. post 8vo, 13s.

Historical Essays. By Earl
STANHOPE. Post 8vo, 3s. 6d.

French Retreat from Moscow,
and other Essays. By the late Earl
STANHOPE. Post 8vo, 7s. 6d.

The Papers of a Critic. Selected from the Writings of the late
C. W. DILKE. 2 vols. 8vo, 24s.

Gleanings of Past Years. I.
The Throne, Prince Consort, Cabinet,
and Constitution. II. Personal and
Literary. III. Historical and Speculative. IV. Foreign. V. and VI. Ecclesiastical. VII. Miscellaneous. By
the Right Hon. W. E. GLADSTONE,
M.P. Small 8vo. 2s. 6d. each.

Lavengro : the Scholar—the
Gipsy—and the Priest. By GEORGE
BORROW. Post 8vo, 5s.

The Romany Rye : a Sequel
to 'Lavengro.' By GEORGE BORROW.
Post 8vo, 5s.

Wild Wales : its People, Language, and Scenery. By GEORGE BOR-
ROW. Post 8vo, 5s.

Romano Lavo-Lil ; Word-Book
of the Romany, or English Gypsy Language ; with an Account of certain
Gypsyries. By GEORGE BORROW. Post
8vo, 10s. 6d.

Field Paths and Green Lanes :
Country Walks, chiefly in Surrey and
Sussex. By L. J. JENNINGS. Wood-
cuts. Post 8vo, 10s. 6d.

Rambles among the Hills ; or
Walks in the Peak of Derbyshire and in
the South Downs. By L. J. JENNINGS.
Illustrations. Post 8vo, 12s.

Livonian Tales. By a LADY.
Post 8vo, 2s.

The Amber-Witch : a Trial for
Witchcraft. Translated by Lady DUFF
GORDON. Post 8vo, 2s.

The Handwriting of Junius.
Professionally investigated by C. CHABOT.
Edited by the Hon. EDWARD TWISLETON.
With Facsimiles. 4to, 63s.

The Literary History of Europe.
By HENRY HALLAM. Library edition,
3 vols. 8vo, 36s. : or Cabinet edition, 4
vols. post 8vo, 16s.

English Studies : Essays by the
late Rev. J. S. BREWER. 8vo, 14s.

Stokers and Pokers, or the
London and North - Western Railway.
By Sir F. HEAD. Post 8vo, 2s.

Specimens of the Table-Talk
of SAMUEL TAYLOR COLERIDGE. Portrait. Fcap. 8vo, 3s. 6d.

The Remains in Prose and
Verse of Arthur Hallam. With Memoir.
Portrait. Fcap. 8vo, 3s. 6d.

Self-Help. With Illustrations
of Conduct and Perseverance. By
SAMUEL SMILES, LL.D. Small 8vo, 6s.

Character. A Companion to
'Self-Help.' By Dr. SMILES. Small
8vo, 6s.

Thrift. A Book of Domestic
Counsel. By Dr. SMILES. Post 8vo, 6s.

Duty, with Illustrations of
Courage, Patience, and Endurance. By
Dr. S. SMILES. Post 8vo, 6s.

Mottoes for Monuments ; or,
Epitaphs selected for General Study and
Application. By Mrs. PALLISER. Il-
lustrations. Crown 8vo, 7s. 6d.

Words of Human Wisdom.
Collected and Arranged by E. S. With
Preface by Canon LIDDON. Fcap. 8vo,
3s. 6d.

Æsop's Fables. A new Ver-
sion. With Historical Preface. By Rev.
THOMAS JAMES. Woodcuts, by TEN-
NIEL. Post 8vo, 2s. 6d.

Letters from the Baltic. By a
LADY. Post 8vo, 2s.

Literary Essays from the
'Times.' By SAMUEL PHILLIPS. Portrait. 2 vols. fcap. 8vo, 7s.

Rejected Addresses. By JAMES
and HORACE SMITH. Woodcuts. Post
8vo, 3s. 6d. ; or fcap. 8vo, 1s.

Lispings from Low Latitudes ;
or, the Journal of the Hon. Impulsia
Gushington. Edited by Lord DUFFERIN.
Plates. 4to, 21s.

An English Grammar. Metho-
dical, Analytical, and Historical. With
a Treatise on the Orthography, Prosody
Inflections, and Syntax of the English
Tongue. By Professor MAETZNER.
3 vols. 8vo, 36s.

POETRY, THE DRAMA, ETC.

The Prose and Poetical Works of Lord BYRON. With Notes by SCOTT, JEFFREY, WILSON, GIFFORD, CRABBE, HEBER, LOCKHART, etc., and Notices of his Life. By THOMAS MOORE. Illustrations. 2 vols. royal 8vo, 15s.

Poetical Works of Lord Byron. Library edition. Portrait. 6 vols. 8vo, 45s.

Poetical Works of Lord Byron. Cabinet Edition. Plates. 10 vols. fcap. 8vo, 30s.

Poetical Works of Lord Byron. Pocket Edition. 8 vols. bound and in a case. 18mo, 21s.

Poetical Works of Lord Byron. Popular edition. Plates. Royal 8vo, 7s. 6d.

Poetical Works of Lord Byron. Pearl Edition. Post 8vo, 2s. 6d.

Childe Harold. By Lord Byron. 80 Engravings. Crown 8vo, 12s.

Childe Harold. By Lord Byron. 2s. 6d., 1s., and 6d. each.

Tales and Poems. By Lord Byron. 24mo, 2s. 6d.

Miscellanies. By Lord Byron. 2 vols. 24mo, 5s.

Dramas. By Lord Byron. 2 vols. 24mo, 5s.

Don Juan and Beppo. By Lord Byron. 2 vols. 24mo, 5s.

Beauties of Byron. Prose and Verse. Portrait. Fcap. 8vo, 3s. 6d.

Oliver Goldsmith's Works, edited by PETER CUNNINGHAM. Vignettes. 4 vols. 8vo, 30s.

Agamemnon. Translated from Æschylus. By the EARL of CARNARVON. Small 8vo, 6s.

Argo: or the Quest of the Golden Fleece, a Metrical Tale in ten books. By the Earl of CRAWFORD and BALCARRES. 8vo, 10s. 6d.

Vie de Seint Auban: a poem in Norman-French, ascribed to Matthew Paris. Edited, with Notes, by ROBERT ATKINSON. Small 4to, 10s. 6d.

The Vaux-de-Vire of Maistre Jean le Houx, Advocate of Vire. Trans-lated b   Illustrations

Life and Poetical Works of Rev. GEORGE CRABBE. Plates, royal 8vo, 7s.

Life and Works of Alexander Pope. Edited by Rev. W. ELWIN. Portraits. vols. 1, 2, 6, 7, 8. 8vo, 10s. 6d. each.

Iliad of Homer. Translated into English blank verse. By the EARL of DERBY. Portrait. 2 vols. post 8vo, 10s.

The Odyssey of Homer. Rendered into English Blank Verse. Books I.—XII. By General SCHOMBERG, C.B. 8vo, 12s.

Poetical Works of Bishop Heber. Portrait. Fcap. 8vo, 3s. 6d.

Hymns adapted to the Church Service. By Bishop Heber. 16mo, 1s. 6d.

The Sonnet; its Origin, Struc-ture, and Place in Poetry. With Translations from Dante and Petrarch. By CHARLES TOMLINSON. Post 8vo, 9s.

The Fall of Jerusalem. By Dean MILMAN. Fcap. 8vo, 1s.

Horace. By Dean MILMAN. Illustrated with 100 Woodcuts. Post 8vo, 7s. 6d.

Ancient Spanish Ballads. Historical and Romantic. Translated by J. G. LOCKHART. Woodcuts. Crown 8vo, 5s.

Remains in Prose and Verse of Arthur Hallam. With Memoir. Portrait. Fcap. 8vo, 3s. 6d.

Rejected Addresses. By James and HORACE SMITH. With Biographical Notices. Portraits. Post 8vo, 3s. 6d. ; or fcap. 8vo, 1s.

An Essay on English Poetry. With short lives of the British Poets. By THOMAS CAMPBELL. Post 8vo, 3s. 6d.

Poems and Fragments of Ca-tullus. Translated in the Metres of the Original. By ROBINSON ELLIS. 16mo, 5s.

Poetical Works of Lord Houghton. New Edition. 2 vols. fcap. 8vo, 12s.

Gongora's Poetical Works. With an Historical Essay on the Age of Philip III. and IV. of Spain. By Archdeacon CHURTON. Portrait. 2 vols. small 8vo, 12s.

Poetical Remains of the late

NAVAL AND MILITARY WORKS.

Army List. (Published by Authority.) With an Alphabetical Index. Monthly. 16mo, 2s.

Navy List. (Published by Authority.) Quarterly, 16mo, 3s. Monthly, 1s. 6d.

Nautical Almanack. (Published by Authority.) 8vo, 2s. 6d.

Hart's Army List. (Published Quarterly and Annually.) 8vo.

Admiralty Publications, issued by direction of the Lords Commissioners of the Admiralty.

Admiralty Manual of Scientific Enquiry, for the use of Travellers. Edited by Sir J. HERSCHEL and ROBERT MAIN. Woodcuts. Post 8vo, 3s. 6d.

A Dictionary of Naval and Military Technical Terms. English-French, French-English. By Colonel BURN. Crown 8vo, 15s.

Our Ironclad Ships : their Qualities, Performances, and Cost, including Chapters on Turret Ships, Ironclad Rams, etc. By E. J. REED, C.B. Illustrations. 8vo, 12s.

Manual of Naval Architecture for Officers of the Royal Navy, Mercantile Marine, Yachtsmen, Shipowners, and Shipbuilders. By W. H. WHITE. With 130 Woodcuts. 8vo, 24s.

Modern Warfare as Influenced by Modern Artillery. By Col. P. L. MACDOUGALL. Plans. Post 8vo, 12s.

Naval Gunnery ; for the Use of Officers and the Training of Seaman Gunners. By Sir HOWARD DOUGLAS. 8vo, 21s.

The Royal Engineer and the Royal Establishments at Woolwich and Chatham. By Sir FRANCIS B. HEAD. Illustrations. 8vo, 12s.

The Principles and Practice of Modern Artillery, including Artillery Material, Gunnery, and Organisation and Use of Artillery in Warfare. By Lieut.-Col. C. H. OWEN. Illustrations. 8vo, 15s.

The Administration of Justice under Military and Martial Law, as applicable to the Army, Navy, Marine, and Auxiliary Forces. By C. M. CLODE. 8vo, 12s.

History of the Administration and Government of the British Army from the Revolution of 1688. By C. M. CLODE. 2 vols. 8vo, 21s. each.

Constitution and Practice of Courts-Martial, with a Summary of the Law of Evidence, and some Notice of the Criminal Law of England with reference to the Trial of Civil Offences. By Capt. T. F. SIMMONS, R.A. 8vo, 15s.

Origin and History of the First or GRENADIER GUARDS, from Documents in the State Paper Office, War Office, Horse Guards, Contemporary History, Regimental Records, etc. By Sir F. W. HAMILTON. Illustrations. 3 vols. 8vo, 63s.

History of the Royal Artillery. Compiled from the Original Records. By Major FRANCIS DUNCAN, R.A. 2 vols. 8vo, 18s.

The English in Spain. The True Story of the War of the Succession in 1834-1840. Compiled from the Reports of the British Commissioners with Queen Isabella's Armies. By Major FRANCIS DUNCAN, R.A. Illustrations. 8vo, 16s.

Wellington's Supplementary Despatches and Correspondence. Edited by his SON. 15 vols. 8vo, 20s. each. An index. 8vo, 20s.

Wellington's Civil and Political Correspondence, 1819-1831. 8 vols. 8vo, 20s. each.

Young Officer's Companion ; or, Essays on Military Duties and Qualities, with Examples and Illustrations from History. By Lord DE ROS. Post 8vo, 9s.

Lives of the Warriors of the Seventeenth Century. By Gen. Sir EDWARD CUST. 6 vols. post 8vo. 1st Series.—THE THIRTY YEARS' WAR, 1600-48. 2 vols. 16s. 2d Series.—THE CIVIL WARS OF FRANCE AND ENGLAND. 1611-75. 2 vols. 16s. 3d Series.—COMMANDERS OF FLEETS AND ARMIES, 1648-1704. 2 vols. 18s.

Annals of the Wars of the 18th and 19th Centuries, 1700-1815. Compiled from the most Authentic Histories of the Period. By Gen. Sir E. CUST. Maps. 9 vols. fcap. 8vo, 5s. each.

Deeds of Naval Daring ; or, Anecdotes of the British Navy. By EDWARD GIFFARD. Fcap. 8vo, 3s. 6d.

RURAL AND DOMESTIC ECONOMY, ETC.

A Popular Account of the Introduction of Peruvian Bark from South America into British India and Ceylon, and of the Progress and Extent of its Cultivation. By CLEMENTS R. MARKHAM. With Maps and Woodcuts. Post 8vo, 14s.

Plain Instructions in Gardening; with a Calendar of Operations and Directions for every Month. By Mrs. LOUDON. Woodcuts. Fcap. 8vo, 3s. 6d.

A Geographical Handbook of FERNS. By K. M. LYELL. Post 8vo, 7s. 6d.

Alpine Flowers for English GARDENS. How they may be grown in all parts of the British Islands. By W. ROBINSON. Illustrations. Crown 8vo, 7s. 6d.

Sub-Tropical Garden; or, Beauty of Form in the Flower Garden, with Illustrations of all the finer Plants used for this purpose. By W. ROBINSON. Illustrations. Small 8vo, 5s.

Modern Domestic Cookery, Founded on Principles of Economy and Practice, and adapted for private families. By a Lady. Fcap. 8vo, 5s.

Thrift : a Book of Domestic Counsel. By SAMUEL SMILES. Small 8vo, 6s.

Duty : a Companion Volume to Self-Help, etc. By SAMUEL SMILES. Small 8vo, 6s.

Royal Agricultural Journal (published half-yearly). 8vo.

Bees and Flowers. By Rev. THOMAS JAMES. Fcap. 8vo, 1s. each.

Music and Dress. By a Lady. Fcap. 8vo, 1s.

Choice of a Dwelling ; a Practical Handbook of Useful Information on all Points connected with Hiring, Buying, or Building a House. Plans. Post 8vo, 7s. 6d.

A Small Country House. Brief Directions on the Planning of a Residence to cost from £2000 to £7000. By ROBERT KERR. Post 8vo, 3s.

FIELD SPORTS.

Dog-breaking ; the most Expeditious, Certain, and Easy Method. By General HUTCHINSON. Woodcuts. 8vo, 7s. 6d.

My Boyhood: a Story of Country Life and Sport for Boys. By H. C. BARKLEY, Civil Engineer. With Illustrations by A. C. CORBOULD. Post 8vo, 6s.

Wild Sports and Natural History of the Highlands. By CHARLES ST. JOHN. New and Beautifully Illustrated Edition. Crown 8vo. 15s. ; or cheap ed., post 8vo, 3s. 6d.

The Chase—The Turf—and the ROAD. By NIMROD. Illustrations. Crown 8vo, 5s. ; or coloured plates, 7s. 6d.

Salmonia ; or days of Fly-Fishing. By Sir HUMPHRY DAVY. Woodcuts. Fcap. 8vo, 3s. 6d.

Horse-Shoeing ; as it is, and as it should be. By WILLIAM DOUGLAS. Plates. Post 8vo, 7s. 6d.

Five Years' Adventures in the far Interior of South Africa with the Wild Beasts and Wild Tribes of the Forests. By R. GORDON CUMMING. Woodcuts. Post 8vo, 6s.

Sport and War. Recollections of Fighting and Hunting in South Africa, from 1834-67, with an Account of the Duke of Edinburgh's Visit. By General Sir JOHN BISSET, C.B. Illustrations. Crown 8vo, 14s.

Western Barbary, its Wild Tribes and Savage Animals. By Sir JOHN DRUMMOND HAY. Post 8vo, 2s.

Sport in Abyssinia. By Earl of MAYO. Illustrations. Crown 8vo, 12s.

EDUCATIONAL WORKS.

DR. WM. SMITH'S DICTIONARIES.

A Dictionary of the Bible ; Its Antiquities, Biography, Geography, and Natural History. Illustrations. 3 vols. 8vo, 105s.

A Concise Bible Dictionary. For the use of Students and Families. Condensed from the above. With Maps and 300 Illustrations. 8vo, 21s.

A Smaller Bible Dictionary. For Schools and Young Persons. Abridged from the above. With Maps and Woodcuts. Crown 8vo, 7s. 6d.

A Dictionary of Christian An-tiquities. The History, Institutions, and Antiquities of the Christian Church. With Illustrations. 2 vols. medium 8vo, £3 : 13 : 6.

A Dictionary of Christian Bio-graphy, Literature, Sects, and Doctrines. From the Time of the Apostles to the Age of Charlemagne. Vols. I. & II. Medium 8vo, 31s. 6d. each.

A Dictionary of Greek and Roman Antiquities. Comprising the Laws, Institutions, Domestic Usages, Painting, Sculpture, Music, the Drama, etc. With 500 Illustrations. Medium 8vo, 28s.

A Dictionary of Greek and Roman Biography and Mythology, containing a History of the Ancient World, Civil, Literary, and Ecclesiastical, from the earliest times to the capture of Constantinople by the Turks. With 564 Illustrations. 3 vols. medium 8vo, 84s.

A Dictionary of Greek and Roman Geography, showing the Researches of modern Scholars and Travellers, including an account of the Political History of both Countries and Cities, as well as of their Geography. With 530 Illustrations. 2 vols. medium 8vo, 56s.

A Classical Dictionary of Mythology, Biography, and Geography. With 750 Woodcuts. 8vo, 18s.

A Smaller Classical Dictionary. Abridged from the above. With 200 Woodcuts. Crown 8vo, 7s. 6d.

A Smaller Dictionary of Greek and Roman Antiquities. Abridged from the larger work. With 200 Woodcuts. Crown 8vo, 7s. 6d.

A Latin - English Dictionary. Based on the works of Forcellini and Freund. With Tables of the Roman Calendar, Measures, Weights, and Monies. Medium 8vo, 21s.

A Smaller Latin-English Dic-tionary. With Dictionary of Proper Names, and Tables of Roman Calendar, etc. Abridged from the above. Square 12mo, 7s. 6d.

An English-Latin Dictionary, Copious and Critical. Medium 8vo, 21s.

A Smaller English-Latin Dic-tionary. Abridged from the above. Square 12mo, 7s. 6d.

A Mediæval Latin-English Dic-tionary. Founded on the Work of Ducange. Illustrated and enlarged by additions, derived from Patristic and Scholastic Authors, Mediæval Histories, &c., Ancient and Modern. By E. A. DAYMAN, B.D., and J. H. HESSELS. *[In Preparation.*

MARKHAM'S HISTORIES.

A History of England, from the First Invasion by the Romans. With Conversations at the end of each Chapter. By Mrs. MARKHAM. With 100 Woodcuts. 12mo, 3s. 6d.

A History of France, from the Conquest by the Gauls. With Conversations at the end of each Chapter. By Mrs. MARKHAM. Woodcuts. 12mo, 3s. 6d.

A History of Germany, from the Invasion of the Kingdom by the Romans under Marius. On the Plan of Mrs. MARKHAM. With 50 Woodcuts. 12mo, 3s. 6d.

Little Arthur's History of Eng-land. By Lady CALLCOTT. Continued down to the year 1872. With 36 Woodcuts. 16mo, 1s. 6d.

MURRAY'S
STUDENT'S MANUALS.

A Series of Historical Class Books for advanced Scholars. Forming a complete chain of History from the earliest ages to modern times.

Student's Old Testament History,
from the Creation to the Return of the Jews from Captivity. With an Introduction by PHILIP SMITH. Maps and Woodcuts. Post 8vo, 7s. 6d.

Student's New Testament History.
With an Introduction connecting the History of the Old and New Testaments. By PHILIP SMITH. Maps and Woodcuts. Post 8vo, 7s. 6d.

Student's Manual of Ecclesiastical History of the Christian Church,
from the Times of· the Apostles to the full Establishment of the Holy Roman Empire and the Papal Power. By PHILIP SMITH. Woodcuts. Post 8vo, 7s. 6d.

Student's Manual of English
Church History, from the Time of Henry VIII. to the Silencing of Convocation in the 18th Century. By Canon PERRY, M.A. Post 8vo, 7s. 6d.

Student's Ancient History of
the East. Egypt, Assyria, Babylonia, Media, Persia, Phœnicia, &c. By PHILIP SMITH. Post 8vo, 7s. 6d.

Student's History of Greece,
from the Earliest Times to the Roman Conquest; with the History of Literature and Art. By Dr. WM. SMITH. Woodcuts. Post 8vo, 7s. 6d.

Student's History of Rome,
from the Earliest Times to the Establishment of the Empire; with the History of Literature and Art. By Dean LIDDELL. Woodcuts. Post 8vo, 7s. 6d.

Student's History of the Decline
and Fall of the Roman Empire. By EDWARD GIBBON. Woodcuts. Post 8vo, 7s. 6d.

Student's History of Modern
Europe. From the End of the Middle Ages to the Treaty of Berlin. Post 8vo.
[*In Preparation.*

Student's History of England
from the Accession of Henry VII. to the Death of George II. By HENRY HALLAM. Post 8vo, 7s. 6d.

Student's Hume: a History of
ENGLAND from the Invasion of JULIUS CÆSAR to the Revolution in 1688. New edition. Continued to the Treaty of Berlin, 1878. By J. S. BREWER. With 7 Coloured Maps and Woodcuts. Post 8vo, 7s. 6d.

Student's History of Europe
during the MIDDLE AGES. By HENRY HALLAM. Post 8vo, 7s. 6d.

Student's History of France,
from the Earliest Times to the Establishment of the Second Empire, 1852. By Rev. W. H. JERVIS. Woodcuts. Post 8vo, 7s. 6d.

Student's Manual of Ancient
Geography. By Canon BEVAN. Woodcuts. Post 8vo, 7s. 6d.

Student's Manual of Modern
Geography, Mathematical, Physical, and Descriptive. By Canon BEVAN. Woodcuts. Post 8vo, 7s. 6d.

Student's Manual of the Geography of India. By Dr. GEORGE SMITH. Post 8vo.

Student's Manual of the English
Language. By GEORGE P. MARSH. Post 8vo, 7s. 6d.

Student's Manual of English
Literature. By T. B. SHAW. Post 8vo, 7s. 6d.

Student's Specimens of English
LITERATURE. By T. B. SHAW. Post 8vo, 7s. 6d.

Student's Manual of Moral
Philosophy. By WILLIAM FLEMING. Post 8vo, 7s. 6d.

DR. WM. SMITH'S
SMALLER HISTORIES.

A Smaller Scripture History of
the Old and New Testaments. Woodcuts. 16mo, 3s. 6d.

A Smaller Ancient History of
the East, from the Earliest Times to the Conquest of Alexander the Great. With 70 Woodcuts. 16mo, 3s. 6d.

A Smaller History of Greece,
from the Earliest Times to the Roman Conquest. 74 Woodcuts. 16mo, 3s. 6d.

A Smaller History of Rome,
from the Earliest Times to the Establishment of the Empire. Woodcuts. 16mo, 3s. 6d.

A Smaller Classical Mythology.
With Translations from the Ancient Poets, and Questions on the Work. With 90 Woodcuts. 16mo, 3s. 6d.

A Smaller Manual of Ancient
Geography. 36 Woodcuts. 16mo, 3s. 6d.

A Smaller History of England,
from the Earliest Times to the year 1868. With 68 Woodcuts. 16mo, 3s. 6d.

A Smaller History of English
Literature; giving a Sketch of the Lives of our chief Writers. 16mo, 3s. 6d.

Short Specimens of English
Literature. Selected from the chief Authors, and arranged chronologically. 16mo, 3s. 6d.

DR. WM. SMITH'S EDUCATIONAL WORKS.

ENGLISH COURSE.

A Primary History of Britain for Elementary Schools. Edited by Dr. WM. SMITH. 12mo, 2s. 6d.

A School Manual of English Grammar, with Copious Exercises. By Dr. WM. SMITH and T. D. HALL. Post 8vo, 3s. 6d.

A Primary English Grammar for Elementary Schools. Exercises and Questions. By T. D. HALL. 16mo, 1s.

A Manual of English Composi- tion. With Copious Illustrations and Practical Exercises. By T. D. HALL. 12mo, 3s. 6d.

A School Manual of Modern Geography, Physical and Political. By JOHN RICHARDSON. Post 8vo, 5s.

A Smaller Manual of Modern Geography, for Schools and Young Persons. Post 8vo, 2s. 6d.

LATIN COURSE.

The Young Beginner's First Latin Book ; Containing the Rudiments of Grammar, Easy Grammatical Questions and Exercises, with Vocabularies. Being Introductory to Principia Latina, Part I. 12mo, 2s.

The Young Beginner's Second Latin Book ; Containing an Easy Latin Reading Book, with an Analysis of the Sentences, Notes, and a Dictionary. Being Introductory to Principia Latina, Part II. 12mo, 2s.

Principia Latina, Part I. A First Latin Course, comprehending Grammar, Delectus, and Exercise Book, with Vocabularies. With Accidence adapted to the Ordinary Grammars, as well as the Public School Latin Primer. 12mo, 3s. 6d.

Appendix to Principia Latina, Part I. ; Additional Exercises, with Examination Papers. 12mo, 2s. 6d.

Principia Latina, Part II. A Latin Reading Book, an Introduction to Ancient Mythology, Geography, Roman Antiquities, and History. With Notes and Dictionary. 12mo, 3s. 6d.

Principia Latina, Part III. A Latin Poetry Book, containing Easy Hexameters and Pentameters, Eclogæ Ovidianæ, Latin Prosody, First Latin Verse Book. 12mo, 3s. 6d.

Principia Latina, Part IV. Latin Prose Composition, containing the Rules of Syntax, with copious Examples, and Exercises. 12mo, 3s. 6d.

Principia Latina, Part V. Short Tales and Anecdotes from Ancient History, for Translation into Latin Prose. 12mo, 3s.

A Latin-English Vocabulary : arranged according to subjects and etymology ; with a Latin-English Dictionary to Phædrus, Cornelius Nepos, and Cæsar's "Gallic War." 12mo, 3s. 6d.

The Student's Latin Grammar. Post 8vo, 6s.

A Smaller Latin Grammar. Abridged from the above. 12mo, 3s. 6d.

Tacitus. Germania, Agricola, and First Book of the Annals. English Notes. 12mo, 3s. 6d.

GREEK COURSE.

Initia Græca, Part I. A First Greek Course : comprehending Grammar, Delectus, and Exercise-book. With Vocabularies. 12mo, 3s. 6d.

Appendix to Initia Græca, Part I. Being additional Exercises, with Examination Papers and Easy Reading Lessons, with the Sentences analysed, serving as an Introduction to Part II. 12mo.

Initia Græca, Part II. A Greek Reading Book, containing Short Tales, Anecdotes, Fables, Mythology, and Grecian History. Arranged in a systematic progression, with Lexicon. 12mo, 3s. 6d.

Initia Græca. Part III. Greek Prose Composition : containing a Systematic Course of Exercises on the Syntax, with the Principal Rules of Syntax, and an English-Greek Vocabulary to the Exercises. 12mo, 3s. 6d.

The Student's Greek Grammar. By Professor CURTIUS. Post 8vo, 6s.

A Smaller Greek Grammar. Abridged from the above. 12mo, 3s. 6d

Greek Accidence. Extracted from the above work. 12mo, 2s. 6d.

Elucidations of Curtius's Greek Grammar. Translated by EVELYN ABBOTT. Post 8vo, 7s. 6d.

Plato. The Apology of So- crates, the Crito, and Part of the Phædo ; with Notes in English from Stallbaum, and Schleiermacher's Introductions. 12mo, 3s. 6d.

FRENCH, GERMAN, AND ITALIAN COURSE.

French Principia, Part I. A
First French Course, containing Grammar, Delectus, Exercises, and Vocabularies. 12mo, 3s. 6d.

Appendix to French Principia,
Part I. Being Additional Exercises and Examination Papers. 12mo, 2s. 6d.

French Principia, Part II.
A Reading Book, with Notes, and a Dictionary. 12mo, 4s. 6d.

Student's French Grammar:
Practical and Historical. By C. HERON-WALL. With Introduction by M. Littré. Post 8vo, 7s. 6d.

A Smaller Grammar of the
French Language. Abridged from the above. 12mo, 3s. 6d.

German Principia, Part I. A
First German Course, containing Grammar, Delectus, Exercises, and Vocabulary. 12mo, 3s. 6d.

German Principia. Part II. A
Reading Book, with Notes and a Dictionary. 12mo, 3s. 6d.

Practical Grammar of the German Language, with an Historical development of the Language. Post 8vo, 3s. 6d.

The Italian Principia, Part I.
A First Course, containing a Grammar, Delectus, Exercise Book, with Vocabularies, and Materials for Italian Conversation. By Signor RICCI. 12mo, 3s. 6d.

Italian Principia, Part II. A
Reading-Book, containing Fables, Anecdotes, History, and Passages from the best Italian Authors, with Grammatical Questions, Notes, and a Copious Etymological Dictionary. 12mo, 3s. 6d.

SCHOOL AND PRIZE BOOKS.

A Child's First Latin Book,
comprising a full Praxis of Nouns, Adjectives, and Pronouns, with Active Verbs. By T. D. HALL. 16mo, 2s.

King Edward VI.'s Latin Accidence. 12mo, 2s. 6d.

King Edward VI.'s Latin Grammar. 12mo, 3s. 6d.

Oxenham's English Notes for
Latin Elegiacs. Designed for early proficients in the art of Latin Versification. 12mo, 3s. 6d.

Hutton's Principia Græca : an
Introduction to the study of Greek, comprehending Grammar, Delectus, and Exercise Book, with Vocabularies. 12mo, 3s. 6d.

Buttman's Lexilogus; a Critical
Examination of the Meaning and Etymology of Passages in Greek Writers. 8vo, 12s.

Matthiæ's Greek Grammar.
Revised by CROOKE. Post 8vo, 4s.

Horace. With 100 Vignettes.
Post 8vo, 7s. 6d.

Practical Hebrew Grammar ;
with an Appendix, containing the Hebrew Text of Genesis I. VI. and Psalms I. VI. Grammatical Analysis and Vocabulary. By Rev. STANLEY LEATHES. Post 8vo, 7s. 6d.

First Book of Natural Philosophy : an Introduction to the Study of Statics, Dynamics, Hydrostatics, Light,

Elements of Mechanics, includ-ing Hydrostatics. By Prof. NEWTH. Sm. 8vo, 8s. 6d.

Mathematical Examples. A
Graduated Series of Elementary Examples in Arithmetic, Algebra, Logarithms, Trigonometry, and Mechanics. By Professor NEWTH. Small 8vo, 8s. 6d.

Progressive Geography. By
J. W. CROKER. 18mo, 1s. 6d.

Æsop's Fables, chiefly from
Original Sources, by Rev. THOS. JAMES. With 100 Woodcuts. Post 8vo, 2s. 6d.

Gleanings in Natural History.
By EDWARD JESSE. Fcap. 8vo, 3s. 6d.

Philosophy in Sport made
Science in Earnest; or Natural Philosophy inculcated by the Toys and Sports of Youth. By Dr. PARIS. Woodcuts. Fcap. 8vo, 7s. 6d.

Puss in Boots. By OTTO SPECK-TER. Illustrations. 16mo, 1s. 6d.

The Charmed Roe. By OTTO
SPECKTER. Illustrations. 16mo, 5s.

Hymns in Prose for Children.
by Mrs. BARBAULD. Illustrations. Fcap. 8vo, 3s. 6d.

A Boy's Voyage Round the

The Home & Colonial Library.

Class A—BIOGRAPHY, HISTORY, &c.		Class B—VOYAGES and TRAVEL.	
1. DRINKWATER'S Gibraltar.	2s.	1. BORROW'S Bible in Spain.	3s. 6d.
2. The Amber Witch.	2s.	2. BORROW'S Gipsies of Spain.	3s. 6d.
3. SOUTHEY'S Cromwell and Bunyan.	2s.	3, 4. HEBER'S Indian Journals	7s.
4. BARROW'S Sir Francis Drake.	2s.	5. Holy Land. IRBY & MANGLES.	2s.
5. British Army at Washington.	2s.	6. HAY'S Western Barbary.	2s.
6. French in Algiers.	2s.	7. Letters from the Baltic.	2s.
7. Fall of the Jesuits.	2s.	8. MEREDITH'S New S. Wales.	2s.
8. Livonian Tales.	2s.	9. LEWIS' West Indies.	2s.
9. Condé. By Lord MAHON.	3s. 6d.	10. MALCOLM'S Persia.	3s. 6d.
10. Sale's Brigade in Affghanistan.	2s.	11. Father Ripa at Pekin.	2s.
11. Sieges of Vienna.	2s.	12, 13. MELVILLE'S Marquesas	7s.
12. MILMAN'S Wayside Cross.	2s.	14. ABBOT'S Missionary in Canada.	2s.
13. Liberation War in Germany.	3s. 6d.	15. Letters from Madras.	2s.
14. GLEIG'S Battle of Waterloo.	3s. 6d.	16. ST. JOHN'S Highland Sports.	3s. 6d.
15. STEFFENS' Adventures.	2s.	17. The Pampas. Sir F. HEAD.	2s.
16. CAMPBELL'S British Poets.	3s. 6d.	18. FORD'S Spanish Gatherings.	3s. 6d.
17. Essays. By Lord MAHON.	3s. 6d.	19. EDWARDS' River Amazon.	2s.
18. GLEIG'S Life of Lord Clive.	3s. 6d.	20. ACLAND'S India.	2s.
19. Stokers and Pokers. By Sir FRANCIS HEAD.	2s.	21. RUXTON'S Rocky Mountains.	3s 6d
20. GLEIG'S Life of Munro.	3s. 6d.	22. CARNARVON'S Portugal.	3s. 6d.
		23. HAYGARTH'S Bush Life.	2s.
		24. ST. JOHN'S Libyan Desert.	2s.
		25. Letters from Sierra Leone.	3s. 6d.

DR. WM. SMITH'S ANCIENT ATLAS.

AN ATLAS OF ANCIENT GEOGRAPHY, BIBLICAL AND CLASSICAL. Intended to illustrate the 'Dictionary of the Bible,' and the 'Dictionaries of Classical Antiquity.' Compiled under the superintendence of WM. SMITH, D.C.L., and GEORGE GROVE, LL.D. Folio, half-bound, £6 : 6s.

1. Geographical Systems of the Ancients.	21. Greece during the Persian Wars.
2. The World as known to the Ancients.	22. Greece during the Peloponnesian War.
3. Empires of the Babylonians, Lydians, Medes, and Persians.	23. Greece during the Achæan League.
4. Empire of Alexander the Great.	24. Northern Greece.
5, 6. Kingdoms of the Successors of Alexander the Great.	25. Central Greece—Athens.
7. The Roman Empire in its greatest extent.	26. Peloponnesus.—With Plan of Sparta.
8. The Roman Empire after its division into the Eastern and Western Empires.	27. Shores and Islands of the Ægean Sea.
9. Greek and Phœnician Colonies.	28. Historical Maps of Asia Minor.
10. Britannia.	29. Asia Minor.
11. Hispania.	30. Arabia.
12. Gallia.	31. India.
13. Germania, Rhætia, Noricum.	32. Northern Part of Africa.
14. Pæonia, Thracia, Mœsia, Illyria, Dacia.	33. Ægypt and Æthiopia.
15. Italy, Sardinia, and Corsica.	34. Historical Maps of the Holy Land.
16. Italia Superior.	35, 36. The Holy Land. North and South.
17. Italia Inferior.	37. Jerusalem, Ancient and Modern.
18. Plan of Rome.	38. Environs of Jerusalem.
19. Environs of Rome.	39. Sinai.
20. Greece after the Doric Migration.	40. Asia, to illustrate the Old Testament.
	41. Map, to illustrate the New Testament.
	42, 43. Plans of Babylon, Nineveh, Troy, Alexandria, and Byzantium.

INDEX.

Lightning Source UK Ltd.
Milton Keynes UK
UKHW02f2043140818
327243UK00012B/770/P